Tombstone, Deadwood, and Dodge City

Tombstone, Deadwood, and Dodge City

RE-CREATING THE FRONTIER WEST

Kevin Britz and **Roger L. Nichols**

UNIVERSITY OF OKLAHOMA PRESS: NORMAN

Publication of this book is made possible through the generosity of Edith Kinney Gaylord.

Library of Congress Cataloging-in-Publication Data

Names: Britz, Kevin Mark, 1954– author. | Nichols, Roger L., author.
Title: Tombstone, Deadwood, and Dodge City : Re-creating the Frontier West / Kevin Britz and Roger L. Nichols.
Description: First edition. | Norman, OK : University of Oklahoma Press [2018] | Includes bibliographical references and index.
Identifiers: LCCN 2017049022 | ISBN 978-0-8061-6029-0 (hardcover : alk. paper)
Subjects: LCSH: Heritage tourism—West (U.S.)—History. | Historical reenactments—West (U.S.)—History. | Historic sites—West (U.S.) | Historical museums—West (U.S.) | Frontier and pioneer life—West (U.S.) | West (U.S.)—History, Local.
Classification: LCC G155.U6 B75 2018 | DDC 338.4/79178—dc23
LC record available at https://lccn.loc.gov/2017049022

1 2 3 4 5 6 7 8 9 10

For my brother Mike, who would have liked it, and for Kate
—KB

Contents

Illustrations

FIGURES

MAP

☞ Preface

This book has had an unusual genesis. Kevin Britz was a PhD student of mine some twenty years ago. The duties he performed as a longtime museum professional included preparing displays for the visiting public, and he wanted to examine how Tombstone developed its historical displays as his dissertation topic. When I suggested a comparative approach incorporating several additional towns, he chose Deadwood and Dodge City. He progressed slowly because of his full-time professional duties and completed the dissertation less than a month before the Graduate College was to end his doctoral study program. Thus he assembled the last several chapters hurriedly, but with every intention of revising them for publication later. Unfortunately, he died in 2011 before completing the revisions.

Kevin's research included impressive archival work on how each of the three towns developed its historical identity. It analyzed the roles of entertainment and popular culture in the development of American ideas about western history and then related them to early town boosterism, efforts at local economic development, and the way in which those elements fit into the growing national tourism. These issues are important and interesting, and the work seemed too good to remain virtually hidden from all but a few scholars. So I decided to try to get it published and wrote to Chuck Rankin at the University of Oklahoma Press, volunteering to edit, rewrite, and incorporate scholarship that had appeared after Kevin completed his work. He agreed, and the press accepted the project. Since then I have edited the manuscript thoroughly, working to reduce the usual repetition and extra data found in most dissertations. Rewriting it has been a challenge because Kevin liked long, involved sentences (four to six lines), while

I use shorter ones. Often his paragraphs ran to a full page, occasionally a bit longer, compared to mine, which are usually about half that length.

Our prose styles differ too. He preferred to use quotations to carry the narrative, while I use them to add color. The resulting narrative includes many fewer quotations than Kevin used but many more than I like. Repetition tends to be unavoidable in comparative studies, and dissertations often have more overlap and data than necessary. While retaining Kevin's general organization and stress on ideas such as historical memory, authentication, and public historical presentation, I switched the positions of his first two chapters. Next I rewrote most of the prose, tried to give each town equal space and attention, redid all of the endnotes and much of the bibliography, and incorporated the major scholarship of the last fifteen to twenty years related to the issues that he considered. The result is a combination of his broad ideas and my organization and additions, editing, and rewriting in what I hope brings together an effective analysis of the central themes.

I thank Chuck Rankin for his support, Thomas Krause for his early editorial work in improving and bringing this manuscript into print, and the other staff members at the University of Oklahoma Press, including Bethany Mowry, Emily J. Schuster, Amy Hernandez, and copy editor Kathy Lewis, for their help. David Webb of the Kansas Heritage Center and Jeanne Ode of the State Historical Society of South Dakota made illustrations available. Kate Bentham Britz has been interested and supportive in all phases of the process and has my deep gratitude. Portions of this work originally appeared in Kevin Britz, "'Boot Hill Burlesque': The Frontier Cemetery as Tourist Attraction in Tombstone, Arizona, and Dodge City, Kansas," *Journal of Arizona History* 44:3 (Autumn 2003): 211–42; Kevin Britz, "A True to Life Reproduction: The Origins of Tombstone's Helldorado Celebration," *Journal of Arizona History* 42:1 (Winter 2001): 369–408; and Kevin Britz, "Deadwood's Days of '76: The Wild West Show as Community Celebration," *South Dakota History* 40 (Spring 2010): 52–84, copyright © South Dakota State Historical Society. Thanks to Bruce Dinges of the Arizona State Historical Society and Nancy Koupal of the State Historical Society of South Dakota for their help with permissions. I hope that Kevin would have been satisfied, even happy, with the results.

Roger L. Nichols
Tucson, Arizona

Acknowledgments

I would like to thank Roger Nichols, Katherine Morrissey, Susan Crane, and Nancy Parezo for their sustained interest, thoughtful comments, and continual support throughout this project. Each advisor's insights, criticisms, and nuts-and-bolts advice provided welcome stimulation. A number of local archivists, librarians, and museum administrators provided valuable assistance. I am especially grateful to Noel Awry and Darleen Smith of the Kansas Heritage Center in Dodge City; Mary Kopco, the director of the Adams Museum in Deadwood; Art Austin, manager of the Tombstone Courthouse State Historic Park; and Mario Einaudi of the Arizona State Historical Society. My unending gratitude goes to Joann Cordis, the director of interlibrary loans at the Central Oregon Community College, whose willingness to locate any source anywhere was a crucial part of this project.

Kevin Britz

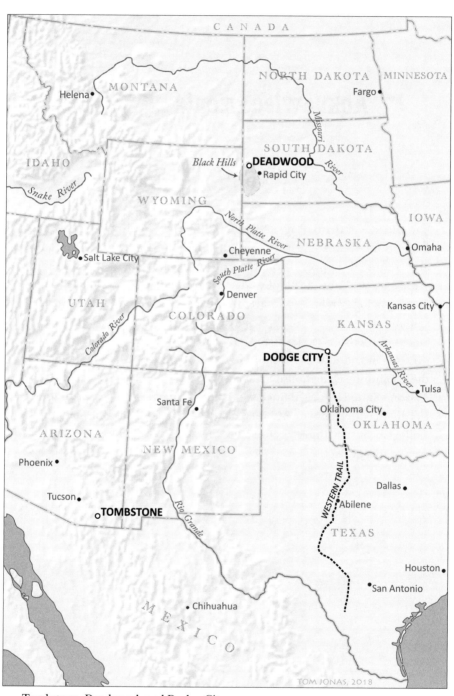

Tombstone, Deadwood, and Dodge City.
Map by Tom Jonas.

Tombstone, Deadwood, and Dodge City

☞ Introduction

Tombstone, Arizona, the "Town Too Tough to Die," attracted national attention in October 2015. One of its Vigilantes (reenactors who perform the gunfight at the OK Corral for tourists) shot another Vigilante using real ammunition during the performance. Instead of blank cartridges, his .45 caliber six-shooter carried all live rounds. When the smoke cleared, only one cartridge remained unfired. His wounded colleague was flown to Tucson for medical attention. Fortunately, the shooting only slightly injured one bystander. The Tombstone marshal's office began an immediate investigation and initially classified the incident as a possible aggravated assault with a deadly weapon. Mayor Dusty Escapule reacted with shock. Calling the shooting unprecedented, he assured the public that "Tombstone takes pride in the safety and security of its townspeople and tourists alike."[1]

Local officials suspended the Vigilante reenactments for three months while authorities conducted their investigation. On January 12, 2016, the town council enacted a new ordinance that required businesses to have permits before starting shooting reenactments, but it applied only to the free performances in the historic district. The four businesses performing daily gunfights on private property continued their shows without permits.[2] Five months after the shooting, apparently hoping to avoid hurting the booming tourist business, the Cochise County attorney's office announced that the shooting was accidental and that it would not file any criminal charges. Apparently that failed to comfort potential spectators, because one disgruntled businessman complained about the drop-off in tourism. He called for action and charged that "anyone who can't tell the difference between a blank and a live round recoil has no business ever having a gun in his hand again."[3]

Although shocking and unexpected, the incident reveals how seriously this small western town takes its historical image. Tombstone, like its Wild West counterparts Deadwood, South Dakota, and Dodge City, Kansas, has constructed a historical identity from a brief past era. The histories that these communities present to the public share a common thread. They all focus on their origins and violent boomtown eras. For Tombstone, the "Helldorado Days" celebration highlights the silver mining boom era of the early 1880s, when the Earp brothers and Doc Holliday defeated the McLaury brothers and the Clantons in their gunfight near the OK Corral. In its "Days of '76" event Deadwood celebrates stories about Wild Bill Hickok and Calamity Jane and the notoriety of the fictional Deadwood Dick from its gold rush era. And Dodge City holds an annual "Last Round-Up" that incorporates lawmen such as Wyatt Earp, Bat Masterson, and Luke Short. The event features fictional officers like Matt Dillon, who fought crime and violence on television, as a way to remember its early heritage.

This book compares and contrasts how and why these three communities, more than many of the other western American boomtowns, came to focus on their disorderly pasts. It demonstrates how the efforts of a few local leaders and national media-created images played off each other to produce the Wild West identities of the three towns. That, in turn, motivated the three towns to fuse fact and fiction about their places in western history to encourage tourism.

All three communities share a common pattern of historical development. Each had an early and brief boomtown era. For Deadwood it was the gold discovery of the mid-1870s. Tombstone enjoyed a silver mining rush just a couple of years later, while Dodge City welcomed the Texas cattle drivers at the same time. All three struggled with rapid growth, violence, and weak law enforcement. In a decade or less the boom period faded and each community faced economic hardship. Dodge City, with its larger population and broader economic base, suffered least, and Tombstone fared the worst. Shortly after the towns appeared, novelists, reporters for eastern newspapers, and magazines focused national attention on people who became famous for actions in each. By the early twentieth century millions of Americans thought of these communities as exciting places of violence and disorder. That image plagued the towns' boosters trying to attract new residents and business investments. To present their cities as modern, promoters tried to deny that picture or to present it as just

Longhorn statue on Front Street, Dodge City, Kansas, 2008.
Photo by Gerald B. Keane, courtesy Wikimedia Commons.

an early step in local development. Those efforts failed. Although each community had serious debates about its unsavory past, by World War I local leaders had decided to accept and use the mythology surrounding their towns to build a colorful tourist industry. This book examines how each of the three towns developed and used its historical image.

If you asked residents today what made these places special, many would refer to the past. Often they would proudly identify their communities as having been among the wildest spots on the American frontier, where law and order stood aside temporarily. Miners and cowboys expressed their rowdy passions in saloons and dance halls, settling their differences with fists or guns. While describing early life in their community, these same residents would caution listeners that each town had a civilized element that coexisted with its colorful outlaws and famous lawmen. Those people farmed, ran businesses, raised families, built schools, and went to church just like citizens elsewhere. According to this view, the transients moved on once the mining, cattle, or railroad booms ended, leaving the solid citizens to create the modern towns of today.

Although aware of that more nuanced image, boosters recognized that it was the turbulent era with its agents of disorder and unsettled and immoral setting that continues to attract tourists. At one time, the very thought of celebrating the disorderly frontier moments repelled leaders of all three communities. While trying to rebuild their societies after the earlier booms had collapsed, Progressive Era leaders wanted to craft new images that presented each place as morally upstanding, law-abiding, economically sound, and politically stable. By the early twentieth century town leaders and boosters had come to depend on modern practices and outlooks to attract the investors and new residents, whom they saw as critical. That effort forced business and social leaders to ignore or divert attention away from the earlier disorderly reputations that journalists and dime novelists had fastened on their towns, replacing them with an image of a stable, prosperous modern society.

Ultimately the emerging power of the mythology of the American West and the important roles that their towns had played in that saga defeated these efforts. The incorporation of Tombstone, Deadwood, and Dodge City into the evolving mythology of the American West resulted from a national obsession with frontier events dating back to the colonial era and the Puritans' Indian captivity narratives. Later American interest in the conquest of the wilderness focused on actual heroes like Daniel Boone, Davy Crockett, and Kit Carson as well as fictional characters like James Fenimore Cooper's Natty Bumppo. After the Civil War a new generation of authors writing for mass audiences crafted a different narrative. This one established vivid images of frontier towns as wilderness communities beset with rampant immorality: excessive drinking, prostitution, gambling, violence, and political corruption. Writers, Wild West show operators, and later Hollywood filmmakers and TV producers used those elements to create fictional lives of actual people or imaginary characters as heroes who brought justice and order to the West.

Literary historian T. K. Whipple considered the Old West to be America's defining myth and highlighted the impact of frontier events on the national imagination. "The story of the West," he wrote, "is our Trojan War, our Volsunga Saga, our Arthurian Cycle, or Song of Roland." In his view the central strength of the myth lay in the values of primitive individualism so essential to Americans: "physical vigor, physical courage, fortitude, sagacity, and quickness." By "remembering the West as an heroic age," he reasoned,

"Americans embodied and preserved . . . the values of a simpler world."[4] Encouraged by the power of this national myth, Tombstone, Deadwood, and Dodge City took on new meaning that went beyond the change from primitive to modern. They became part of the larger process of inventing and then marketing America's western frontier heritage. Studies by Richard Slotkin, Roderick Nash, David Wrobel, Edward Bruner, and Kara McCormack analyze these ideas effectively.[5]

Over time, community business, political, and social leaders embraced and even welcomed a past that they once detested, although its images ran counter to their own values of morality and community stability. Two factors fostered this shift. First, leaders in each place strove to develop local tourist attractions. Second, a flood of books, magazines, and newspaper accounts as well as later movie and TV shows also played a role in the change. Each dramatization of the Old West erased the stigma attached to that era and transformed the towns' national and self-images forever. Local governments, chambers of commerce, and other civic boosters now debated whether or how to use the earlier negative reputations that they had spurned. Once they accepted the images of a violent past, they moved to reinvent their historical reputations. Each place sought exciting commodities to attract and entertain tourists. As they redefined their self-images, town leaders developed annual celebrations and local sites to present this Old West heritage for their new customers.

Civic leaders in Tombstone, Deadwood, and Dodge City responded directly to a burgeoning number of tourists looking for aspects of the Old West that they had read about and seen in theaters or in Wild West shows. The visitors' expectations demanded that they see the traditional images that had evolved into standard descriptions of the Old West, including saloons, gunfights, lynching trees, horses, stagecoaches, false-front buildings, outlaw cemeteries, and occasionally Indians. To satisfy visitors looking for these expected elements, each town marked and advertised its Wild West sites, staged reenactment of events, preserved vintage buildings or replicated new versions of frontier structures, established museums, and even constructed ersatz graveyards. By the end of the twentieth century, led by Tombstone, each had become a living monument to Americans' perceptions of the Old West.

In recent years scholars have begun to analyze western historical celebration and reenactments as moves to generate tourism. Some of them tend to overlook the local decision-making processes. Others do not consider how the flood of outside ideas about the West persuaded town boosters to accept and use the early negative images of their communities (as this book does), with several exceptions. Bonnie Christensen's study *Red Lodge and the Mythic West* analyzes how that Montana community replaced its messy coal-mining past with a more "authentic" western image using cowboys and ranching. Michael Elliott's *Custerology* shows how the Battle of the Little Bighorn continues to attract reenactors and tourists, while creating a seemingly never-ending stream of books and articles about it. Kara McCormack's *Imaging Tombstone* focuses on that community's preservation story, while Robert R. Dykstra and Ann Manfra's *Dodge City and the Birth of the Wild West* examines that community. In another instance citizens in central and western Kansas tried to fit Francisco Vásquez de Coronado's sixteenth-century hunt for the legendary Quivira into their local historical celebrations to attract visitors.[6]

These examples demonstrate how town leaders used memories of real and fictional local characters and events to place their communities into a historical context to stimulate tourism. Certainly the commemorations in Deadwood, Dodge City, and Tombstone fit this pattern. In all three the local efforts grew out of pressing, even desperate economic circumstances. Each town developed its official memory as one response to its sagging commercial and business climate, hoping to harness tourism for survival. Both Deadwood and Tombstone faced ruin, so attracting visitors became crucial for survival. Dodge City, however, boasted a stronger business and economic base. It looked to the Wild West as just another opportunity too potentially lucrative to ignore. In each case the key to developing a successful tourist industry, promoters soon discovered, lay in meeting the expectations of travelers seeking an interesting and exciting portrait of the Old West.

The way in which local communities created notions of authenticity to meet this goal is essential for understanding the content and presentation of Old West celebrations. Literary critic Jenni Calder described the West as "a hub around which reality and legend spin in colourful confusion."[7] As a central element in the country's defining myth, the region had a continuing power to attract and hold audiences both in America and abroad. At the same time, purely fictional accounts undermined the myth's accuracy and diminished its status. Writers, publishers, showpeople, and Hollywood producers gradually all came to understand the need for some truth. They strove to make their products at least seem somewhat accurate, including using real figures and places. Leaders in these three communities clearly sought to benefit from the search for an exciting past.

Americans traveled to these three towns in the twentieth century, looking for remnants of the Old West. Their expectations, however, depended largely on images perhaps based on a grain of truth but more likely embellished and dramatized by outsiders. Town leaders responded quickly once they realized that visitors often came looking for fictional images. They created historical or fictional characters to match potential visitors' expectations—a necessity for successful tourism. They held parades, marked important sites, and built museums. Moving beyond those elements, they fabricated select past moments that they rationalized as being "true" to the spirit of the times. Their authenticity remains a topic of ongoing debate. In these three towns, just as on the national stage, impassioned arguments among historians, preservationists, and business or political leaders over the definition of the true West continue.

That question in turn raises a larger one about authenticity itself. It is beyond the scope of this study to describe how the concept developed, but we should recognize people's need to verify the truth of important cultural ideas. Walter Benjamin, an early twentieth century German philosopher, believed that authenticity rested on the authority of originality related to the history of the object or event. He called this the "aura" of an object and theorized that it faded or even disappeared if later reproduced or (in the case of the West) turned into fiction.[8] Tourism promoters in Tombstone, Deadwood, and Dodge City collected and exhibited artifacts in museums and celebrations to demonstrate their historic legitimacy. Early local museum curators and celebration organizers called these items "relics" and used them, just as Roman Catholics preserved the bones of saints, as tangible evidence to support the truth of their belief in the existence of the Wild West.

Today scholars debate how tourists perceive such offerings. Dean MacCannell and later Eric Cohen challenged Daniel Boorstin's contention that tourists could be gratified by what he called "pseudo-events." They both argued that travelers do indeed seek real experiences and in fact are able to perceive the degree of credibility of events and objects.[9] Sociologists Gianna Moscardo and Philip Pearce surveyed tourists at two fabricated Australian theme parks. Their data suggest that the degree of satisfaction depended on visitors' perception of reality and how what they saw met their expectations. Visitors who thought their experiences were genuine had the most satisfaction.[10] The implication of Moscardo and Pearce's contention that authenticity is a social construction has a direct bearing on this study. Much of the commemoration of the Old West in Tombstone, Deadwood, and Dodge City is based on perceptions and images generated by outsiders—earlier showpeople, authors, publishers, and Hollywood. However, operators of historical re-creations cannot afford to overlook tourists' expectations. For example, as Edward Bruner points out, in 1989 tourists found the lack of colored lights and decorated Christmas trees at New Salem, Illinois, so disappointing that the celebration was not held the next winter. The visitors had imposed their modern expectations for holiday decorations on the past.[11]

As this book shows, the evidence makes clear that local boosters realized during the 1920s that they had to use their towns' historical notoriety to develop local attractions that would lure visitors to the community. Promoters discovered that, unlike other industries, successful tourism depended on wide community involvement. To achieve that they persuaded citizens to help them create an official identity based on their Wild West past. In most instances newspaper editors led the effort, calling for public support by sponsoring beard-growing contests and offering prizes for authentic period dress. They ballyhooed the virtues of tourism, printed pictures of pioneer families, and published reminiscences by locals. Often hyperbolic and sometime sentimental, their efforts validated national images and rallied public support. This work reveals, however, that memorialization of the frontier moment did not come easily or without debate. At times promoters faced public apathy and even opposition from their own communities. In fact many people abhorred the picture of the West presented by the media and their city leaders and rejected it as unauthentic and a distortion of actual western settlement.

The commodification of Old West memories and related debates over authentication in the three towns involved a complex set of factors. Of the three towns, Deadwood and Tombstone had close parallels because of their similar size, shared history as mining boomtowns, and severe economic slumps when mining ended. By contrast Dodge City had a larger population: its boom period grew out of buffalo hunting and then serving as a railroad terminal for cattle drives. Because of these differing environments, actors, and varying levels of national attention, creating a tourist-driven memory evolved sporadically over decades in each community. During the process, public celebrations, museum displays, media attention, and preservation efforts all cross-fertilized the commemorations. This comparative study analyzes the similarities and differences among the three towns topically as each struggled to become an embodiment of the Old West.

While promoters tailored their historical presentations to new audiences, they all faced the same question: should they offer an accurate or exciting view of the past? Few could answer. Local groups' efforts to preserve the memory of the Old West called attention to the complex and fickle nature of historical authenticity. Each town sought to offer physical proof of its importance as a site of America's Western past. As various groups used museums and restored or replicated old buildings, it became apparent that behind the scenes they held vastly differing ideas about the need for accuracy. Conflicts between the contending interests underscored what had become obvious by the end of the twentieth century: authenticity was a metaphysical exercise, not a practical endeavor. The Old West clearly became a cultural, social, and economic construction, a virtual reality where the present folds over into the past. In Tombstone, Deadwood, and Dodge City the past is not a separate country but a place deeply intertwined with the present that can be visited and experienced, bought and sold.

This introduction ends with a final illustration showing how the commodification of the past ultimately failed to transform Tombstone. In 1993 a group of studio executives visited the town, hoping to use it as a location for a new version of the Wyatt Earp film *Tombstone*. After looking over the city, they decided that it was too modern and lacked the historical elements that they needed. Rather than shooting their film there, they moved to Mescal, a Western movie set east of Tucson. Although it was only a Hollywood-built replica, to them it offered a more realistic version of the past. Rather than being disappointed, many locals expressed relief. They felt that the studio officials had demanded too much when they called for city residents to hide their paved streets and curio stores. That would have disrupted their businesses during the filming. Despite their failure to persuade the filmmakers to use their town, the result pleased local promoters. They had the best of both worlds. Now they could avoid the disruptions of filming while benefiting from a new round of free publicity for their community

1 ✒ Exciting and Violent Towns

Many present-day Americans think about the Wild West as a place with action, danger, and excitement. Creating those images became a business over a century ago, as historian Ann Fabian points out. It had "an economics and history of its own."[1] Based on heroes and adventures, that effort began before the Civil War and expanded dramatically between 1865 and 1900 as millions of Americans moved west. It included the work of dime-novel publishers, popular magazines, newspapers, biographers, historians, and showmen such as William "Buffalo Bill" Cody. In the twentieth century, radio, motion pictures, and television added new images and excitement to the old stories. These businesses came to rely on each other as they replicated and overlapped standardized plots, characters, and images. Publishers and entertainers all understood the attraction of western stories for a national market. Blending fact and fiction skillfully, their portrayals brought the epic of conquering the frontier to their customers' imaginations. As the western industry gained sophistication, it created powerful literary and visual images of a "Wild West" that sold well across the country.

As businesspeople, producers of American literature and entertainment looked for subjects with wide appeal. From the earliest days of settlement, the frontier or Old West had offered reliable and profitable topics. In the mid-nineteenth century the California gold rush and the repeated mineral discoveries that followed lured hundreds of thousands of people west. Miners and those hoping to mine them moved repeatedly, establishing dozens of small, isolated communities. At the same time, railroads crisscrossed the land, attracting cattle drives and less exciting homesteaders. This spread of people created other towns, many of which survive as small quiet communities scattered across the West today. Unlike nearly all of those settlements, Tombstone, Deadwood, and Dodge City became modern tourist centers. They achieved this status for three interrelated reasons. First, the history of each included colorful, exciting, and violent events. Second, national writers and entertainers brought repeated attention to their real and imagined Wild West experiences. Third, each of these communities eventually chose to build tourist-based economies using the real and fictional stories and events that gave them national reputations.

Their rise to prominence grew from early western fiction. The cattle and mining towns of the 1870s gave dime novelists good settings for their stories and eastern reporters plenty of material for their columns. Often writers set their novels in isolated small settlements populated with seedy characters involved in gambling, prostitution, and random violence. Many western communities shared those features during their formative years because they attracted mostly mobile working-class young men. That group had generated conflict in communities across the country as early as the eighteenth century, which continued a hundred years later.[2] Gradually the local elites used town ordinances, questionable lawmen, vigilante action, and prohibition to remove the troublemakers and bring calm to their towns. Then they established schools, churches, and other elements of a stable society. Once that happened, the towns lost the colorful and dangerous people who had given them notoriety. Rather than being "wild and woolly" places they resembled dozens of other rural small communities across the country.

Fiction writers and journalists ignored or missed those social changes but kept their focus on the earlier situations even beyond the frontier era, giving readers the excitement that they had come to expect. For them Tombstone, Deadwood, and Dodge City had plenty of exciting stories and fascinating characters. With overblown prose featuring brave heroes and colorful plots, they helped create national reputations for each town. Although based on repeated tales of disorder and violence these perceptions had only a slight factual basis. Yet these ideas refused to die because, like all myths, they often contained at least some element of truth. Stories of these towns' actual newsmakers (Wild Bill Hickok, Calamity Jane, Wyatt Earp, Doc Holliday, and Bat Masterson) helped each of the three communities develop an appealing historical identity with a solid market value.

Changing public attitudes helped to shift the towns' identities from the edges to the center of popular fiction. Americans began to realize that their society had mostly overcome the wilderness. At that point one literary historian wrote that "the prairie had disappeared into farm land and few wild spaces remained even on the high plains. The West was now a farm. . . . You can't fool Americans about farm life—they know better."[3] So did the publishers. By the 1860s dime-novel plots were shifting their locations quickly. Authors moved their settings from earlier eastern frontiers to the turbulent new western towns with the color and excitement that readers wanted.

Tombstone, Deadwood, and Dodge City stood at the center of that change. While their individual histories differed, all three shared the same general pattern of early development. Each experienced boomtown conditions with violence and disorder brought by miners, hunters, or cowboys. They all had law enforcement officers or famous gunfighters in their streets. In each case those individuals caught the attention of writers and reporters who spread their fame. Eventually all three of the three communities used their violent past to develop a thriving tourist industry.

Deadwood gained fame before the other two towns because of rumors of gold discoveries in the Black Hills. National officials hoped to avoid a major war with the Sioux, who considered the Black Hills their sacred land. When tribal leaders threatened to kill any whites who went there, the army tried to prevent would-be miners from entering the region and to remove those who were already there.[4] However, George Armstrong Custer's 1874 expedition into the Black Hills confirmed prospectors' rumors of gold. The army could not halt the thousands of miners who rushed into the area. Despite this invasion, the Sioux refused to leave the Black Hills. By 1876 large numbers of them had joined camps led by Sitting Bull and Crazy Horse. That summer western army commanders received orders to force the Indians onto reservations. In the summer 1876 campaign that followed Lieutenant Colonel Custer led the Seventh Cavalry into a reckless attack on a Sioux and Cheyenne camp of several thousand people. At the resulting Battle of the Little Bighorn or Greasy Grass the warriors destroyed most of Custer's command.[5]

The disaster captured national attention and persuaded the government to force the Sioux bands out of the Black Hills and onto reservations. In August 1876 the federal government sent the Manypenny Commission west to negotiate. The comissioners were to extract an agreement from the Sioux that would give the Black Hills to the United States and legally

Deadwood in 1876.
Courtesy U.S. National Archives and Records Administration.

open the land for the miners. They ignored the earlier provisions of article 12 of the 1868 Fort Laramie Treaty requiring that "at least three-fourths of the adult male Indians" had to sign any further land cession. To get an agreement the negotiators threatened to withhold promised food rations unless the Lakota Sioux accepted the new boundaries. Although all of the Indian leaders opposed the cession and most spoke against it, they had little choice and signed the papers giving the Black Hills to the United States.[6]

News of Custer's defeat and the land cession attracted dozens of reporters into Deadwood to get the details. There they found a series of local mining districts scattered along the creeks running through small Black Hills valleys. By April 1876 the discovery of rich surface deposits of placer gold had attracted miners to Deadwood Gulch, reportedly clogged with downed timber that gave the camp its name. Merchants, teamsters, assayers, lawyers, saloonkeepers, gamblers, and prostitutes followed quickly. As people rushed in during April 1876, leaders organized and platted the town. By summer's end it boasted 173 businesses, including hotels, drugstores, general stores, a theater, a newspaper, temporary churches, and even two small schools. Residents built a Congregational church in November of that year and a Catholic church the next spring. At its peak, during the boom summer of 1876, Deadwood may have had as many as 10,000 residents.[7]

The boom faded after miners had taken all the profitable claims, almost as quickly as it had begun. By autumn 1876 the population had fallen to about 3,000 as miners drifted away to nearby strikes at Lead, Spearfish, Custer, Hill City, Belle Fourche, Sturgis, and elsewhere. Although violence occurred, including the murder of Wild Bill Hickok, local leaders quickly established a working government. It tried to deal with fire hazards from shoddy construction, a smallpox epidemic, and ongoing disorder. The leaders held an election, organized a provisional government, and reduced crime effectively.[8] They appear to have succeeded. Two years later, in 1878, Louis Janin, a visiting mining engineer, reported that the town was "by no means the rough mining camp that exists in the imagination of many. On the contrary, it is one of the pleasantest of all mining localities I have visited, and in no other district is justice more ably administered, or greater security afforded to life and property."[9]

The rush of miners lasted less than two years, as they exhausted the easily located surface ore. The underground or lode mining that followed required major investment and scientific engineering skills that few of the itinerant miners had. Most of them left, with little desire to work as underground laborers. The hardrock mining that followed required expensive stamp mills to crush the ore and reduce it for gold extraction. In 1878 Deadwood had 47 mills that produced $404,000 of gold each month.[10] These mills and the smelters that went with them helped the community to become a banking and supply center for the area. In 1890 the first railroad arrived. By then the town *Directory* listed 20 percent of the residents as business owners, 12 percent as business employees, and 18 percent with skilled trades or professions. Only 18 percent were listed as unskilled laborers. At the turn of the century, most of the population worked for businesses that served the local mining enterprises.[11] By then the mining boom had long ended.

Most journalists and writers who visited Deadwood during the early mining rush gave the town its violent reputation. Many sharply criticized it as a center of lawlessness and depravity. A visiting French author looking for book material commented on Deadwood: "like all towns of the frontier, this one has had a boisterous infancy. The rising tide of civilization, like the sea, has a foam of scum, and it is by this scum that it announces its arrival."[12] Some visiting American journalists had the same impression. Writing for *Scribner's Magazine*, Leander Richardson wrote: "I never in my life saw so many hardened and brutal-looking men together—Every alternate house was a gambling saloon and each of them was carrying on a brisk business."[13] James Butler Hickok, already made famous as a gunman by novelists, reached Deadwood in 1876. His murder there that same year gave the town a local western hero that it has used ever since.

A reporter for Wisconsin's *Manitowoc Pilot* observed that "every man in Deadwood carries about fourteen pounds of firearms hitched to his belt. The fellow that gets his gun out first is best man, and they lug off the other fellow's body." He guessed that "the average deaths amount to about one hundred men a month."[14] The town's reputation for violence persuaded a Cheyenne newspaper to suggest changing its name from Deadwood to Deadman.[15] News reports that filtered east reinforced this vicious image. A *New York Times* column entitled "Deadwood Described: A Disorderly, Sinful, Sickly City" concluded that "there is no such place anywhere" and criticized it as the worst example of the "fast and flash American trait." The author wrote that the town had "about 1,500 houses and huts, and hundreds of tents up the hill-sides." The column warned readers that Deadwood was a place "where the few prey on the many" and thousands live in poverty and crime. The reporter assumed that most of the business owners expected to leave town quickly, because they had the saloons and stores put up in sections "ready to be taken apart at a day's notice." Few real homes existed, and the families that he saw looked as if they were "waiting for the next train" out of town. "There is not much law or order in Deadwood," the reporter noted. "Courts have just been established, and the city is policed; but Police happen to be in league with the gamblers, who rule the town and so criminals are apt to go unwhipped by justice."[16]

Not all newspapers agreed. A correspondent for *Frank Leslie's Illustrated* labeled Deadwood fascinating. "The frailty of human nature," he observed, "is illustrated in the buildings which grace its sides. These are a curiosity in modern architecture, and their light construction is a standing insult to every wind that blows." He did agree with his *Times* counterpart that "a keen-eyed, money-grubbing set of men make up the population," but he argued that "they are far from the blood-thirsty scoundrels the average newspaper correspondent would make them out." Rather than seeing the dangerous and violent town portrayed by the *Times* reporter, the *Leslie's Illustrated* correspondent observed that "shooting is not frequent, fighting only occasional, and property is perfectly secure."[17]

This kinder and milder picture had little impact on other would-be writers. The idea of Deadwood as a violent, corrupt, and wide-open town made it attractive as a dime-novel setting. Shortly after the August 1877 *New York Times* piece appeared, Edward L. Wheeler placed his Deadwood Dick series in the boomtown. In *Deadwood Dick, the Prince of the Road* he built directly on the early negative reports. Describing the scene in August 1877, the narrative began: "The streets are swarming with constantly arriving newcomers; the stores and saloons are literally crammed at all hours; dance-houses and can-can dens exist—all along the gulch are strung a profusion of cabins, tents and shanties." The novel focused on the town's disorder: "Saloons, dance houses, and gambling dens keep open all night and stores do not close until a late hour. . . . Fighting, stabbing and hideous swearing are some of the features of the night; singing, drinking, and dancing and gambling are the others."[18]

Wheeler's *Deadwood Dick* became an overnight success and helped make the town a favored locale for other authors. The stories proved so profitable that in 1885 his publisher created a Deadwood Dick Jr. series to cash in on the character's popularity. Even while enjoying the strong sales of his Deadwood Dick stories, in 1879 Wheeler tried to capitalize on the town's popularity with a second hero based there. His new character appeared in *Rosebud Rob; or Nugget Ned* but lacked Deadwood Dick's attraction. After only after three novels the author dropped the series later that same year.[19]

Although Wheeler's stories continued to use the Wild West image, other reports gave a different picture. In an 1879 article entitled "No Idling at Deadwood" the *New York Times* noted that "times have quieted down a good deal" and that the "surplus population has pretty much all departed, . . . and while times are not very dull, yet there is not the buoyant feeling that existed two years ago." In place of the wide-open and dangerous scenes presented earlier, now the paper described a stable community. Idlers no

Copyright 1877-1884, by Beadle & Adams. Entered at Post Office, New York, N. Y., as second class matter. Mar. 15, 1899.

No. 1. | *Issued Weekly.* March 15, 1899. | M. J. IVERS & CO., Publishers, (James Sullivan, Proprietor,) 379 Pearl Street, New York. | *Price 5 Cents.* $2.50 *a Year.* | Vol. I.

DEADWOOD DICK,
THE PRINCE OF THE ROAD;
Or, The Black Rider of the Black Hills.

BY EDWARD L. WHEELER.

"Ha ha ha isn't that rich, now? Ha! ha! ha! arrest Deadwood Dick if you can!"

Cover of *Deadwood Dick, the Prince of the Road; or, The Black Rider of the Black Hills* by Edward L. Wheeler.
Courtesy Edward T. LeBlanc Collection, Rare Books and Special Collections, Northern Illinois University.

longer thronged the streets and "the keno men, tramps, and sharpers of all classes who infested Deadwood and the other camps two years ago have left for more promising fields of operation." The *Times* assured its readers that it "is as orderly as any Eastern city of its size, . . . the haunts of vice have been rooted out," replaced by "sociables, sing schools, and literary clubs." In fact, Deadwood had become a city with respectable citizens, "well-attended Congregational, Episcopal, and Catholic churches, and good schools."[20] Although this rosy view of the community may have been accurate, church-loving citizens did not sell newspapers or dime novels. Tales of gore and adventure were popular, so most writers continued to emphasize the wild and lawless events in Deadwood history well into the twentieth century.

Deadwood refocused its view of historical events in 1931 when Stuart Lake's *Wyatt Earp: Frontier Marshal* included a chapter on Earp's experiences there, linking it to Dodge City and Tombstone. While this was a timely connection, the Dakota community already had a long-established Wild West reputation because of the popularity of Deadwood Dick, Wild Bill Hickok, and Calamity Jane. The three remained a permanent part of the town's identity, and their stories gave it prestige as an Old West setting. Renewed attention to Hickok during the 1920s and 1930s brought the mining-boom era back into public view. That, in turn, encouraged a shift away from using local accounts to underscore progress to emphasizing pioneer-era disorder. The memoirs of townspeople echoed what popular literature said: the town's formative period became the foundation of its identity. Deadwood, like Tombstone and to a lesser degree Dodge City, became a monument to its past.

However, this took a while. At the beginning of the 1920s the editor of the *Deadwood Daily Pioneer-Times* continued to stress town progress and stability. He remarked that at some point the "real history of the Black Hills will be written." By that he meant an account that included founding the Women's Club and the Bar Association, starting the fire department, and building schools and churches. Still, he realized that market demands overshadowed this need for an accurate community history. "The reading public," he complained, "seems to demand the recital of the doings of the notables and the writers are supplying their wants." He hoped that "by and by, the public would be fed up on it, as are the old timers now are."[21] He was clearly swimming against the current: in 1923 Emerson Hough's best-selling novel *North of 36 and* William S. Hart's use of Deadwood as the setting for his film *Wild Bill Hickok* brought renewed attention to early violence in the community. What the editor failed to realize was that few people cared about the history of common institutions or events. Instead they wanted tales of the Old West and the exciting figures who had lived in Deadwood. To his disappointment, most writers of the 1920s and 1930s repeated stories about Wild Bill and Calamity Jane.

Before that happened both Tombstone and Dodge City gained fame and became the settings for violent western adventures of their own. As another mining town, Tombstone had its own rags-to-riches saga that resulted from almost instant wealth, the overnight flood of fortune hunters, and the usual disorder that followed each new mineral discovery. These events made it a prime setting for dime novels and lurid reporting. Its story began in 1878, just two years after Deadwood's founding, when Ed Schieffelin, a veteran of earlier western mining rushes, ventured into Apache-dominated southern Arizona. Ignoring friends' warnings that the only thing he would find in Apache country would be his tombstone, he proved them wrong. He avoided hostile Indians and discovered large silver deposits near the San Pedro River. Responding to the earlier predictions, Schieffelin named the find Tombstone. In August 1878 his brother Albert and Richard Gird, an assayer, joined him. With backing from territorial governor A. K. Safford the men returned to the site and incorporated their properties as the Tombstone Mill and Mining Companies. The next year, as Ed Schieffelin and Gird worked the mine, brother Al went east to sell company stock. He succeeded: in March 1880 Philadelphia investors bought the brother's interests for $600,000.[22]

News of the rich strike attracted hundreds of men, and in 1878 the Tombstone and Tucson Express began stagecoach service to the camp and the nearby Southern Pacific Railroad siding. Large-scale mining operations had developed by late 1879. Local citizens formed a town-site company, laid out its borders, and organized a government. By then the settlement had a population of about 6,000 people. At first most of its buildings reflected its overnight growth: many of the miners lived in adobe shacks, tents, or brush huts, because the nearest timber was in the Chiricahua and Huachuca mountains some miles away.[23] That changed within another year or two, as attractive hotels, expensive restaurants, and clothing stores opened. A bowling alley, tennis courts, and ice cream parlors quickly followed, although it took some time for the miners' tents and rude early dwellings to disappear.[24]

Tombstone's boom period echoed that of other mining towns. Unskilled workers poured in, and a wave of business owners hoping to make a profit from the miners followed. As the hub of regional mining, the town dominated banking and mercantile activities, serving the mineral industry as well as surrounding ranches and nearby military posts. It also paralleled Deadwood by suffering devastating fires during the early 1880s. Rebuilt quickly, the town soon boasted all the trappings of a modern community, with two newspapers, hotels, restaurants, four theaters, two bakeries, clothing and shoe stores, six Chinese laundries, five physicians, two dentists, eight attorneys, schools, and four churches.[25] The telegraph arrived in 1880, and four years later Tombstone had a waterworks and a fire department. An Arizona booster observed that "the streets are regular and the whole place laid out, and . . . there is an air of permanence and substantiality rarely noticed in new mining camps." Early estimates of the town population varied from 6,000 to 10,000.[26] Because of its rapid growth and distance from Tucson, which it depended on for county services, the territorial legislature created Cochise County in 1881, making Tombstone the county seat.

Much of the early civic disorder passed quickly but not without major violence and bloodshed. During the first several years a bitter feud pitted local ranchers, led by the Clanton and McLaury families and their outlaw allies Bill Brocius and John Ringo, against the four Earp brothers and Doc Holliday. For a time the town elite led by Mayor John Clum and mining magnate E. B. Gage supported the Earps and hired some of them as law officers. Matters came to a head on October 26, 1881, at the so-called gunfight at the OK Corral. When the smoke and dust cleared, two of the McLaury brothers and one of the Clantons lay dead and two Earps and Doc Holliday had been wounded. Some of the townspeople denounced the victors as murderers. Soon a wave of reprisals left Morgan Earp dead, Virgil Earp disabled, and the brothers under indictment for murder. They left town before legal action against them began.[27]

Like Deadwood's, Tombstone's economy soon depended on large-scale underground mining operations. This left almost no opportunities for individual prospectors or unskilled miners, so they left quickly. By 1883 workers in the three major mines all hit water. At first that seemed positive.

It allowed the companies to process the ore in town and also provided a reliable water supply. While the flooding blocked mining in the lower levels, two of the companies installed massive pumps to drain the water. Work resumed for several years. In May 1886 a fire destroyed one of the pumping facilities, then a few months later another fire hit another mining plant. Tombstone's boom era ended abruptly when the companies failed to agree on paying the costs of rebuilding and abandoned their mines. With no work, miners left, businesses closed, and the population dwindled, so that by 1900 only 646 people remained.[28] The town experienced a short-lived rebirth from 1901 through 1910, when a new group of investors consolidated all the larger mining operations and tried to pump the water out of the mines. When that effort failed, the town limped along, supported by small-scale mining, nearby ranches, and income from its role as the county seat.

Most descriptions of Tombstone during its mining heyday differed little from those of Deadwood. They depicted a whiskey-drenched town that never slept and swindlers and dangerous criminals preyed on the unwary. A *Chicago Tribune* correspondent's negative sketch written after a visit in the winter of 1879 described "the principal street lined with adobe buildings, large tents, and frame structures," noting that "nearly every other building is a saloon." The customers included "rough-looking men, miners and others with a sprinkling of red-nosed, bloated looking gentry." The gambling halls operated "in a stifling atmosphere of stove-heat, unwashed humanity, whiskey fumes, and a cloud of tobacco-smoke." The itinerant miners' actions appalled the reporter, who labeled those men "debauched and depraved." Moving from one camp to another, they are "the sticks, straws and scum born onward by the rising human tide."[29] Another visitor, shocked by the heavy drinking as men moved from one saloon to another, claimed that "every house is a saloon and every other house is a gambling hell."[30]

William Bishop, writing for *Harper's New Monthly*, actually counted sixteen saloons and gambling places on one of the major streets and stressed the absence of banks. He inferred that all the cash in town moved from hand to hand so quickly that nobody had time to save any. Bishop's account described the large numbers of firearms that the men carried, commenting that "whiskey and cold lead are named as the leading diseases of Tombstone." Later he contradicted himself, wondering how despite the constant drinking and "the universal practice of carrying deadly weapons . . . cold-lead disease should claim so few victims."[31]

These descriptions gave Tombstone all the elements needed to become a dime-novel setting. Paralleling Deadwood, the new camp attracted writers' attention soon after the early newspaper descriptions appeared. In 1879 Edward Willett's *The Gray Hunter; or, The White Spirit of the Apaches: A Tale of the Arizona Mountain Placers* presented a generalized Arizona backdrop taken from stories about Tombstone that had filtered eastward. The town itself first appeared as a central locale in 1881 when Edward L. Wheeler moved his Deadwood Dick south from the Black Hills to the Southwest in *Deadwood Dick's Dream; or, The Rivals of the Road: A Mining Tale of Tombstone.* The novel pictured the town as a "new Eldorado," where "as rough and uncouth a crowd of humans as Dick had met in many a day" filled both sides of the streets. Wheeler, who never saw either place or any of the West for that matter, described Tombstone in terms that fit Deadwood better. A small place only a few months old, it had "a couple score of log cabins scattered about on either side of the creek, a grocery store, [and a] milling establishment where quartz was crushed." The Eureka Saloon and a second saloon that also had a dance hall operated "full blast night and day."[32]

Tombstone never had any log cabins and was not located on a creek. Joseph Badger's *The Old Boy of Tombstone; or, Wagering a Life on a Card* (1883) gave a more accurate description. He wrote that the town got its name from a "jest by the bold explorers whose friends declared they were prospecting for a tombstone instead of a fortune," as they discovered silver in present Cochise County, Arizona. To spin a marketable tale, Badger quickly set the novel's tone. In Tombstone people had "cold meat for breakfast, dinner and supper, with an occasional free lunch of dead men sandwiched in between the regular courses by way of an appetizer, and to break the dull monotony."[33]

In *The Dashing Diamond Dick; or, The Tigers of Tombstone* (1898) W. B. Lawson repeated earlier stories of explosive growth, instant wealth, and seediness. His narrative focused on a "wild, breathless struggle from morning till night, in which the strong dominated the weak and the weak went under, and men went mad in their insane greed for gold." While mistaking Tombstone's silver deposits for gold, Lawson declared that violence was inevitable. "For men in this mad scramble after fortune forgot the meanings of the ages, and descended to primeval savagery, stalking about with weapons openly displayed and ever ready to fight at the slightest provocation—real or fancied."[34] Other writers also used Tombstone as a setting. While most of their tales lacked the descriptive detail of either Wheeler or Badger's stories, all depicted Tombstone as a town full of dangerous characters where violent death occurred frequently. Despite this focus on violence, however, early writers ignored the OK Corral incident until the twentieth century.

Of the three communities, Dodge City received the least attention from dime novelists. Certainly it had many of the same elements (disorder, saloons, gambling, and hurriedly slapped-together buildings), but it lacked the dramatic rush that the mining towns experienced. Located in western Kansas, Dodge City got its start before the other two towns as a shipping terminal for the harvesting of buffalo hides and later as a terminus for the Texas cattle drives. Neither of those offered the allure of instant wealth of the gold and silver strikes that had brought thousands of miners to Deadwood and Tombstone. Located on the Santa Fe Trail, Dodge City became a logical place to locate U.S. soldiers in order to protect wagon trains headed west. In 1865 the army established Fort Dodge, which attracted army suppliers and buffalo hunters during the early 1870s. Town-site developers, including army officers from the fort, contractors, local merchants, and Atchison, Topeka, and Santa Fe Railroad officials, formed the Dodge City Town Company early in 1872. As in the other two communities local leaders platted what became the new town of Dodge City in July of that year.[35]

Railroad access boosted the market for buffalo hides, offering easy transport to the East. A leading Dodge City merchant reported that the railroads had carried 200,000 hides to eastern markets between 1872 and 1873. The hide boom attracted both hunters and merchants. Local businessman Robert Wright later compared Dodge to early days in the mining camps that he had visited. Yet his account stressed opportunity rather than violence. He wrote that "I never saw any town to equal Dodge," where a man could earn one hundred dollars a day. That attracted an army of buffalo hunters who killed nearly all of the animals in just a few years, ending the hide boom quickly. Facing town collapse and desperate for new opportunities, Dodge City merchants and business owners turned to the Texas cattle trade as a replacement.[36]

Their hopes fit directly into Atchison, Topeka, and Santa Fe Railroad plans. By then the farming population near the railroad's terminal at Wichita had grown, and impending quarantines on Texas longhorns to prevent the spread of disease to local cattle herds became inevitable. As a result railroad planners selected Dodge as their new western shipping center. The town became the terminus in 1876, and cattle from Texas began arriving. The next year the city shipped 22,940 animals east, leaving competing towns far behind. For another decade the city prospered from the stock trade, government freighting, and the buffalo bone trade. In July 1884 the railroad shipped 239,324 cattle from Dodge. Two years later the town's population had grown to 2,656.[37]

The cattle drives brought the cowboys who drove the animals north from Texas to the railroad each summer. Once they delivered the herds to town, the cowboys got their wages and spent much of the cash in local stores. This "transient market" provided food, clothing, barbering, boots, and entertainment. The predominant male markets such as saloons, gambling dens, dance halls, and houses of prostitution vied to empty the visitors' pockets and quickly became central in the town economy. The cowboys' free spending, heavy drinking, gambling, and fighting proved an unwelcome result, and often town fathers hired seasoned gunmen to keep order. Within a few years the invasion of Texas cowboys had ended. When more farmers moved into the area, they established their own cattle herds. Worried that the trail animals would infect their animals with Texas Fever, they joined townsfolk who opposed the cowboys' disorderly actions. Together they lobbied the legislature for a quarantine of the Texas animals. By the late 1880s the trail herds had shifted farther west and north. The boom and its related violence had ended.[38]

Writers exaggerated the period of open disorder in Dodge City as they had for both the other towns. According to the most extensive study of Kansas cowtown violence, Dodge had fifteen gun-related murders between 1876 and 1885, which averaged no more than Abilene, Ellsworth, Wichita, or Caldwell.[39] Most of the shooting victims did not die in gunfights: many of them were unarmed. In reality Dodge City showed little tolerance for civil disorder and took strong measures to limit it. In 1874 the city government passed a strict gun-control ordinance that prohibited everyone but law officers from carrying or discharging firearms within the city limits. Tombstone had similar regulations. A police force of as many as five officers, including Wyatt Earp and Bat Masterson, enforced these local controls. In Dodge City the business community suppressed violence while it welcomed and profited from the disorderly cattle trade.[40]

Despite that effort the town, like both Deadwood and Tombstone, got a far different reputation. As the community boomed, journalists focused their remarks on its transient market. Several writers even referred to it as the "Deadwood of Kansas." In 1877 one chronicler compared it to "other frontier towns" with "fast men and fast women" by the "score, seeking whom they may devour, hunting for a soft snap, taking him in for cash, and many is the Texas cowboy who can testify as to their ability to follow up successfully the calling they have embraced in the quest of money."[41] Others echoed this criticism. One labeled the town the "wickedest city in America" and "a hell on the great plains."[42] The *Washington Evening Star* echoed that sentiment, telling its eastern readers that "Dodge City is a wicked little town . . . marked for special providential punishment." Much of its disorder came from the Texas cowboys, who "loiter and dissipate, sometimes for months, and share the boughten dalliances of fallen women."[43]

Another writer made no biblical references but noted that the number of saloons in the town outnumbered other businesses by three to one. Their customers filled the night with "clamorous profanity and ribald songs and laughter."[44] A *New York Times* reporter described the streets as "thronged with swaggering, swearing cowboys, and oily confidence men." If any of his fellow travelers wanted to see the night life, "all the billiard halls, concert saloons, and keno dens" remained open for them. He remarked that the community had an air of transience because "pretty much all the buildings, which are of frame, lurch to the west as if impatient to move on, the effect of high prairie winds."[45]

Virtually all of the visiting writers labeled the all-night transitory towns as natural settings for violence and anarchy. In 1883 reports that violence in Dodge City had led to mob rule repeated an earlier similar charge about Deadwood. On May 10 the *New York Times* front page announced: "A City in the Hands of a Mob." It described Dodge City as being "one of the few points in Kansas where the saloons are run openly and gambling is legitimate." The report described a feud between those trying to shut down the saloons and gambling halls and those who operated or supported them.[46]

On May 11, 1883, New Yorkers learned that the "lawless element in Dodge City, Kansas became so obnoxious that the authorities have determined to drive them out." The town council rounded up the "gamblers and prostitutes" and put a "number of these persons on a train" headed out of town. At the same time the reporter assured his readers that no bloodshed had occurred and that the "affair amounts to nothing more than a determination on the part of law-abiding citizens to establish order."[47] A month later the *Times* denounced the community members who complained that suppressing gambling had hurt other businesses too. Soon the paper gave more details about the Dodge City War. This dispute over the forced closure of the Long Branch Saloon and other "sinful" businesses ended when the heavily armed "Dodge City Peace Commission," including "ex-sheriffs" Bat Masterson, Wyatt Earp, and Charles Bassett, reached a "compromise" with town leaders, who allowed them to reopen the gambling halls and saloons. These events prompted the reporter to contrast western immaturity with eastern sensibilities.[48]

The annual cattle drives and the cowboys' unruly actions made Dodge City a good locale for novelists. The town provided the setting in 1877 when Edward Wheeler introduced *Wildcat Bob*'s adventures with buffalo, bandits, and gamblers. It got more notoriety when Prentiss Ingraham reintroduced Wild Bill Hickok to the Kansas plains four years in his *Wild Bill, the Pistol Dead Shot; or, Dagger Don's Double.* Dodge City became the primary setting in A. K. Simms's novel *The Dandy of Dodge; or, Rustling for Millions* (1888). By the time this book appeared the author admitted that the town's violent era was over: "I write of the days when Dodge City was the great cattle town of the West," but "those days are past." That admission caused him to shift the focus to the Bedrock Bower, the town's leading all-night saloon and gambling spot. At that point he made Dodge the backdrop as a rough, no-nonsense town with plenty of saloons but also with a growing number of citizens working to build a stable successful community.[49]

Dodge City gained renewed notoriety in 1929 when William MacLeod Raine published his book *Famous Sheriffs and Western Outlaws*. This included articles that he had written earlier for *Liberty Magazine*, including "Hell Roaring Dodge." Unlike his portrayal of Tombstone as serene, his Dodge City was "a wild and uncurried prairie wolf, and it howled every night and all night long. . . . One might justly use many adjectives about it, but the word respectable is not among them."[50] Within this hell-roaring setting, Raine highlighted the careers of sheriffs Bill Tilghman and Bat Masterson and the string of outlaws who passed through the city. A year later he and co-author Will Barnes published *Cattle*, in which Dodge City played a major part as the end of the line for the trail drives. Both of these books

Interior of the Long Branch Saloon in Dodge City, Kansas.
Photographer unknown, courtesy Wikimedia Commons.

kept the unwanted Wild West image alive; but unlike either Deadwood or Tombstone, the town still lacked a major Old West hero who might attract national attention.

Stuart Lake's *Wyatt Earp: Frontier Marshal* (1931) changed that dramatically. It replaced Bat Masterson with Wyatt Earp as the town's central figure and by doing so forged a permanent link between Dodge City and Tombstone. *Wyatt Earp* became an overnight bestseller. Almost a third of the narrative took place in Dodge City, which the author described in dime-novel Old West terms. "Gamblers, gunmen, thieves and thugs gathered from the corners of the earth and with them the hardier of the scarlet sisterhood. . . . By the time Wyatt Earp reached the camp, some seventy or eighty argumentative visitors had been buried with their footgear in place—Dodge had lost accurate count."[51] After the lawman tamed Dodge City with the help of his brothers and friends, Doc Holliday and Bat Masterson, he traveled to Tombstone, the "howling wonder of the Western world," to establish order there as deputy marshal. Literary historian C. L. Sonnichsen credited Lake with having played the most important role in making the Earp legend because he described him as a folk hero, presenting him to the movies and television as an "embodiment of our dream of the frontier."[52] By focusing on the sensational events in the three boomtowns, early writers created powerful visual images that helped their readers define the frontier and Old West. To gain a wide popular reputation, towns needed random violence and disorder. Usually this came from the actions of the large numbers of underemployed transient underclass men and women living in them. Many of the plots depicted actual places and included both real and fictional characters. Certainly newspapers and magazines seemed to add some authenticity to dime-novel narratives by including living people, but the dime novels shaped popular ideas about life in the West. Beginning in 1860, the publishers printed at least 101 series with as many as a thousand titles in each. The first printing of every novel included 60,000–70,000 copies. Many appeared in ten to twelve printings in a single year. There was almost no escape from this flood of junk fiction, which continued to shape American ideas about the West for generations.[53] For example, just before the outbreak of World War I a tourist from St. Paul recalled his trip to Deadwood after reading everything that he could find about "Deadwood Dick and other notable characters in the vicinity." While he was eager "to mix in the turmoil and trouble" that he expected, finding a corpse hanging from a flagpole near the city hall came as a distinct shock. To his relief he learned that it was only a straw dummy of a local politician hung in effigy by his opponents.[54]

When Frederick Niven, an English writer and avid dime-novel reader, came west to visit the region he remembered that the first mining camps he saw "kept reminding me, in the most insistent way, of the covers of those cherished booklets." He even considered buying a lot in Deadwood, the home of his hero Deadwood Dick.[55] As late as 1941 Percy Waxman, a *Cosmopolitan* editor from England, recalled in that the western novels had given him "an intense desire to visit the United States and meet as many" Americans as possible.[56] The adventure stories actually persuaded some readers to move west rather than just visit. In his book *Hard Knocks* (1915) Harry Young wrote that the dime novels had filled his head with "'hair raising' stories of Indians, hunters, trappers, and other denizens of the Wild West" and that he decided to go there and "assist in the extermination of the Noble Red Man."[57] The flood of books and articles set in the West stirred so much curiosity about the region that by 1883 travel guides such as *The Pacific Tourist* listed both Deadwood and Tombstone as places to visit.[58]

Although the colorful images remained attached permanently to the three towns, they applied to many other boomtowns across the West too. The histories of places like Miles City, Butte, Prescott, Jerome, Wickenberg, Wichita, Hays City, Bisbee, Silver City, Virginia City, Coeur d'Alene, Helena, Cripple Creek, Leadville, and Aurora all shared at least some boomtown experiences. A few of them even appeared in dime novels, but most of them depended on easily forgotten fictional characters, not the actual heroes who walked the streets of Deadwood, Dodge City, and Tombstone. The reputations of those towns, based largely on erroneous news stories and cheap fiction, remained alive because they included a grain of truth and gave a natural setting for the real western figures associated with them.[59]

Accounts of wild, colorful towns with real heroes sold dime novels, magazine articles, and newspapers to mass audiences. Across the country these accounts presented a moment frozen in time—an unwashed world of vice, sin, violence, and corruption. Following their relatively brief periods of disorder, all three communities moved beyond that moment as they tried to build stable political, economic, and social infrastructures. Having done that, they sought to attract new residents and outside investment. At that point having national reputations based on lower-class sordidness, violence, and crime was the last thing they wanted. To them, the Wild West and people who symbolized its glory held only negative memories, best forgotten.

2 ✍ Creating Wild West Heroes

A mericans' fascination with stories of the Wild West rested on two things. Small western towns became the stage and people who walked their streets the characters in highly publicized violent events. Most of the actors came from the ranks of criminals, lawmen, soldiers, Indians, cattlemen, or town leaders. Only a few women gained a place among them. While many exciting events filled the pages of western history, only relatively few individuals became known as "heroes" nationally. This chapter analyzes four interrelated questions about prominent western figures: Who became famous? What did they do to get that status? What roles did the national media and entertainment industries play in publicizing their actions? How did these "heroes'" notoriety help each town create its public reputation?

In all three places the historical events that received the most national attention related to persons involved in law enforcement or public violence. Even when they were not the most important people in each community's history, their actions brought national media attention to incidents that later helped these towns to develop their western identity. Use of frontier tales of violence and adventure began during the earliest days of settlement. As far back as the seventeenth century, narratives of the Puritans' wartime experiences and surviving Indian captivity became the first American popular literature. A hundred years later a new type of hero emerged: the buckskin-clad pioneer who lived on the frontier between the Indians and civilization. In 1784 John Filson introduced Daniel Boone to his readers as a living example of the wilderness adventurer. A good story bears repeating, and in 1813 Daniel Bryant published *The Adventures of Daniel Boone*. Twenty years later Timothy Flint offered a biography of the pioneer. During the 1820s and 1830s these stories translated easily into James Fenimore Cooper's widely popular fictional Leatherstocking Tales.[1]

Those successes inspired a flood of pioneer-style western fiction during the next thirty years.[2] Later writers who used Cooper's frontier settings transformed his Indian allies into savage killers. They increased the bloodshed and set the pattern for a new wave of violent adventure stories. Robert M. Bird's *Nick of the Woods* is the most graphic example. His hero had little in common with Cooper's noble scouts. This frontiersman, appropriately named Nathan Slaughter, bounded through the forests killing Indians at nearly every step. To justify these barbaric acts Bird depicted his Native American victims as depraved savages who deserved to be killed by the hero. In 1846 Charles W. Webber followed Bird's pattern in his *Jack Long; or, Shot in the Eye* and subsequent novels. His heroes' exploits filled the pages with adventures and gore as they repeatedly killed Indians.[3] While other authors wrote adventure stories during these decades, Bird and Webber's novels set the stage for the flood of dime novels that followed after mid-century.

Some authors recognized the market for quasi-reality and put their fictional characters in real places or used real people in fictitious places. The crossover from nonfiction to fiction fit best when using an actual person. Some of Daniel Boone's successors, including Davy Crockett and Kit Carson, fit this mold. Crockett, a true self-promoter, vaulted to fame as a frontier hero with his 1834 autobiography, *Narrative of the Life of David Crockett*. Martyrdom at the Alamo sealed his reputation. Carson gained public attention a decade later through Jesse Benton Frémont's rewriting of her husband's exploration journals. *The Life and Adventures of Kit Carson* by DeWitt C. Peters soon followed. Looking for a large market, Peters added so much color and excitement that Carson reputedly commented that he had "laid it on a leedle too thick."[4]

For writers during the 1840s and 1850s the growing number of literate adults—over 90 percent in the northern states—offered a vast potential market. Crockett's and Carson's adventures appealed to this public market and brought large profits. By then the gradual introduction of the steam rotary press had begun to cut book production costs dramatically. Entrepreneurs offered popular stories to the ever-growing literate population. Wilson and Company of Boston became one of the first to use the new technology in 1839 when it issued a weekly serial in newspaper format.

In the next decade popular novelettes priced at only fifteen to twenty cents appeared. Aspiring writers hurried to submit texts for the weekly serials, and by the 1850s publishers had developed standard plot formulas reflecting popular demands for stories of America's recent past.[5]

A decade later the new dime novels transformed the publishing business. These cheap, action-packed stories appealed directly to readers of all ages. Claiming to blend fact and fiction, they gained wide popularity in 1860 after the New York City firm Beadle and Company published Ann S. Stephens's *Malaeska, the Indian Wife of the White Hunter.* An immediate success, it sold 65,000 copies in just a few months.[6] That encouraged the publishers to issue *Seth Jones; or, The Captives of the Frontier,* by twenty-year old Edward Ellis. It appeared later in 1860 after a broad advertising campaign and enjoyed almost overnight sales of 60,000 copies. Eventually the public bought 600,000 copies of the book, as Ellis became one of the most successful dime-novel authors.[7]

Recognizing the public enthusiasm for Ellis's cheap fiction, Beadle and Adams rushed other novels into print. They varied widely and included sea, detective, adventure, and frontier narratives. The publishers judged the potential market correctly and sold nearly 5 million dime novels between 1860 and 1865. That rapid success attracted five major rivals, all based in New York City. Each of them targeted the large numbers of working-class readers, and by 1890 at least fourteen publishers were issuing dime novels.[8] Over the years the increasing competition for sales led the businesses to change their format and content. Soon nearly all of these short books had eye-catching illustrations and crude visual images that included scenes of action and violence. Gunfights, lynchings, horse chases, and enraged heroes all became frequent book-cover sights. Seen and read by millions of readers, the drawings and plots created and responded to public expectations.[9]

Despite their need to find new heroes for marketing reasons, publishers kept some of their stories slightly anchored in fact. Their sales suggested that readers responded to stories set in historic locations, and many novels accurately depicted settings from Kentucky to Texas and Oregon. At the same time, authors appealed to nationalistic feelings, by fusing their narratives with events such as the American Revolution, Indian conflicts, mineral rushes, railroad building, and cattle drives. "If on the one hand they were a trifle hectic," one writer observed, "they were on the whole splendidly calculated to promote interest in authentic facts and personages connected with United States history."[10]

Having real people as characters often helped sell dime novels too. The rival publishers knew that stories about famous Americans sold well. With their marketability proven decades earlier, Daniel Boone, Davy Crockett, and Kit Carson now reemerged as heroes. Yet by the late 1860s the urgent need to find new subjects, fresh settings, and exciting events prompted writers and publishers to look at the newly opened plains and beyond. Soon they were using real-life figures such as Wild Bill Hickok, Calamity Jane, and Buffalo Bill Cody. In this process the writers helped create and popularize the reputations of these people. As no biographies of them existed, the novelists had nearly total freedom to invent adventures for their subjects.

Yet it took more than authentic heroes to sell stories; lurid imagery helped too. The dime-novel prose appealed to the fantasies of a broad public much as twentieth-century comic books, radio soap operas, movies, and television did later. Writers offered their readers color, excitement, and adventure along with stock characters, predictable plots, and fast action. In many of the early stories the wilderness and Indians represented danger. The author of *The Red Warrior* had the heroine tied to a stake while "faggots were heaped about" her feet. At that point, "with a blazing torch in his hand the chief] approached from the circle of yelling demons that surrounded her." As he set the brush afire, rescuers dashed into the village to save the girl.[11] Although most authors never gave their characters more than two dimensions, enemies had to look dangerous. In another story the villain Single Hand is described as "a man of gigantic mold, with a face cut like a Roman cameo, a nose hooked like the beak of a vulture and with black eyes full of savage fire."[12]

With hundreds of stories written in this lurid style, the West became central in much popular fiction after the Civil War. Almost from the start journalists writing for major newspapers and national magazines like *Scribner's* or *Harper's New Monthly Magazine* recognized that they were competing with dime novelists for good copy.

Early in 1867 George Ward Nichols, a writer for *Harper's*, traveled to Springfield, Missouri, where he found a perfect subject, James Butler Hickok, later known as "Wild Bill." This former Union Army soldier and scout had become known as a feared gunfighter after leaving the military.

Tall, with a slender physique, long hair, buckskin clothes, and a demonstrated skill with pistols, Hickok had all the elements that the writer needed to make him a western hero.[13] After their interview Nichols wrote an almost totally fictional account of how the gunman killed ten men while they tried to kill him. Hickok reportedly told him that after shooting seven of the attackers "I got hold of a knife . . . and I was wild, and struck savage blows . . . striking and slashing until I knew that everyone was dead."[14]

Nichols's wildly exaggerated account, "Wild Bill," appeared in the February 1867 issue of *Harper's New Monthly Magazine* and propelled Hickok to national fame. It also encouraged other writers on the subject. Two months later Henry M. Stanley wrote an article about Hickok for the *St. Louis Democrat*. The author focused on the scout's gunfighting skills and claimed that Hickok had killed "considerably over a hundred men," each of them "with good cause."[15] Stanley's exaggerated version of Hickok attracted dime novelists, and that same year *Wild Bill the Indian Slayer* and then *Wild Bill's First Trail* appeared. Although Hickok was known to have fought repeatedly without his pistols, those incidents got little attention because, as one biographer said, "that sort of fighting detracts from his reputation as a mankiller."[16]

These lurid descriptions of the gunman drew mixed reviews. Nichols's colorful prose brought heated responses when local newspaper editors complained that the exaggerated stories whitewashed Hickok and maligned their towns. A reporter for the *Atchison (Kansas) Champion* protested that the author's description of Hickok made him unrecognizable. Rather than being a hero, the reporter said, Hickok "was simply a desperado." Later the paper conceded the accuracy of the description of the gunfighter's appearance but repeated its charge that he bore no resemblance to the man in the article. Other papers agreed. Worry that Hickok's portrait as an heroic gunfighter made the Missouri town look bad led a reporter for the *Springfield Patriot* to criticize Nichols's article heatedly. He wrote that it had slandered the "city and citizens so outrageously by its caricatures, that it will deter some from immigrating here, who believe its representations of our people."[17]

The new hero soon attracted the interest of Edward Judson (Ned Buntline), a sensationalist writer also looking for new material. He hoped to depict Wild Bill as an Indian fighter but changed focus after meeting the charismatic and talkative former scout William "Buffalo Bill" Cody.

James Butler "Wild Bill" Hickok.
Courtesy Wikimedia Commons.

He chose Cody as his hero but also included Hickok as a minor figure. Buntline's December 1869 *New York Weekly* series, "Buffalo Bill, the King of the Border Men," published in England as well, reached wide audiences.[18] In the original story he killed off Wild Bill, but Hickok's popularity caused publishers to resurrect the character, who appeared in other Wild Bill novels for the next two decades. In the world of dime novels, where fiction and reality seemed to blur, all things were possible.

Hoping that people who loved to read about real heroes might also pay to see them in person, Hickok and Cody went east. In 1870 Hickok tried to capitalize on his own fame. He staged a buffalo hunt in Niagara Falls, New York, but lost money when it failed.[19] Buntline wrote a play based on his earlier series entitled *Scouts of the Plains* that same year and persuaded Cody to perform with him in Chicago. Two years later Cody joined Buntline in a New York City production, *Buffalo Bill, King of the Border Men*. Cody, in turn, persuaded Wild Bill to play himself on the stage. Although easterners seemed pleased to have a genuine frontier figure in their midst, Hickok's celebrity embarrassed some westerners because of his poor image. One reporter wrote that "Wild Bill's star has been ascending and now the credulous New Englanders have an opportunity to interview in person the man who has shot down in cold blood [men] by the scores and is as big a criminal as walks the earth. . . . Bill is making money showing himself, so they say."[20] Together Hickok and Cody entertained eastern audiences off and on for two years with mostly poor drama and bad acting. Their manager Hiram Robbins recalled that Hickok got mostly secondary roles because he "had a voice like a girl."[21] Even if true, that did nothing to weaken his image as a brawler and gunfighter. Hickok's modest acting continued until his habit of "firing blank cartridges" at the legs of fellow performers, "often burning them severely," ended it.[22]

Leaving the theater, Hickok drifted west into Deadwood, then a rough new mining camp. It was just one of many isolated frontier towns until Hickok's August 12, 1876, murder there. On that Wednesday afternoon Jack McCall shot him in the back of the head while he played cards in Saloon Number 10. According to the local stories, the assassin rushed out the door as the dying Hickok slumped in his chair. McCall tried to escape, but his poorly tied saddle slid under the horse. He fled on foot to a nearby butcher shop, where the bystanders captured him. A miners' court tried the shooter but surprisingly acquitted him when he claimed that he shot Hickok in revenge because the gunman had killed his brother earlier in Kansas. McCall left Deadwood soon after the trial, but in March 1877 the federal court in Yankton, South Dakota, ruled that the Deadwood miners had no legal jurisdiction to decide the case. Yankton authorities then arrested, tried, convicted, and hanged McCall. After the shooting the Deadwood citizens interred Hickok's body in the local Inglewood cemetery. The day of the funeral all of the town's business, saloons, and dance halls closed out of respect, in the words of one participant, for "the greatest character of his day."[23] In 1879 authorities moved Hickok's grave to Deadwood's newly opened Mount Moriah Cemetery.

Hickok's murder did little to end dime novelists' interest in him. Prentiss Ingraham, best known as Buffalo Bill Cody's biographer, began to publicize Hickok by including him in some of the Buffalo Bill stories. In 1882 he began a new Wild Bill series with *Wild Bill, the Pistol Dead Shot*. Rival Street and Smith's Campfire Library and the Nugget Library retold some more of Hickok's adventures later. In 1891 Ingraham published the first in what became a long list of historical biographies entitled *Wild Bill, the Pistol Prince*. A writer later described the book as an attempt to create a believable character by the liberal "interspersion of fact with fiction." Hickok's exploits also continued to live on the stage. Actor Julian Kent

"Wild Bill's Monument." John C. H. Grabill, photographer.
Courtesy Library of Congress Prints and Photographs Division, #LC-DIG-ppmsc-02687.

portrayed him in an 1881 play called *Wild Bill, King of the Border Men.*[24] It substituted "Wild Bill" for "Buffalo Bill" in the title of the play that the two men had co-starred in nearly a decade earlier.

Unlike either Dodge City or Tombstone later, in addition to Hickok, Deadwood had an entirely fictional dime-novel hero, Deadwood Dick. He first appeared as a dashing fighter for justice in Edward Wheeler's novel *Deadwood Dick, the Prince of the Road; or, The Black Rider of the Black Hills.* The series proved so popular that it ran until 1885 and then as *Deadwood Dick Jr.* for another dozen years. Deadwood Dick first appeared in the Black Hills town, but his adventures soon took him across the West. While Dick was purely the product of Wheeler's imagination, readers had little reason to doubt his existence because so many dime novels used the names of actual people. Edward Senn, publisher of the *Black Hills Times* and an avid reader of Deadwood Dick adventures, remembered being disappointed when he arrived in town and learned from old pioneers that the "first they ever heard of him was when the novels, published in the east, filtered back to Deadwood."[25] After repeatedly being asked about Deadwood Dick by tourists, John McClintock, one of the town's longest residents, answered gruffly in his memoir: "There was no such character."[26]

Often stories about Wild Bill Hickok and Deadwood Dick became intertwined with the community's other real-life celebrity, Martha Canary: Calamity Jane. She had become a renowned dime-novel heroine and Wild West icon by the time she was twenty-one years old. The only woman to gain that stature (except for Annie Oakley, who became famous by performing in Buffalo Bill's shows), Calamity Jane did so primarily because she often dressed like a man and took jobs usually seen as masculine at the time. In many ways her story as a frontier character paralleled that of Hickok. Both of them appeared as fictional characters in dime novels that made them national celebrities during their lifetimes. Calamity Jane's experience differed significantly from his, however, in that she lived far longer and her real life markedly contradicted her fictional one. Unlike Hickok, she could not separate herself from her fictional reputation. As her life faded, she tried to become a sympathetic figure, far removed from her real story.[27]

In 1877 Edward Wheeler introduced the fictional Calamity Jane to American readers as the female counterpart of Deadwood Dick in the first of his novels with that name. After that she appeared in the series regularly and as the central figure in the author's 1878 *Deadwood Dick on*

Martha Canary (Calamity
Jane), ca. 1895.
*Courtesy Library of Congress
Prints and Photographs
Division, #LC-USZ62–50004.*

Deck; or, Calamity Jane, the Heroine of Whoop-Up. While described as a woman,
Wheeler's Calamity Jane was a boisterous, cigar-smoking match for any
man. "She was mounted on her thoroughbred cayuse . . . well-armed
with a sixteen-shot Winchester, and a brace of holster revolvers, besides
those she wore in her belt."[28] Throughout the *Deadwood Dick* novels, she
had a shifting relationship with its hero. Sometimes she was in love with
someone else; at other times she and the road agent intended to marry,
and they did so twice in the novels. Other authors paired her with Wild
Bill Hickok. This fictitious relationship formed the central theme for stage
plays. Years later she added to future biographers' puzzlement when she
suggested that the relationship was not platonic but romantic as well.[29]

The real Calamity Jane had little in common with the ennobled heroine of the dime novel world. According to James McLaird, her "career offers an outstanding case study in legend-making." In his view minor events in her life became major adventures; as a result, her reputation "bore little resemblance to reality."[30] She was born Martha Canary. Her parents died sometime in the 1860s, while she was still a young girl. She made a living in different places as the consort of soldiers, railroad workers, and miners, which, as one Deadwood writer observed, "caused her to become a parody on womanhood, shorn of all decency and most womanly attributes."[31] Another writer complained about the fame that she received. "A hundred waiter girls and mop squeezers in this gulch are her superior in anything," he wrote.[32] Along the way Calamity Jane gathered a variety of "husbands" and a reputation as a loud, hard-drinking person who dressed and swore like a man. She spent much of her time in saloons and jails, drifting back and forth between Deadwood and nearby army posts, while making her living as a bull-whacker, prostitute, hotel manager, and bartender. Eventually she became so controversial that one writer suggested that "the veil of oblivion should be drawn" over her memory.[33]

During the 1890s a ghostwriter helped prepare an autobiographical pamphlet entitled *Life and Adventures of Calamity Jane by Herself*, a sort of dime-novel version of her life. Calamity Jane lived her final years near Deadwood working as a brothel cook, peddling copies of her life and postcards that portrayed her as a scout or standing next to Hickok's grave. By that time, pathetic and homeless, she wandered among the Black Hills communities of Deadwood, Spearfish, and Terry. She died on August 1, 1903, at the age of forty-seven. Her body became the object of morbid curiosity as locals rushed to get a last look at the dime-novel celebrity. After onlookers began to cut locks of her hair as souvenirs, authorities placed a wire screen over her head to prevent townspeople from taking any more mementos from the corpse. When the funeral service ended, a long line of carriages and a band escorted the hearse to Mount Moriah Cemetery. There the funeral workers placed her coffin in a plot next to Hickok's grave.[34]

In contrast to Deadwood's Wild West heroes, at first neither Dodge City nor Tombstone had anyone with a reputation to rival either Hickok or Calamity Jane or any long-term popular fictional character resembling Deadwood Dick. Tombstone and to a lesser extent Dodge served as an occasional setting in cheap late nineteenth century fiction, but their characters lacked any real-life authority. Wyatt Earp, Bat Masterson, and Doc Holliday, associated with both towns, all gained wide notoriety later. Following the 1890 announcement by the director of the census that the frontier had closed, a host of writers began a feverish search for people to illustrate the heroic aspects of the earlier West before it disappeared entirely. This growing interest in the end of an era prompted actual participants such as Wyatt Earp and Bat Masterson to step forward with their stories.

Turn-of-the-century writers ultimately focused their efforts to preserve western history on each town's actual public figures. They believed that the full significance of the West demanded that they elevate it above the fictional accounts of the dime-novel era. Theodore Roosevelt had suggested this after having lived on a North Dakota ranch for several years.[35] Two other prominent easterners, Owen Wister and Frederic Remington, agreed. After his first western travels in the 1890s, Remington began to publish his artistic impressions in popular magazines. Following a visit to Wyoming in 1891, Wister decided to join Roosevelt and Remington's efforts. Later he wrote that "Roosevelt had seen the sage-brush true" and "had felt its poetry," as did Remington, who "illustrated his articles so well."[36] Still, he asked, what had fiction accomplished? Wister wanted to elevate the West above the dime novels and pulps—"to disperse the Alkali Ikes," as he called them.[37] He succeeded in 1902 when he published *The Virginian*, a book that most scholars regard as the first serious Western novel. Zane Grey and Emerson Hough followed with their own stories in that same decade. In 1903 Charles Siringo's nonfiction memoirs and Andy Adams's fictional recollections came out. Adams described his experiences on cattle drives from Texas to Kansas and devoted an entire chapter to the cowboys' raucous visits to Dodge City saloons and dance halls.[38]

New authors, coupled with changes in the publishing industry, helped expand the market for more nearly authentic westerns. The depression of the 1890s, competition from cheap magazines, and low postal rates had combined to end the dime novels as the source for popular regional images. By 1900 only two major publishers, Frank Tousley and Street and Smith, still published them.[39] During the early twentieth century that genre evolved into pulp westerns. At the same time, a new magazine format known as the "slick" changed much of the publishing business. Unlike pulps, they used high-quality paper that allowed them to print better illustrations and attract advertisers, who became their main source of profit. Within just a few years *Colliers'*, *Saturday Evening Post*, *Ladies' Home Journal*, and *McCall's* came to dominate the market for middle-class and lower-class readers. Driven by advertisers sensitive to their customers' tastes and the intense competition among the publishers, these magazines found that western fiction brought readers and income.

Those market developments called for more sophisticated westerns and a new orientation toward adults and gave Alfred Henry Lewis his chance. As the writer most responsible for introducing Tombstone and Dodge City to eastern readers, he focused attention on Bat Masterson and Wyatt Earp. Lewis used his personal experiences effectively in his western stories. although trained as an attorney, he had worked on his uncle's ranch for a time. During his eight years in the West he labored as a wagon freighter and ranch hand in western Kansas and southwestern Arizona, living in both Tombstone and Dodge City. His experiences in the West gave him a clear knowledge of everyday life in those frontier communities. Described as an accepted member of the "cowmen and sporting fraternity" in Kansas, "he rode the range, bucked the numerous faro banks in Dodge City in those days, and danced in the cowboy dance halls."[40] Between 1883 and 1885 Lewis spent time in Tombstone, absorbing its local color. Tired, as he put it, of "mule and steer, mesquite and cactus," he returned to Kansas City, where he practiced law and became a real-estate dealer.[41]

In 1889 Lewis published his first western short story, "The Old Cattleman Talks," under the pen name Dan Quinn. That introduced his nameless "Old Cattleman," who spun yarns about people and events in a dusty southwestern Arizona town that the author named Wolfville. The success of those stories gave Lewis his start. In 1891 he ended his law practice and began writing western fiction and muckraking political articles full time, which gained him a position as the Washington correspondent for the *Kansas City Times*. In 1894 Lewis became the head of William Randolph Hearst's Washington Bureau of the *New York Journal*. There he became friends with Theodore Roosevelt, who urged him to compile his stories into a book.[42]

Published in May 1897, with Roosevelt serving as editor, *Wolfville* included illustrations by Frederic Remington. The book brought Lewis national fame and appeared in fourteen printings and five sequels between 1902 and 1913. The narrative, often considered to be a portrait of Tombstone, blended stories of that town and Dodge City. It intertwined

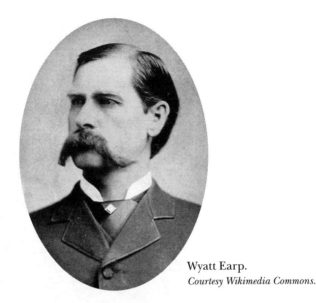

Wyatt Earp.
Courtesy Wikimedia Commons.

actual landmarks and living people with fictional ones from each place. Tombstone shared adobe buildings, Boot Hill, the Bird Cage Theatre, and a New York Store with his fictional town, while Wolfville included the Lady Gay Theater from Dodge City. Supposedly a mining town, it resembled a cowtown. Lewis also introduced some of the men who lived in both communities, often mixing fact and fiction about them. In one case he put Doc Holliday in an epic poker game against Cherokee Hallo, one of his fictional characters.

Just before Lewis offered his humorous Wolfville experiences, Wyatt Earp stepped forward with a different portrait of life in Tombstone and Dodge City. In 1896 *San Francisco Examiner* editor Andrew Lawrence persuaded the former lawman to write a series based on his experiences. The first article, Earp's version of life as a frontier peace officer in Tombstone, appeared in August that year. Entitled "How I Routed a Gang of Arizona Outlaws," it gave his first retelling of the Earps versus the McLaurys and Clantons shootout fifteen years earlier. Other pieces narrating events in Dodge City followed, all depicting his friends, Doc Holliday, Luke Short, and Bat Masterson as heroic fighters for justice.

Earp presented himself as a moralistic avenger who used force only when the legal system had collapsed. After apologizing to readers for having

Luke Short.
Courtesy Wikimedia Commons.

"too much blood" and "too much of myself in my story," he reminded them that he wrote from "half a lifetime on the frontier."[43] Affirming Earp's accuracy, the editor of the *Examiner* contrasted the lawman's account with Lewis's fictional account. "You may know your Bret Hart and your Dan Quinn from beginning to end, but you will never know the frontier until you have read Wyatt Earp," he bragged. "Why there is nothing in fiction to compare with the cold record of this man's experience." He added that Earp had "the reputation of being the bravest fighter, squarest gambler, best friend and worst enemy ever known on the frontier."[44]

Lewis quickly responded to Earp's series in the *New York Journal*, calling the aging gunman "grim, game and deadly" and an unsavory man well past his time. During the 1920s other writers depicted the gunman more positively. Gathering material for a book on Tombstone, Chicago journalist

Walter Noble Burns decided to write a biography of Earp. His timing was bad because Earp and his friend John Flood had already begun work on their own biography of the gunfighter. Disappointed, Burns talked about a book on Doc Holliday. Later Earp mentioned that he and Flood might want Burns to take over the project if his manuscript failed to get published.[45] For months the writer questioned Earp about people and events. During his visit to Tombstone. Burns interviewed Lorenzo Walters, a Tucson policeman, who told him to write about the Earp-Clanton fight because of its market value. An exciting episode, Walters told him, it "will make interesting reading for the public who are craving the wild and wooly stuff."[46]

When the book appeared in 1927, it described Tombstone in ways that sound familiar today. The roaring boomtown included all of the usual disorderly characters that readers had come to expect. Burns crafted his narrative as an Arthurian drama. He posed Wyatt Earp as Sir Galahad and his brothers and Doc Holliday as Knights of the Round Table, fighting the climactic battle against the McLaurys and Clantons, who threatened peace and needed to be conquered. Despite Earp's fears about how Burns might depict him, the author presented the gunman as a defender of law and order and promoted him as a true western hero. In fact his masculine Earp set a pattern for other writers and went a long way toward making him a commercially successfully western icon. The book is also responsible for many of the errors about Earp's actions and career.

Meanwhile two competing authors, William Breakenridge and William MacLeod Raine, challenged Burns's positive characterization of the Arizona lawman. Breakenridge, the only surviving law officer from the OK Corral era other than Earp, saw the gunman differently. Writing to Burns, who was gathering information about the events, the old deputy labeled the Earps as a violent gang and argued that peace did not come to Tombstone until the citizens had run the brothers out of town.[47] Raine directed readers' attention to the town's violence. He presented the local disorder as growing out of the bitter rivalry between two competing gangs. According to Breakenridge one consisted of cowboy rustlers who stole cattle in Mexico and "in the main were easy-going, likeable young fellows," led by John Ringo and Curly Brocius. The narrative pitted them against "a rival town gang led by Wyatt Earp and his brothers, who, even though they were law officers, knew more about stage robberies than they admitted."

Their antagonism created a deadly feud, led to what has come down to the present as the Gunfight at the OK Corral, and ended only when reprisals for the murders of the cowboys drove the Earps out of town.[48]

While the Earps continued to receive much negative attention, Bat Masterson overcame his negative past after moving to New York City. There he reconnected with Alfred Henry Lewis. The two men had known each other in Dodge City years earlier, when Masterson had a reputation as an Indian fighter, buffalo hunter, newspaper editor and writer, town marshal, and professional gambler. Masterson also knew Earp in Dodge City and later followed him to Tombstone. He returned to Dodge City to avenge the death of his brother Edward and supported Luke Short in the so-called Dodge City civil war. After that Masterson drifted north to Colorado and worked as town marshal, prize fight promoter, referee, and sports writer for *George's Weekly*, a Denver paper. In 1902 he moved to New York and became a sports columnist for the *New York Morning Telegraph*. Working with Lewis's brother William brought the gunman and the novelist back together.[49]

Masterson gained national attention as an actual Wild West figure soon after moving to New York. In 1902 E. C. Little published an article entitled "The Round Table of Dodge City" in *Everybody's Magazine*. It portrayed Masterson as a western Roland, "a man of chivalric tendencies" who "held as the sovereign principle of his career absolute loyalty to his friends."[50] A year later Andy Adams described him as a tough Dodge City marshal and a prankster. In his *Log of a Cowboy* Adams recalled an old cowman's advice to the cowboys to behave because "Dodge's officers are as game a set of men as ever faced danger." That warning referred to Wyatt Earp, Bat Masterson, and Doc Holliday. "The puppets of no romance ever written," Adams wrote, "can compare with these officers in fearlessness."[51]

When Masterson's reputation as a wild westerner grew, Lewis acted as an unofficial press agent for the old Dodge City lawman. He depicted Masterson as a western hero and urged him to publish his memoirs. In 1904 Lewis published four articles about Masterson's Dodge City exploits and another about Wild Bill Hickok in slick magazines. A year later he combined the original four into *The Sunset Trail*, the first full-length biography of Masterson. He claimed that his goal was to document "a phase of American existence that, within the touch of present time, has passed away." In the introduction Lewis told readers that "in doing this I have

Doc Holliday.
Courtesy Wikimedia Commons.

seized on [the story of] a real man and, in its tragedy at least told what really happened."[52]

Based on the author's experiences and Masterson's recollections, *The Sunset Trail* gave a rambling, disconnected outline of Masterson's life in Dodge City and marked the first historic description of the town. Despite his claim to be writing serious biography, Lewis described Dodge City with dime-novel prose. He wrote that the town was "a volcano; an eruption might occur at any time! The air to-day was wholesome; to-morrow it might be as full of lead as the Ozarks!" The narrative depicted the gunfighters like Masterson as honorable, loyal men adhering to a moral western order. Clearly, by this time he had changed his view of the Earps and Doc Holliday. Influenced by Masterson, Lewis elevated them to noble status. He painted Holliday as a "well-bred" gunfighter who, after leaving Dodge City, made his way to Tombstone. There he met the Earp brothers, who "were all splendid shots and sterling folk of standing, character and force. The brothers Earp and Mr. Holliday became friends at sight."[53]

Reviewers saw the book either as hero worship of Masterson or as an accurate if shocking picture of western life. Despite this mixed response, Lewis's fascination with gunfighters grew, as did his patronage of Bat Masterson. In 1905 he became editor of *Human Life*, a slick journal based in New York City. Two years later he persuaded Masterson to write a series of sketches entitled "Famous Gunfighters of the Western Frontier" for the magazine. Lewis introduced the articles, stressing the passing of a "dangerous" era and Masterson's role as an actual participant. "Mr. Masterson is singularly well equipped for the task at hand," because he "witnessed stirring times, and stood for many years a central and commanding figure in a dangerous day that has gone."[54]

Between February 1907 and March 1908 Masterson penned sketches of western men that he actually knew: Ben Thompson, Luke Short, Doc Holliday, Bill Tilghman, and Wyatt Earp. In November Lewis added an article entitled the "King of the Gun-Players" in answer to a "tempest of inquiries touching Mr. Masterson himself." In these stories nearly all of the action took place in either Dodge City or Tombstone. Throughout the series the two authors underscored their protagonists' virtues as shooters and friends and the lost times with a chivalric sense of honor. Masterson's Earp was a particularly flattering picture of the gunman, in an effort to protect his friend's reputation. The name "Wyatt Earp," he wrote, "has excited, by his display of great courage and nerve under trying conditions, the envy and hatred of those small minded creatures with which the world seems to be abundantly peopled." He continued: "I have known him since the early seventies and have always found him a quiet, unassuming man, not given to brag or bluster, but at all times and under all circumstances a loyal friend and an equally dangerous enemy."[55]

The self-promotion of historic figures and the efforts of writers and publishers to profit from the western past gave Deadwood, Dodge City, and Tombstone plenty of famous Wild West characters to use when they began to re-create their pasts a decade later. The narratives of famous gunmen had exceptional resiliency throughout much of the twentieth century as journalists, novelists, popular historians, movie makers, and later television producers told their stories repeatedly. In contrast, Deadwood Dick, the lone fictional character, faded when the dime-novel era passed, and Calamity Jane, the single woman of note, became little more than a minor character in most accounts until the mid-twentieth century (when she became the title character in the western musical *Calamity Jane*, played by Doris Day; she also appeared in the gritty television series *Deadwood* from 2004 to 2006). Ultimately, the gunmen provided the most exciting stories and became major sources of the three towns' historical identities.

Hickok, Calamity Jane, Earp, Masterson, and Doc Holliday became celebrities because they met a number of social needs. One was economic. Western heroes made good business. At another level they offered legitimate proof of American exceptionalism growing out of the frontier experience to a mass audience. They presented larger-than-life figures who illustrated that great epic. As long as Americans saw the frontier West as an identifier of national character, real-life western hero-figures had key roles in the narrative. At first, however, these celebrated figures did not meet the needs of the communities that they came to represent. In fact the town boosters often saw them not as positive symbols of a romantic frontier history but rather as negative reminders of an unsavory past. They hoped to put that era, characterized by immorality and civil disorder, behind them. While each of the three towns struggled toward modernity after the turn of the century, they carried the burden of an infamous Wild West reputation created and perpetuated by the same sources that gave them their equally undesired heroes.

3 ☞ Rewriting Town Histories

The early mining and cattle booms in the three towns faded quickly and left each of them facing a local depression. By the 1890s, or soon after, their leaders looked for ways to revive their slumping economies. All shared the challenges of isolation and dwindling population in an era of rapid urbanization and industrialization with dozens of other small towns across the country. At the same time, each of them had an additional problem that limited their efforts to attract investors and new residents. By then all three faced national reputations as centers of frontier violence and lawlessness. Civic leaders and town boosters had to find ways to blunt or overcome that negative image. At first they all tried to distance themselves from the popular stereotypes about their past by ignoring or rejecting them. When that failed, they tried to present the violence as just an early step on the way to civil maturity. Over time those efforts had little impact. The communities experienced continuing stagnation with few prospects for growth. Town boosters who earlier had sought to ignore or paper over the lawless, colorful events and violent people associated with their histories gradually changed their views. Once they recognized that their violent history might have economic value, they began to accept the Wild West images as positive for their towns.

Before that switch happened, the boosters shared a common vision of what the ideal progressive city needed if it hoped to attract new residents and grow along with other postfrontier western communities. Their list of positive elements included a responsible local government that provided civic services such as police, fire protection, and a reliable water system, all necessary for economic and social stability. Every town needed good housing, roads or rail links to the rest of the country, and a positive climate for business activity. To ensure continuing growth and morality, the boosters called for strong schools and well-established churches as well as social clubs, lodges, and other voluntary groups to help hold the community together. At the end of the nineteenth century local leaders throughout the West repeatedly called for civic solidarity and a moral, family-oriented atmosphere.[1]

The strong and growing public interest in the towns' colorful and lawless histories ran head-on into their efforts to downplay their past violence. By the end of the nineteenth century the heyday of dime novels and other pulp fiction that had created lurid pictures of each town had passed. Yet, as local leaders sought to establish modern communities, the early twentieth century version of popular fiction begun by Owen Wister, Emerson Hough, and others complicated their efforts. In fact a growing popular interest in memorializing what remained of the nation's western heritage before it all disappeared undermined their efforts. That resulted in yet another flood of western fictional and nonfictional descriptions of these towns. Once again public opinion focused on their exciting pasts and famous lawmen.[2] Still, at first most civic leaders tried to ignore those developments and worked stubbornly to get out from under their raucous past.

As town boosters struggled to revitalize their sagging economies, they emphasized investment opportunities and continued potential for growth. In Deadwood and Tombstone promoters concentrated on mining, while Dodge City stressed agriculture, calling its location the "garden spot of western Kansas." Persuaded that a modern city needed to attract newcomers, local business elites worked closely with town newspapers to generate or coordinate virtually all promotional activity. Deadwood boosters had organized a Board of Trade as early as 1881. It dissolved but reappeared with several names until 1929, when it became the Deadwood Chamber of Commerce. Dodge City had three booster groups that merged in 1921 to become its chamber of commerce. Tombstone experienced a similar process as leaders there worked to coordinate their activities. In all three towns civic and business groups, rather than the local governments, carried out most of the promotional activities. Leaders in each town looked for ways to replace past images of lawlessness and general immorality that the popular press continued to offer. To do that they highlighted institutions that demonstrated solid family values and local stability. Churches, schools, and civic organizations got the most attention. A 1911 Dodge City poster bragged about the six churches there and commented that "no prudent or cultured person will consider any community or city for a permanent home" that lacks either churches or schools.[3]

Deadwood had made a similar claim a few years earlier when a booster listed a Catholic church, four Protestant congregations, and a synagogue. One local writer bragged that the community valued education so much that it had built, "at great expense, six modern brick school buildings."[4] Tombstone joined the rush to claim social progress in a 1903 promotional circular that boasted about its four "well attended" schools. The author made the dubious claim that many of the excellent local faculty had "occupied professorships in some of the country's most prominent universities."[5]

In 1904 Deadwood promoter George Baldwin reported that "several women's clubs . . . hold weekly meetings and add to the social features of the city." He went on to list a dizzying array of lodges and civic groups for both men and women, including the Masons, Elks, Eagles, Odd Fellows, Knights of Pythias, Knights of Columbus, Grand Army of the Republic, Daughters of the American Revolution, and Women's Relief Corps.[6] Dodge assured future residents that its women's social and literary clubs offered "educational advantages to the ladies" that equaled those available anywhere. It also promised that "especial attention is given to new-comers and a few days' residence here is sufficient to make them feel at home and that they are among friends."[7]

To overcome visions of random vice, drunkenness, and crime, the promoters stressed that their local governments took full responsibility for ensuring law and order. Tombstone depicted its officials as "public-spirited citizens of intelligence, who occupy their official positions wholly to serve the better interests of the community that has become their pride through long association."[8] Deadwood bragged that it had a "well organized and vigilant" government whose "internal improvements are modern in character."[9] In a similar vein Dodge City publicity asserted that "no better government has been devised and no better can be found" than there.[10] Another source assured readers that because the town had so little violence its sheriff had served six terms and spent much of his time "doing all in his power to make Dodge grow."[11] In 1888 Kansas extended its state prohibition laws to Dodge and closed all of the remaining saloons. Town leaders rushed to take credit for erasing most of its public disorder.

No longer rough camps with only cabins, shanties, tents, or cheap and hastily thrown up false-front structures, the towns pointed to their modern buildings as symbols of stability and solid business potential. Deadwood claimed to be the "biggest little city in the world," with "many of the elements of metropolitanism usually found in a city of 100,000 inhabitants." A booster pointed to the volume of business that its banks and stores enjoyed to support that assertion.[12] Coming into Dodge City, a "visitor is at first impressed by the imposing Santa Fe station and the Fred Harvey Hotel." The commentator highlighted the "immense traffic conducted by the Santa Fe" and the "modern spirit and activity" of the local businesses.[13] Tombstone had Wolcott's Department store, a substantial and architecturally attractive building, as well as the Can-Can restaurant, "elegant and in artistic taste."[14] To be certain that no interested people missed this point, all the towns used highly illustrated materials with photographs, drawings, and maps in their material.

In the boosters' thinking, well-kept homes illustrated another side of stability and community success. The towns clearly had moved far from their disorderly beginnings and now offered places of natural beauty and physical well-being. For example, Deadwood boasted that the Black Hills offered "a place of natural intimacy. There one feels in touch with every hill and mountain, and that he can reach out and grasp it." In an early appeal to easterners' growing interest in regaining health and vigor in the West, an 1883 article stated that "the air is so saturated with piney odors that it builds up an invalid in the most magical way."[15] Having regained full health, people could enjoy the chances for investment and profit that the region offered. Tombstone's dry climate and "distant purple mountain landscapes" promised good health to visitors. Its weather was described as "unquestionably superb, and its superiority proclaims Tombstone as a natural sanitarium" that would provide "ethereal nourishment."[16]

Dodge City ignored the lack of mountains and desert air in making its own claims. At an elevation of 2,500 feet its plains location provided plenty of excellent water in an area well suited for agriculture. One spokesman lauded the climate and stated that "many persons afflicted with lung trouble . . . come for relief and in many instances a complete cure is effected."[17] Occasionally promoters made exaggerated claims in their efforts to tout health and climate. For example, a Dodge City writer bragged that "we have never had anything approaching a cyclone in Western Kansas and compared to what is called a blizzard in the north, we do not know what it means."[18] His mention of the two varieties of negative weather events raises the suspicion that the town had experienced both.

Despite these repeated efforts to build identities as modern communities, frustrated town leaders could not avoid or dismiss tourists' expectations. For decades millions of Americans had seen Wild West shows and read the thousands of dime novels and frequent newspaper accounts about Wild Bill Hickok and Calamity Jane, the gunfight at the OK Corral, riotous cattle drives, and multiple boot hill graveyards. Now people wanted to see evidence of them. Their demands left the boosters few options. They faced the dilemma of having to reconcile their goal of civic progress with the older and increasingly popular notorious images without destroying the potential for developing tourist business. Some boosters tried to deny the violent past. "At no time in its history could Deadwood be classed as a 'gross town.' It has ever been singularly free from the bad element that has made other western and frontier towns notorious," one writer claimed. Any negative ideas about it arose because "writers of blood and thunder stories have frequently laid the scenes of their fiction within her portals."[19] Occasionally town promoters ignored this sensitivity at their own risk. Jess Denious, the new editor of the *Dodge City Globe*, learned this quickly. When he reprinted some old articles about Wyatt Earp and Bat Masterson, people warned him that city residents did not welcome any negative reminders of the town's past.[20]

Gradually people realized that they could neither ignore nor deny the past, and all three towns chose a third way to reconcile it with the present. They decided to make their colorful era just the beginning chapter in the ongoing story of community development. A Dodge City writer said that "the pioneer days are of the dim past and [now it] stands as the largest and most prosperous city west of Hutchison, in Kansas."[21] Another criticized those who chose "to emphasize the riotous side" of Dodge City's past rather than focusing attention on "her industrial and commercial supremacy."[22] Tombstone publicists dismissed its early violence as a natural outcome of the frontier situation. One wrote that "the characters who made Tombstone famous . . . who kept the pot aboiling . . . will never return . . . for the conditions which made them possible was past."[23] At the end of the nineteenth century town leaders came to regard their violent history as just another step on the path to the present. They tried to show it as a rite of passage in which the pioneers overcame the frontier challenges to establish a prosperous modern life. Whether they ignored, denied, or incorporated the past, leaders in each town identified it as a safe place to visit, live, or manage a business.

In three pre–World War I town histories longtime residents used their personal experiences and adopted the boosters' approach. They pushed early violence into the background and emphasized the real story: dedicated, hard-working pioneers had built their communities. Rather than ignoring the disorderly past, they tried to give it truthfully and end the fictional uses that they regarded as harmful. Deadwood's writers began nearly a generation before those in the other towns. In 1895 the Reverend Peter Rosen, pastor of St. Ambrose Parish during most of the 1880s, published *Pa-Ha-Sa-Pah*. Focused mainly on the nearby Dakota Indians, it included anecdotal accounts of Deadwood's history as well. The priest's account used a sin to salvation approach. Although he did not live there until after the boom era ended, much of his narrative featured Wild West actions told in dime-novel prose. "The thirst for gold overcame all difficulties, and brought thousands to these wilds," he began. Yet he moved beyond that and presented the citizens' responses to the fire of 1879 and the 1893 flood as proof that their "dauntless will and energy could not be subdued."[24] He concluded that the city's progress since those events resulted from having overcome difficult frontier experiences.

In her 1899 memoir *The Black Hills* Annie Tallent gave a dramatic account of living in Deadwood. Rather than focusing on fictional sensational accounts of the past, she drew attention to average people, describing them as the "chief great civilizing force employed in achieving our present civilization." Although she lived in Deadwood during its boom days, proper young women had avoided the seedier parts of town. As a result it seems likely that her descriptions of events came from dime novels rather than from personal experiences. In 1875, before either of them had arrived in Deadwood, she met Wild Bill Hickok by chance. Her narrative described him as looking like a "Quaker minister with side-arms." She reported that he told her he had killed men but only "in absolute self defense, or in the performance of an official duty." Tallent's narrative used a wilderness to civilization theme, and she noted the "remarkable absence of disorder in the streets of Deadwood during its pioneer days." When that era ended, street widening, a sewage system, electric lights, and permanent brick buildings marked the movement toward stability.[25]

Dodge City's first memoir appeared in 1913 when Robert Wright published his recollections as *Dodge City: The Cowboy Capital and the Great Southwest in the Days of the Wild Indian, the Buffalo, the Cowboy, Dance Halls, Gambling Halls, and Bad Men.* He based it on having been a part of the early cowtown scene. Despite its dime-novel title, he tried to write a comprehensive history of the town. A former bull-whacker on the Santa Fe Trail, a leading merchant, and then a state legislator, he wrote from close personal experience with the city's famous gunmen Bat Masterson, Luke Short, and Wyatt Earp. Like the authors discussed above he too used the city's progress from frontier to modern circumstances as his central theme.

To gain credibility and distance his work from earlier dime-novel fiction, Wright claimed that friends had asked him to give a true story of the town's early days. His account blamed the early violence on "the newness of the territory, the conditions of life, the dangers and associations of a western frontier, and the daring and reckless spirit that such conditions engender." After a lengthy description of Dodge City's reputation for violence, he defended the town as "not the worst place on earth." His narrative described the actions of people from saloon owners to bankers and showered praise on the local lawmen. He labeled Bat Masterson, his favorite, as "one of the most notable characters of the West." According to Wright, Masterson was not only "a leader of men and a natural born general" but "high-toned and broad-minded, cool and brave," and a "most loyal man to his friends."[26]

Wright's narrative demonstrated how frontier adversities had equipped the townspeople with "courage and a sense of prudence," as they moved toward progress and stability. In his view the Santa Fe railroad helped bring the town's early prosperity. Dodge had stood on the brink of permanent growth and prosperity when the Kansas quarantine of Texas cattle had toppled the economy. Then, as in the other boomtowns, fires destroyed many of the flimsy early buildings. His narrative showed how those two events tested the citizens' character. The community gradually regained some of its earlier prosperity, and by 1912 Ford County had become the second leading wheat producer in the state.[27] Wright concluded that, having overcome adversity, the townspeople gained courage, prudence, and a sense of stability, characteristics that made Dodge City the chief commercial city in western Kansas.

Despite the early boosters' claims and participants' efforts to show each of the towns as successful and nonviolent, their detailed narratives of the boom era reinforced popular ideas about the towns. Many of the local citizens clearly wanted to play down their violent past, but many other Americans craved something else. To them modernization meant loss, not gain. They objected to western small towns' becoming like their eastern counterparts. That signaled the end of the frontier and of American exceptionalism and identity. They wanted the Old West to remain, at least in vivid memory.[28] While the *Overland Monthly* told eastern readers that "no such characters as the average cowboy of fiction ever lived, either in the Old West or elsewhere," it assured them that wide open spaces still remained because the "nature of the country makes its complete occupation by the farmer impossible." A Deadwood paper later echoed this idea, reporting that South Dakota lands would always "continue as examples of the old west of Kit Carson and Buffalo Bill."[29]

At the end of World War I several new books promised that the pioneering spirit would survive. The editor of Deadwood's *Black Hills Weekly* addressed this issue directly. "The blood of pioneering ancestors still stirs restlessly in our veins," he wrote, "and we are, unconsciously, a little homesick for days that this planet will never see again." One way to keep those memories alive was to limit the "Old West" to its early frontier era, a time of "simple days that had a glamor and hardship and danger, but lacked the spider-web of problems which mere modern living involves us."[30] Jazz-age writers-turned-historians echoed these ideas. They ignored the actual West and instead looked to the earlier frontier days.

This growing nostalgia for what appeared to be simpler times brought a renewed focus on the Old West. In 1928 a reviewer for *Sunset* magazine commented that "the country—or the book publishing business of the country at least—had become 'west conscious,' and the publishers have decided that if the public wants the old west they'll give it the old west and plenty of it."[31] Residents of the three towns joined other Americans as avid consumers of westerns. In 1930 the Deadwood city librarian reported that western books were "so much in demand that they are often literally read to pieces." Most of the time her readers wanted local histories and "there was always a waiting list for volumes concerning early day Deadwood and its characters."[32] This outpouring of public interest persuaded memoir authors and pioneers that they had been part of a glorious era, and many shaped their recollections to fit that idea. In doing so people in Tombstone, Dodge City, and Deadwood began to redefine their history to meet national ideas rather than local ones.

In 1922 Frederick Bechdolt published *When the West Was Young*, which focused on Tombstone. His narrative traced the Earps' actions in Dodge City and reminded his readers that "whatever else may be said about them, they were bold men and there was something Homeric in their violence." Rather than showing how the community had moved from violence to peace and stability as writers of the preceding era had, *When the West Was Young* shifted the emphasis. Now the Old West ceased being a stepping stone toward modern times. Instead its history ended when order and stability arrived. The departure of its basic elements—"the bad man and frontier officer, Indian fighter, cow-boy, stage driver, trooper, and faro-dealer"—marked its demise. Recognizing the nostalgia of many Americans for the Old West during the 1920s, he deplored its passing.[33]

Other writers looking for Old West topics traveled west to gather information. In August 1926 Chicago journalist Walter Noble Burns came to Tombstone looking for new material. His recently published success *The Saga of Billy the Kid* had persuaded him that western narratives continued to enjoy wide sales. "People now demand high class work both in pictures and stories of the old West," he told a Tombstone reporter.[34] Although interested in a biography of Wyatt Earp, he broadened his goal to a history of Tombstone. He poured through back issues of the town newspaper, interviewed aging pioneers, and pestered Earp so often for material that the gunfighter worried that Burns was trying to write a biography that would compete with his own account.

To prevent that, Earp wrote the publisher in 1927, warning him of having been duped by the writer and refused to give permission to use his material. "The story of Wyatt Earp, or any portion of it, if it is to be written must be written, only by Wyatt Earp," he directed.[35] After several publishers had rejected their manuscript, John Flood, his prospective co-author, wrote to Burns secretly to ask if he was still interested in becoming Earp's biographer. By then the writer rejected the offer because his Tombstone book was far along. He considered Flood's book a "dud."[36] Meanwhile Doubleday, Page and Company, his publisher, sought to avoid a lawsuit by offering editorial rights to Wyatt. Burns responded angrily: "He [Earp] has no earthly claim on any part of my book."[37] As Andrew Isenberg demonstrates, the aging gunman quarreled fiercely with both writers and publishers over his self-proclaimed right to control the publication of his biography until he died at the end of the decade.[38]

Earp's objections had little impact on Burns, who saw potential film rights that might follow publication as more important than the book itself. He reminded the editor that his account portrayed Tombstone and that Earp appeared in only a third of the narrative. To prevent "future trouble," however, he recommended that the lawman receive 25 percent of prospective film rights and a flat $1,000 fee. When Wyatt rejected the offer, Doubleday assured him that the book was "highly flattering to you and states several times that you were the greatest force for law and order during your residence in Tombstone." The publisher's letter repeated the author's contention that the book was a history of the town, not an Earp biography. It reminded Earp that "as a public official" there "your acts automatically became a matter of public record" and reaffirmed their final offer.[39] The Burns narrative followed Bechdolt's earlier story line, showing that when the violence ended Tombstone became "a sociable, hospitable community," which signaled the end of an era. He concluded: "Once it was romance, now it's a town."[40]

In July 1927, just months before Burns's book appeared, William MacLeod Raine had published an article entitled "Helldorado" in *Liberty Magazine*. It opened with a markedly different view of Tombstone's past than other writers had given. Raines claimed that it was not a bad town. "There were no hold-ups or burglaries. People who minded their own business were left strictly alone by the gunmen." Readers needed to realize that "the gamblers were good citizens, and the wives of some of them were leaders in the church: for professional gambling was as legitimate a business as selling groceries."[41] Having used this placid description, Raine faced the same dilemma as local boosters did. They wanted tourists and he wanted book sales. He realized that this peaceful view of the town would not sell many books.

Raine became the ghost-writer for William Breakenridge's 1928 full-length memoir *Helldorado: Bringing Law to the Mesquite*. This firsthand account made no pretense of giving a history of progress from disorder to stability as Wright had done for Dodge City a decade earlier. It traced Breakenridge's career as a Tombstone deputy sheriff, deputy U.S. marshal, and a claim agent for the Southern Pacific Railroad. It gave special attention to his early 1880s role as an Old West law officer in the town. By centering on that era, his account moved away dramatically from the earlier memoir writers' efforts to build a sense of community. Instead he and Raine worked to authenticate Tombstone's "Wild West" moment and the old deputy's part in it.

Helldorado earned wide acclaim at least in part because of its heightened sense of reality, based on Breakenridge's actual participation in the events being described. The *Tombstone Epitaph* called it "true insofar as exciting data and man's memory can make it." *Sunset* called it "the real article," because Breakenridge "was there; all of it he saw and pretty near all of it he was."[42] Others agreed. Frederick Bechdolt commented that it "proves that western stories are based on a fundamental truth" and that "its first-hand portrayal of frontier sheriffs is a refreshing thing in this day when the popular conception of frontier types emanates from Hollywood." J. Frank Dobie, the prominent western folklorist, saw it as complementing Burns's *Tombstone*. "Together [they] give a picture of desert mining towns that have long since decayed and that will always have associations with romance," he wrote. "They depict a class of men as extraordinary as they were bloody. My taste may be debauched but I like to read about such devils."[43]

Later that same year (1928) Lorenzo Walters published the fourth book on the town, *Tombstone's Yesterdays*. The author said that he wanted to answer the "eastern tourist's question: 'What became of all of the bad men who used to live in and around Tombstone in an early day?'" His book included a disconnected set of biographies and gave the Earps plenty of attention. As others had, Walters wrote that he wanted to get at the "real truth" about the most colorful events in Tombstone's past. To do that he cast the Earps as heroes despite the conflicting evidence. He also sought to give the public a "wild and woolly" book. He brushed off the issue that multiple versions of events existed and claimed that most of the participants had forgotten local events. When they said that Tombstone was not a bad town or that there were not many killings there, he explained that as resulting from their bad memory. "It is not believed that such statements were made with any misleading intentions," he wrote, "but that in those days human life was held with such light regard that many killings actually took place that were quickly forgotten."[44]

The growing national focus on their town's violence angered many residents who thought that the outside writers had stolen and distorted their past. Some defended its reputation vigorously. The editor of the *Tombstone Epitaph* feared that the growing flood of Wild West stories would undermine the community-building efforts of the preceding decades. "Men who would hang today for a fraction of the crimes they committed in the early days are becoming heroes in our distorted vision," he warned. The fact that "hundreds of men who shed their blood in an effort to develop our state are now being passed over and forgotten . . . because the renegade's story makes better reading is more reason why we should guard more closely the true story of our western growth."[45]

Former county judge William Monmonier warned his audience at the Tombstone Luncheon Club not to "believe all you read" about the town's "wild days, instead of cut-throats and bandits the citizens were the 'salt of the earth.'" He admitted that "there were a few bad men," but that "they predominated or were even much noticed at the time is a falsehood born in the heads of fiction writers."[46] The town's first mayor, John Clum, echoed these ideas and charged that "clever and colorful writers have added much to the wild and wooly reputation"; in reality, he contended, the town was as "orderly and law-abiding as any community of equal size."[47] Despite those objections and complaints, the four books and another by Lewis a generation earlier all helped to create a legitimate Wild West identity for the community. By continuing the dialogue about the Earps' role as either ruthless killers or successful law officers in Tombstone's history, the writers focused attention on the past violence.

Tombstone's growing fame as a true representative of the Old West shared close ties with people and events in Dodge City. The pre–World War I writings of Bat Masterson and Alfred Henry Lewis had given that town a solid Old West reputation. The tie between Tombstone and Dodge City reappeared, this time in Eddie Foy Jr.'s 1928 memoir *Clowning through Life*. As a young performer, Foy had traveled a vaudeville circuit to many frontier boomtowns, including both Dodge City and Tombstone. As a public entertainer who worked in dance halls and theaters throughout the West, Foy remembered each of the two towns quite differently from the other writers. He admitted having dime-novel images of Dodge when he first arrived but soon changed his ideas. A few weeks after his first visit he described Dodge City as "an ugly but fascinating little town," where "a goodly percentage of the buildings on Main Street were devoted to amusement and refreshment of one sort and another." Yet he noted that most of the citizens appeared to be "well-behaved folk." "Women were treated with grave courtesy," and "most dance hall girls" he met "were personally as straight as a deaconess."[48]

Foy's memoir mentioned meeting gunfighters such as Sheriff Bat Masterson. According to Foy he and the sheriff "soon took a liking to each other and were friends thence forward." His account talked about Wyatt Earp, or "'Erb,' one of the city police and a famous gunfighter." Virgil Earp, Luke Short, and Doc Holliday all became acquaintances. The book agreed with the locals that eastern publishers had created Dodge's disorderly reputation. They "spread the impression elsewhere that Dodge was a town where the leading industries were vice and murder, wholesale and retail."[49] Foy's linking of the gunmen in the two towns foretold the close intertwining of their later reputations when they gained notoriety as authentic Wild West icons. His memoir provided an honest account of both towns but deemphasized the dangerous characters and disorder, two main ingredients in most works on the Old West. While the entertainer brought Dodge City some new attention, his book failed to captivate readers as did the earlier ones by Bechdolt, Burns, and Breakenridge.

Stuart Lake's book *Wyatt Earp: Frontier Marshal* (1931) brought new attention to both Dodge and Tombstone. As Lake finished the manuscript, Earp's widow Josephine tried to guard his reputation. While Lake prepared the book for publication, she insisted on editorial rights that frustrated both the author and the publisher. She demanded that the narrative depict her positively and that it play down Earp's role in the violence. Lake responded that her pestering threatened his narrative of "the only *authentic* report of one of the most colorful episodes of frontier history."[50] At one point she wanted the author to include an incident in which she claimed Earp had rescued a disabled woman from a burning building. Events like that, she told the publisher, "were much more satisfactory than those which involved gunplay."[51] Eventually, to pacify her, Lake minimized her role in the narrative and changed the title from *Wyatt Earp: Gunfighter* to *Wyatt Earp: Frontier Marshal*.

In 1930 Lake published the manuscript as a serial in *Saturday Evening Post*. When the book came out the next year it became an immediate best seller. About a third of it pictured Dodge City in lurid, almost dime-novel terms. Early residents included "gamblers, gunmen, thieves and thugs gathered from the corners of the earth and with them the hardier of the

Bat Masterson (*standing*)
and Wyatt Earp, 1876.
Courtesy Wikimedia Commons.

scarlet sisterhood. . . . By the time Wyatt Earp reached the camp, some seventy or eighty argumentative visitors had been buried with their footgear in place—Dodge had lost accurate count." After the lawman had tamed Dodge City with the help of his brothers and friends Doc Holliday and Bat Masterson, he moved to Tombstone, the "howling wonder of the Western world," to establish order there as a deputy marshal.[52]

In Tombstone the book sharpened the ongoing controversy about the Earps, sparking bitter rebuttals to Lake's positive description of the lawman. Anton Mazzanovich, a former town resident and author of *Trailing Geronimo*, launched a blistering attack. Others followed suit, and denunciations of Lake became so intense that Earp's defenders hastened to the writer's defense. Arlington Gardiner, president of the chamber of commerce that was struggling to present the town as a tourist attraction, saw any book about it as helpful. He attacked Lake's critics sharply in the *Tombstone Epitaph* and challenged them to "be prepared to make your criticisms or corrections stick because the 'old gang' [Earp's supporters] is full of fight now so when you see the whites of their eyes, FIRE."[53]

In contrast to Tombstone, Dodge City residents had generally favorable ideas about Earp, perhaps because only a few remembered his brief time there. When Earp died, the *Dodge City Daily Globe* wrote that old-timers remembered him as "a man of courage who was hired to clean up the city and who delivered it in a fearless manner."[54] Others seem to have accepted this view, hailed by one reviewer as exceptionally vivid, colorful, and dramatic. Lake's effort to make it authentic made it "unique among American biographies because of the character, achievements and historical consequences of its subject." Merritt Beeson, the son of Chalkley Beeson, an Earp contemporary, thanked the publisher for enlightening the citizens about their history. "I never realized the important part played by Wyatt Earp in suppressing the bad men of the west," he wrote, adding that "this book should be in every old timer's library."[55]

Lake's book stimulated longtime residents of both towns to write accounts of the old days. As in Tombstone the Dodge City newspapers became a prime source for the growing collection of reminiscences that centered on the town's Wild West moment. The local press printed letters from and interviews with former residents eager to tell their stories. In Dodge City many of them viewed its early history as that of an adolescent community sowing its wild oats before growing up to become a vastly different place. Most of the recollections came from men who took pride in giving their impressions from a young male perspective. Often they dismissed the drinking, fighting, and pranks as natural boyish behavior. One man recalled that the town consisted mostly of saloons and dance halls with stacks of buffalo hides filling the vacant lots, but "no shooting and no rough house." A boarding house operator remembered the Earps and Masterson as having been well behaved when they lived at her place, while another person remembered Dodge as "a town full of cowboys singing civil war songs."[56]

A few mentioned less harmless actions. The Reverend George Durham, a former town minister, described an 1886 midnight burial of a murdered gambler on Boot Hill by some cowboys. One man remembered coming to town on a quiet day and seeing only one "little gunfight in which a gent was killed." Another claimed to have known the famous gunmen, including both Masterson and the Earps. He depicted them as fearless and determined lawmen, any of whom "would have charged hell itself for the man he wanted." The former mayor's wife had a different view of the gunfighters. She remembered her husband leveling a gun at Masterson and ordering him to leave town.[57]

Whether positive or negative, many of these accounts stressed the differences between the old and new Dodge City, reinforcing the idea that the modern town bore little resemblance to its earlier version. A former cattle drover told a reporter that things had changed so much that he could not "even find the old cattle trail he rode once to the city." Another was shocked to realize that the Old Western Hotel was "the only landmark he could remember." A Baptist minister who had preached in the town during 1879 noted what he saw as major positive changes: "prohibition has removed the saloon and other dens of vice. The churches and Schools have improved the morals of the people."[58] Despite these varied experiences, all of them shared a common idea. Although the colorful people and violent events from Dodge's past differed from the present, during that era they made the town a special place.

Deadwood also changed its narrative of its past after Stuart Lake's *Wyatt Earp: Frontier Marshal* linked it to both Dodge City and Tombstone. The town had an established Wild West reputation because of the popularity of Deadwood Dick, Wild Bill Hickok, and Calamity Jane. The three remained a crucial part of the town's Wild West identity. Renewed attention to Hickok during the 1920s and 1930s refocused public attention on the mining-boom era. That brought a shift away from tales of local progress to reemphasizing the violent pioneer era. Gradually the old-timers' memoirs repeated images from popular literature, and the town's formative period became the foundation of its identity.

However, it took a while for this change to occur. At the beginning of the 1920s the editor of the *Deadwood Daily Pioneer-Times continued to* write that real history of the Black Hills would move away from violence to include such the stories of how local civic organizations got started. Still, he recognized that the public "demanded exciting stories of the past, and hoped that their interest in violence would fade."[59] What he failed to realize was that few cared about the history of common institutions or events. They wanted stories of Old West violence and the exciting people who had lived in Deadwood. To his disappointment, most writers of the 1920s and 1930s repeated the old stories about Wild Bill and Calamity Jane.

Hickok, the dean of Old West characters from the town's past, got new attention from Emerson Hough's 1923 novel *North of 36* and William S. Hart's film *Wild Bill Hickok* that same year. Historians and biographers followed closely with a flood of books. Walter Noble Burns began research for a biography on Hickok but shifted his efforts to a biography of Billy the Kid. In 1926 O. W. Coursey published his *Wild Bill*, the first full-length book on the gunfighter since Prentiss Ingraham's dime novel a generation earlier. Two years later Frank Wilstach published *Wild Bill Hickok: Prince of Pistoleers*, which presented Hickok as an uncorrupted hero on the side of law and order.

In 1927 attention shifted to the gunman's contemporary Calamity Jane. That year Duncan Aikman profiled Deadwood's famous heroine in his *Calamity Jane and the Lady Wildcats*. His version depicted her as a pathetic alcoholic and promiscuous drifter, an image that fit well during the prohibition era. These two books whetted public interest in Deadwood, and during the next decade more accounts of the two characters appeared. In all of them the community appeared at a frontier moment, the expected setting given the 1870s experiences of Hickok and Calamity Jane. As in Tombstone and Dodge City, the authors' intentions to give the readers authentic stories about actual people strengthened the popular images of disorder and its associated local characters.

Deadwood's remaining pioneers added four full-length memoirs, far more than in either of the other two communities. All of them focused on the frontier era. One noted that the town's historical significance lay in "the last quarter of the 19th century, a time when the Hills were truly western and still under the spell of frontier enchantment." The authors seemed to think that in order to write "the true and correct story of the pioneers," in Black Hills history, "a picture of the turbulent years must be preserved."[60] Yet whether they knew it or not, this accepted the view of Old West writers like Burns, Lake, and Raine, who all believed that the West ended when civilization arrived. For example, in 1928 Estelline Bennett, daughter of Deadwood's first federal judge, wrote that "for nearly fifteen years it was a stagecoach town and then one cold December morning the railroad came and in that one day the merry young mining camp bloomed into a surprised town with civil and moral obligations."[61]

By the 1930s, if not before, all three of the towns had attracted a renewed public interest in events that the citizens wanted to forget. Vague fears that the dehumanizing processes of the machine world such as mass production and corporatization threatened the earlier "frontier pattern of thought" stimulated a continued focus on the Old West. Popular histories, biographies, pioneer memoirs, and local newspaper accounts all looked back to the frontier era. They defined that time using particular images and heroes. Public fascination with those grew dramatically during the

1920s and 1930s. Romantic, dramatic, and lurid, these near-mythic events and persons came to represent the Old West to many reading Americans. Because the characters had been actual people, their exploits got told and retold in popular fiction and later in the movies and television. Those outlets kept Deadwood, Dodge City, and Tombstone in the nation's eye for generations.[62] Whether the town residents liked it or not, their Wild West histories became their national identity. That had dramatic local effects. Reputations viewed as embarrassing and as barriers to progress now became the attraction for increasing numbers of tourists hoping to experience some part of the Old West. This development challenged town promoters, but gradually they accepted the exceptional roles that most Americans assumed their communities had played during the nation's frontier age. They turned their energies toward questionable history to meet local present and future needs.

4 ☛ Early Tourism

The works of popular historians, local memoir writers, and filmmakers of the 1920s gave each town a chance to transform its unsavory reputation from a liability to a community asset. After World War I the chambers of commerce, whose members had viewed their past with contempt decades earlier, now tried to find ways to convert the national publicity that they received from books and movies into economic benefits for their towns. They seized on tourism as the most obvious way to capitalize on the new wave of notoriety that overtook them. Yet promoters quickly discovered that luring visitors presented vastly different challenges than attracting residents or new businesses to their communities. It required alliances between business and political leaders, newspapers, and the community itself. As town leaders worked to transform their colorful pasts into profitable ventures, they faced both apathy and opposition from many of the citizens. At the same time, they struggled to meet the desires of visitors who hoped to see some part of the exciting Old West that they had read about or seen in early films. To do that town boosters began to identify landmarks and historic buildings that they thought would satisfy tourists' cravings for the authentic past.[1]

During the 1920s all three towns began to develop their tourist attractions. The ailing economies of Tombstone and Deadwood demanded action. Even before World War I any lingering dreams of returning to their former economic success faded, as a collapse followed each minor boom. Tombstone's hopes had revived in 1901 when a group of mine owners established the Tombstone Consolidated holding company, gathered its major mining properties, and resumed pumping operations at several mine sites. This venture lasted only ten years and failed in 1911, unable to afford the enormous costs of removing water from the lower levels of the mines. At that point the Phelps-Dodge Company bought Consolidated's assets and continued small-scale mining as the Bunker Hill Mines Company.[2]

Strategic needs for manganese and lead stimulated production during World War I, but when that conflict ended the demand for those mineral dropped, prices fell, and the mines closed. Phelps-Dodge leased some of its property to small-scale operators who continued to produce lead and silver for another two decades. Between 1922 and 1931 their profits averaged only $180,000 a year, compared to the $1,000,000 a year that the Tombstone mines had earned between 1880 and 1910, showing how far local mining had declined. Tombstone lost its role as the regional leader to nearby Bisbee, a town prospering because of the Phelps-Dodge copper mining operations there. During the 1920s Bisbee's booming economy lured people and businesses away from Tombstone. Bisbee replaced it as the county seat in 1929. Meanwhile Tombstone's economy limped along, offering legal, financial, and general services to the small remaining mining community and nearby ranches and amenities to travelers who arrived on U.S. Highway 80, its main outside connection. By 1930 the town population had dropped to only 849—half the number of inhabitants ten years earlier.[3]

While Tombstone went into a sharp decline, Deadwood fared little better. Between 1898 and 1917 a new cyanide ore treatment process gave mining operations there a boost, but only temporarily. Using this new technology the gold mines produced about $8,000,000 a year. Employment grew: between 1894 and 1903 the number of men employed in Black Hills mining nearly tripled to 1,281. Yet the new process gave only temporary help, and the new mining boom faded. High labor costs and difficulties stemming from the need to work ever less valuable ores at greater depths halted nearly all of the nearby mining. When the war ended in 1918, only the Homestake Mining Company operations in nearby Lead remained in full production.[4]

As Deadwood's mines closed, it service industries faded too. Despite its boosters' images of a morally upstanding town, in 1909 it still had one saloon for every 250 people. Two years later a state-mandated local-option law led several other Black Hills towns to shut down businesses serving alcohol, which brought noticeably more customers to Deadwood saloons. This surge in saloon business gave rise to more attacks and public debate on the issue. It began in 1910 when Edward Senn, editor of the *Deadwood Telegram*, started a campaign against the saloons, gambling, dance halls, and prostitution. Two other papers, the *Deadwood Pioneer-Times* and the *Lead Call*, opposed Senn's crusade. They pointed out that many of townspeople held jobs in what Senn called the "vice industry." He lost that fight temporarily, but in 1917 national prohibition closed the saloons. Added to the downturn in mining, shutting down those businesses hurt the town. By 1920 its population had dropped to 2,400 people, a third fewer than two decades earlier.[5]

Deadwood's shrinking size corresponded to its fading prominence as a Black Hills economic center. Rapid City came to overshadow it just as Bisbee had done to Tombstone. Located between the Black Hills towns and nearby farming-based communities, Rapid City developed a booming trucking industry, becoming the region's leading distribution center and its gatekeeper for tourists coming to the Black Hills. A 1902 fire that destroyed the Gem Theater, Deadwood's once opulent opera house, further reduced the town's attraction. Nearby Lead, with a strong economy based on the Homestake Mine, built a new opera house, the Homestake Theater, in 1914. Even Edward Senn, the boosterish editor of the *Deadwood Telegram*, admitted that the town was in the middle of a downturn. "It is useless to hide what all the world knows—that Deadwood has been steadily retrograding in population and business importance since the flush days following the discovery of gold here. It was an inevitable result of the passing of the boom which brought in thousands of fortune hunters."[6] Outsiders agreed. In a scathing article published by the *American Mercury Magazine*, Duncan Aikman depicted the town as a "backwash," a place that had not been "fully exposed to civilizing influences until the motor tourist age." He claimed that it was "too poor, shabby, and broken spirited to catch up." Members of its despondent population "amble aimlessly" amidst "neglected storefronts" in a "tableau of premature architectural senility."[7]

In contrast to the two mining towns, by the 1920s Dodge City boasted a strong economy and growing population. Construction of a new Santa Fe rail terminal and a Fred Harvey Hotel, as well as the boom in wheat and livestock production during the war, helped the town become the leading shipping, financial, and commercial center in western Kansas. By 1921 the population stood at 6,039, up 17 percent in a single year, allowing it to brag that it was the fastest-growing city in the state.[8] By the end of that

The Gem Theater, Deadwood, ca. 1878. *Courtesy Wikimedia Commons.*

decade Dodge City had grown to 10,000 people. That prompted the Kansas State Board of Agriculture and *Editor and Publisher* Magazine to recognize it as the regional "capital of Southwest Kansas."[9] During this growth spurt the city began developing a fledgling tourist industry for travelers headed to Colorado for vacations. Unfortunately, this local prosperity collapsed. Facing an extended drought that began in 1930, all of western Kansas lay in the middle of the Dust Bowl, an ecological disaster that destroyed the town's agricultural base during that decade. The situation became so serious that by 1940 nearly one-fifth of the population had fled.[10] That left business and political leaders scrambling desperately for solutions, and tourism seemed to offer the boost that they needed.

In their early efforts to attract visitors each of the three towns tried to provide some wayside services for the automobile travelers who began to fill the roads once the war ended. The number of cheap cars available grew quickly during the 1920s, and many people chose to drive when the railroads hesitantly resumed passenger service. The developing state and national highway systems made driving easier and gave motorists a new sense of adventure. Tourism had been established in Deadwood for years. Since 1889 the Burlington and Northwestern Railroad had regularly brought passengers to visit the natural wonders of the Black Hills. The early efforts focused mostly on getting people to dude ranches, fishing lodges, and the health spas of Hot Springs.[11] Aside from occasional visitors to the graves of Calamity Jane and Wild Bill Hickok, the town itself attracted few outsiders.

Hoping to increase tourism leaders in all three of the towns took active roles in the growing national and regional trail associations that lobbied for road improvements. Each of the major trail groups supported building new routes, repairing and improving the surfaces of existing roads, developing standard signage, and publicizing routes and the attractions they offered. Encouraged by chamber of commerce members from many communities, the associations drew attention to local scenes and famous places. Throughout the 1920s and 1930s frequent reminders that "tourists pay" and will become "a growing business" appeared repeatedly in local newspapers.[12] Each of the three towns had at least one person working actively with these groups. Bert Bell, a commercial photographer and president of the Deadwood Chamber of Commerce, represented his town in the Black and Yellow Trail Association. It linked communities from Chicago to the Black Hills and on into Yellowstone Park. Tombstone's Arlington Gardiner served as an active member of the Old Spanish Trail Association, Arizona Good Roads, and later the Boulevard of America Association. He wrote weekly reports for the *Tombstone Epitaph,* warning of potential road hazards or detours for motorists. Chamber of commerce secretary M. W. Drehmer represented Dodge City and took part in the Santa Fe Trail Association's plans to "advertise the trail and encourage its use by tourists to Colorado and other Western States."[13]

Whatever else they supported, the trail associations saw their first order of business clearly. The *Dodge City Daily Globe* reported that the Santa Fe Trail group wanted "to keep the trail in condition to travel, and to prevent travelers from being diverted to many cow paths along" it.[14] Deadwood's accessibility by automobile benefited from local mining activities, which required modern roads. Lawrence County took the lead in road improvements in South Dakota with the 1911 reconstruction of the Deadwood-Spearfish highway. Over the next ten years the county invested over $600,000 in road construction.[15] The town bragged about its modern roads in the *Souvenir Book of Deadwood, Lawrence County, South Dakota* (1915), proclaiming that "all roads lead to Deadwood, the center of good highways in the Black Hills."[16]

Despite that boast, getting paved roads built in rural areas was a slow process. The Good Roads Movement began in 1880 when the League of American Wheelmen (bicycle riders) organized. In the 1890s the U.S. Post Office began experimenting with what it called Rural Free Delivery. It became national policy in 1902 and helped focus attention on the need for improved roads, this time for mail delivery. When the chorus demanding federal support for paved roads grew, Congress passed the 1916 Federal Road Act. The new legislation offered matching dollars to states in its first support for road-building since the National Road had been constructed a century earlier. The Highway Act of 1921 required states to set aside a number of roads to serve as primary highways for a numbered national highway system. Between 1921 and 1930 these acts helped double the number of paved highways and ended the named highways. Signage became standard across the country. This shifted the agendas of highway associations toward regional promotion as members sought to steer travelers onto their particular routes. In 1921 Tombstone allied with Deming, Lordsburg, and El Paso to provide literature aimed at diverting tourists from Phoenix south to the border route. Deadwood joined the Associated Commercial Clubs of the Black Hills, which included chamber of commerce representatives and Good Roads committees, while Dodge City became a charter member of the Southwest Chamber of Commerce.[17]

As the local promoters hoped, tourists brought added income to many towns and encouraged new businesses to help meet their needs. Owners of restaurants, stores offering groceries, souvenirs, and hardware, and service and gasoline stations all benefited almost immediately. In 1919 one Dodge City investor opened one of the first motels. He built fifteen cabins and equipped them with running water, gas burners for light cooking, and beds.[18] Three years later another Dodge City businessman opened a tourist supply store providing surplus army items and camping equipment for visitors seeking an outdoor experience. From the start, the early visitors represented affluence. In 1922 the *Dodge City Daily Globe* reported that the tourists that year were among the "higher type of citizens" and spent their money "more freely than in other years." The account clearly implied that the community's efforts to attract outsiders had succeeded.[19]

Visitors also demanded the best facilities, a frequent challenge for small-town businesses. Fortunately, Dodge City had its new Fred Harvey Hotel and Deadwood had the Franklin Hotel, which catered to wealthy guests. The *Tombstone Epitaph*, however, complained that its town lacked any high-class lodging, in fact almost any lodging at all. In 1920 Josephine Rock tried to fill that gap. She bought an old store, hoping to create a first-class hotel aptly called "The Tourist." Its major attraction was having a restroom on the first floor. Apparently a hotel with a single restroom failed to satisfy visitors, because some years later the *Epitaph* repeated its earlier protest about the lack of a "suitable hotel to care for the traveling public." If the community lacked capital to build a good hotel, the editor hoped that "outside financial interests" might invest in the town.[20]

Certainly hotels attracted wealthy travelers, but what about those with less to spend? Almost from the start towns sought to build tourist camps for them as well. At times they allowed campers to set up their tents in city parks, which they then publicized as auto or tourist camps. By the early 1920s all three towns had established free camps and marketed them aggressively. Deadwood offered a "beautiful, well-sanded and park-like tract" for "travelers who wanted to do their roughing it inside the dry limits." These efforts in each town succeeded: in 1922 the Dodge City campground had 11,000 users.[21] When the number of tourists grew dramatically during the 1920s, promoters tried to improve the camps. Those efforts brought some of the first open community resistance. Critics asked why taxpayers should have to support an industry that benefited only a few townspeople. Facing open criticism, the boosters responded by saying that everyone gained from a healthy local economy. Tombstone's Commercial Club urged residents to give a "pleasant smile" and a "good word" to visitors while helping to improve the campground in order to get more tourist business.[22]

In 1923 the *Deadwood Daily Telegraph* urged support for a new camp because this "city has fallen behind its neighbors in making provisions to attract tourists." It reported that while "many thousands of auto tourists have passed thru the city, few have stopped over night because there is not a suitable place for them to stop." Describing the town camp as "miniature," the editor feared that most of the travelers camped at nearby Spearfish. After a heated debate over the best site for a park and who should maintain it the city bought land at the top of nearby hill in 1924 and christened it Pine Crest Park.[23] Despite this success, boosters had to struggle repeatedly to gain public support. Dodge City voters had the same concerns. In 1923 and again the next year they rejected city efforts to purchase land and establish a tourist park. While the town leaders pointed to the estimated 300 cars that passed through the community each day, the taxpayers feared that they would have to pay the costs of sanitation and maintenance. Apparently the citizens tolerated a camp as long as the politicians promised that it posed no burden for them.[24]

At first civil leaders in Deadwood and Tombstone saw publicity about their lurid histories primarily as a way to attract new residents. To do that they stressed the orderliness and economic well-being of each community. "We want a town that will attract desirable homesteaders and important industries," the *Black Hills Weekly* told its readers. The *Tombstone Epitaph* echoed that sentiment. It hoped that visitors attracted by publicity in magazines and books that focused on "Old Tombstone" would encourage visitors to become permanent residents.[25] Local editors urged their readers to keep their property repaired and attractive to make a good impression on visitors. The *Epitaph* claimed that good appearances affected businesses directly. A "disorderly town" repelled people, and neglected buildings "reflect on all." In Deadwood the papers pleaded with people to keep their homes repaired "for the town's good." One editor informed his readers that more than half a million tourists would visit the Black Hills and that they should do their part to give the visitors "a good opinion of the most famous city in the Black Hills" so that it would be recognized for its "progressiveness as well as its history and romance."[26]

Yet clean and orderly western towns by themselves attracted few visitors, and soon promoters realized that they had to meet tourists' expectations. Most of their visitors wanted to see at least some vestiges of the colorful Wild West era. Without those elements many tourists felt let down and left disappointed. A group of visiting state editorial association members observed that "with all the wild picturesqueness gone—and nothing of the old glamour left one could not see much difference in Deadwood from any other city of the same size." Others repeated this idea, sometimes in almost the same words. When writer James Flagg drove into Dodge City in 1925, he expected to see something of "the fierce romance of the old cow days—where so many herds were driven to and where so many cowpunchers raised their simple hell until their pay gave out." Instead he found nothing but a little town "with lots of cowboys walking the streets in blue overalls."[27] Charles Finger arrived in Tombstone in 1931 prepared for a rollicking Wild West town but instead found a quiet place with a cowboy leaning against a drugstore wall eating an ice cream cone. The first two hours proved "beyond doubt that this town, once so boisterous, has passed from its vivid youth to an age of repose and contentment." A *New York Times* writer supported this impression: "Nowadays the citizens devote only an occasional reminiscent thought to the men who were laid to rest with their boots on in Boot Hill cemetery. . . . Real Tombstoners are now more interested in paving bonds."[28]

Promoters in both Deadwood and Tombstone learned early that the Old West authenticity intrigued visitors most. In economic terms, disappointed visitors equaled unhappy customers. Once they reached this conclusion, editors and chamber of commerce representatives launched efforts to arouse community support for historical tourism. The editor of the *Black Hills Weekly* reminded his readers that "visitors to the West come not to do the usual things, but to rub shoulders with glamour."[29] Outsiders seconded this idea. A doctor visiting Deadwood advised the citizens to stop trying to imitate the East and "keep your West and your western ways," as they are "the most precious thing you have." The *El Paso Herald* pleaded with leaders in Tombstone to stop their efforts to modernize. When a town has an "old pioneer appearance . . . with bad men and Indians and prospectors, gambling halls and the like, it's a pity to modernize it." That would take away "everything the tourist is willing to go far to see" by making it just like 5,000 other towns. Instead of changing, the community should "sell itself to the world as an old time mining camp and Cowtown."[30]

At least some in each community thought that tourists expected their town to resemble the images that dime novel, newspaper, and western history writers had presented. Many visitors certainly arrived expecting to see some of the places they had read about before they went west. Of the three communities Tombstone came closest to offering sites to match visitors' imaginations, with some buildings like the Bird Cage Theatre still standing. In March 1920 F. M. Loomis, editor of *Motor World* and *Motor Age*, and Robert Manger, field secretary of the National Automobile Dealers Association, visited Tombstone on a trip promoting car travel in the West. They reported being "impressed by the quaint appearance of the many old landmarks of pioneer days" and being happy to have visited "the historic mining camp of which they had heard so many stirring tales."[31] Karl Harriman, editor of the western pulps *Blue Book* and *Red Book*, came to see what he knew only through his reading. He found the town to be "the west, the Old West, the glorious West of America's best fiction come to life," before his eyes.[32] Another outsider told the Tucson Lions Club that Tombstone is the "most interesting town remaining in the West today." He predicted that thousands of tourists "looking for the Old West would come and stay if they knew about what could be seen" there.[33]

Deadwood and Dodge City had fewer vintage buildings than Tombstone, but promoters gave visiting journalists tours to persuade them that the Old West remained in spite of modern amenities and new structures. Their efforts brought mixed results. One visiting editor told his Dodge City audience that the community was "rich in historical events" and one of only four "historical" Kansas towns.[34] Another journalist expressed his surprise at how much the town differed from the images created by the "blood and thunder stories that were told" of it. He pointed out that the street fronting the railroad "lined with cafes and billiard parlors," along with some of the town's narrow business streets, still offered relics of its past.[35] While these visitors saw much less of the Old West than they had hoped, their disappointment failed to overcome their desires.

Deadwood visitors hoped to see similar things. One, who looked for "the bright lights, the rush and bluster of the 'never-to-be-forgotten days'—when Deadwood was once the center of the universe," complained that it had become only a quiet country hamlet. At the same time he saw a "shadow of the past in Deadwood wherever you turn."[36] Another commentator agreed that "the eloquent silence of the crumbling frame dwellings tell [sic] stories of adventure, murder and physical prowess that one looks for usually only in books of a highly seasoned variety of adventure."[37] Irwin Aldrich, writing in Sunshine State, saw the South Dakota settlement as a "relic of the old days," whose "history carries the romance and adventure of the wild days without law; without homes; of the days of gold dust, of easy living and quick fortune."[38] Still another commentator said that "Deadwood, while shorn of its 'wild and woolly' scenes, retains many of its pioneer characteristics."[39] Whatever else they said about the towns, they all pointed out that Americans saw each community as representing the now-vanished West.

The continuing interest in their towns' unsavory pasts convinced some Deadwood and Tombstone boosters that their historical fame might help them recall some of the regional leadership that they had lost. In contrast to relatively prosperous Dodge City, leaders in the other communities hoped that the national publicity that their history attracted would help make them centers of regional tourism. The *Deadwood Daily Pioneer-Times* claimed that the town should dominate the area because "Deadwood has been more extensively advertised to this world than any other Black Hills city or town."[40] Tombstone promoters shared that view: "Every day adds more evidence to the fact that the name and fame of Tombstone is a trade-getting traffic asset to the cities and towns located on the Old Spanish Trail and Bankhead Highways." In 1924 the *Epitaph* claimed that the town's "gruesome name, the books of Alfred Henry Lewis, Frederick Bechdolt, and the publicity now being broadcast by the Tombstone Commercial Club" combined to bring new attention to the community.[41]

The growing realization that their histories had market value caused local promoters to see history books and articles about their communities not as literature but as advertisements. Each new novel, biography, history, or film gave them free publicity and proof that the Wild West offered business opportunities. One of the first to promote this idea, Arlington Gardiner became an enthusiastic booster. When Walter Noble Burns's *Tombstone* appeared in 1927, he saw the book as opening a new economic age for the town. Soon after its publication he wrote to the author that "*Tombstone* is going to be the means of bringing many people here from now on who read the book and had no intention of coming this route before they read it."[42] Burns's book appeared in the same year that U.S. Highway 80 came to town. Before the coming of the "great national highway, few if any of its inhabitants dreamed it would ever become a tourist town," the *Epitaph* proclaimed, "but one day the presses of Doubleday, Page and Company gave the world the book *Tombstone* and the next morning the people awakened to the fact that Tombstone was booked to become a tourist town." The editor predicted that the book would draw more visitors than any place in Arizona except for the Grand Canyon.[43]

Soon town promoters welcomed each new book and article about the area as helping them do their jobs. When William Breakenridge's *Helldorado* came out in 1928, the *Epitaph* commented that "the value of this book is incalculable. . . . It will bring hundreds of people to this place and advertise Tombstone to thousands of others."[44] And when the *New York Times* published an article after Wyatt Earp died in January 1929, the *Epitaph* crowed that almost every week some magazine or book publisher prints a story that feeds the interest already there. "America has made up its mind to visit Tombstone. . . . What other cities are spending thousands of dollars to receive we have handed to us on a silver platter."[45] In 1932, after listing all of the books about Tombstone since Lewis's 1898 *Wolfville,* Gardiner praised Burns's *Tombstone* as the most important. It is like a "diamond in the sky" he wrote, because it put the town "on the map."[46]

At the time Deadwood and Dodge City lacked the same level of public attention, so they advertised their pasts through their chambers of commerce. Although Deadwood had some national publicity from the earlier biographies of Calamity Jane and Wild Bill Hickok, it also benefited from being in a desirable vacation area, surrounded by other cities that also wanted to attract tourists. In 1920 the Deadwood Business Club proposed that the competing towns work together to advertise the region, which they soon began to do. Between 1927 and 1935 the Associated Commercial Clubs of the Black Hills of South Dakota and Wyoming published a series of tourist guides. These gave careful attention to the natural and historic sites, and at least one of them suggested what clothes to wear. Each of the guides described Deadwood as a "historic city" and gave special attention to its days of "wild chaos" and its leading characters, Wild Bill Hickok and Calamity Jane. Feeling the need for more professional coordination of its publicity, Deadwood went a step farther. In 1930 it hired a secretary for the chamber of commerce to coordinate publicity and to "play up historic attractions and give the Easterner the thrill of discovery."[47] Meanwhile Dodge City proclaimed in 1926 that "it pays to advertise," and the *Daily Globe* announced that the chamber of commerce had published 6,000 new booklets. These presented the town's early history, location of its historic landmarks, and its civic assets. Distributed to convention visitors and sold to local businesses for distribution, the pamphlets carried the town's story through business contacts.[48]

Having gotten plenty of regional and national publicity, each of the three communities needed specific things to show potential visitors. This forced boosters to reconsider their attitudes toward old buildings and historic sites that many had seen as nothing more than local eyesores. Now promoters searched for ways to meet tourists' expectations. The town leaders realized that the Schieffelin Obelisk in Tombstone and the Roosevelt Memorial in Deadwood needed work to make them attractive tourist sites. At the same time, they selected buildings like Tombstone's Bird Cage Theatre and tried to give them authenticity with signs and plaques that explained their historical importance. In both Deadwood and Dodge local leaders pushed to open city-owned car parks that would encourage travelers passing through to remain and visit the local sites.

This proved harder than tourism advocates expected. Cash-strapped local governments had little money to spend on commemorative programs, and people in each community remained apathetic about increasing tourism. In 1923 and 1924 Dodge City voters rejected city council efforts to enlarge facilities for automobile tourists.[49] Others objected to plans that highlighted past crime and violence. They rejected the lurid descriptions of their communities and countered that they lived in "a nice, quiet, clean town."[50] In order to begin even modest programs such as marking sites and buildings, the promoters had to overcome or get around their fellow citizens' resistance. The *Dodge City Journal* editor complained that only a few people living there "could give him accurate information of many events in the town's early day history."[51] A grumpy Tombstone resident described the local history as "nothing but a macedoine of crime, folly, and bad luck" and stated that "the less history people or places have the better."[52] Similar attitudes in each town thwarted or at least slowed efforts to build a thriving tourist industry.

Promoters started slowly by marketing existing monuments. Prior to 1920 both Tombstone and Deadwood had large memorials dedicated to well-known people, and the boosters turned to them first. Friends and family had erected a granite obelisk to Ed Schieffelin, Tombstone's founder, after his 1897 death. It stood on a nearby hill overlooking the town. When visitors came looking for things to see, the Commercial Club began printing brochures about the prospector. Frederick Bechdolt's book *When the West Was Young* (1922) also described the grave site. That publicity encouraged a group of citizens to hold a "rock rolling day": they cleared a dirt road to the monument so tourists could view it more easily. During the work project major signs of neglect led some people to question whether the pioneer miner's remains were there, but a brief investigation persuaded them that they were.[53]

Like the Schieffelin Obelisk, Deadwood's Theodore Roosevelt Memorial resulted from the efforts of a few citizens, not the local government. Seth Bullock, Deadwood sheriff during the 1870s, headed the 1919 effort to honor his close friend when Roosevelt died. The monument was dedicated on July 4, 1919. Its builders claimed the distinction of having built the

Ed Schieffelin Obelisk in 2007.
Photograph by crbill, courtesy Wikimedia Commons.

first memorial to the former president. Atop Sheep Mountain, which they renamed Mount Roosevelt, it paid tribute to him as Deadwood's most famous neighbor. The sweeping view of the Black Hills and the plains below allowed visitors to see "the country he rode about when a resident of Dakota Territory, a part of which his wise policy of irrigation and reclamation . . . was the means of changing from an arid plain to a most productive and prosperous farming community."[54] Like its Tombstone counterpart, the Roosevelt Monument soon became a major feature in local promotional materials and Black Hills guidebooks.

The new definitions and descriptions of existing buildings were one of the most important results of the scramble for tourists. Dilapidated old

Bird Cage Theatre, Tombstone, Arizona.
Courtesy Library of Congress Prints and Photographs Division, #HABS ARIZ,2-TOMB,18-1.

structures, once taken for granted or scorned, suddenly gained historic value as visitors inquired about them. In Tombstone boosters "discovered" the Bird Cage Theatre as their first useful site. Following its heyday as a major theater on the vaudeville circuit, it had closed in the 1890s, was sold, and became a warehouse. Over the next few decades the building fell into disrepair. Alfred Henry Lewis's Wolfville stories and Frederick Bechdolt's *When the West Was Young* brought it national prominence. This newfound attention persuaded town leaders that they had a marketable roadside attraction. In 1924 Arlington Gardiner included it in a Tombstone Commercial Club brochure. Describing the building as an immortal place because of Bechdolt's and Lewis's writing, he recommended it as a good target for "Kodakers."[55]

Despite Gardiner's enthusiasm, promoters had few ideas about how they could make the building appealing to visitors. Many believed that it ranked among nationally prominent sites and should stand at the center of the town's commemoration of the Old West. "This famous relic of Tombstone's early days should be converted into a museum housing the many valuable exhibits of the days of gold," the *Epitaph* wrote. "Like the Alamo, of San Antonio, Texas, [it] should be for tourists to see and snapshot to their hearts content." The editor went on to call for an effort to turn the warehouse into a museum, because those days would soon be forgotten when the last of the participants died. The Bird Cage museum that boosters envisioned would ensure Tombstone's place in the annals of the Old West. They stressed the structure's violent past. Because only a few "of the old pioneers who reveled in the hilarity and woe of the Bird Cage" remained to give "the first hand tales of its incidents of joy and sorrow," it should "be made into a museum that will stand as an everlasting monument of the time when blood and gold were valued as naught."[56] Outside interest in the Bird Cage affirmed these local ideas. In Tucson the *Arizona Daily Star* remarked that the theater "was the only mark of the early days left," and now the "little county seat has few things to show the gaping tourist."[57]

This interest in the Bird Cage building also fostered a new awareness that the past should be preserved as a tourist attraction. In 1922 some citizens tried to organize a local historical society to support the preservation of Tombstone's history. They identified buildings, pictures, stagecoaches, and other items to be displayed and then proposed forming a corporation to turn the Bird Cage into a museum for "tourists and visitors from all over the world."[58] Both of the town's two newspapers supported the effort. The *Epitaph* wrote that "providence allowed the buildings to remain," while the *Daily Prospector* predicted that the theater would "draw hundreds of visitors" to town.[59] This burst of support faded quickly when it became apparent that the building's owner, town mayor and local real-estate dabbler C. L. Cummings, had his own plans for the Bird Cage. Having gathered a large collection of historic material, he expected to open his own museum there. He died before that happened, but in 1934 his wife opened a private museum and coffee shop in the building.[60]

The tensions between private and public interests surrounding the Bird Cage illustrated some of the difficulties that even well-motivated citizens faced as they tried to market the past. The simplest means of validating a town's historic events and sites could challenge its advocates. Historic designations proved the quickest and least expensive way to commemorate the past when compared to building monuments or opening museums. Even efforts to create and install signs and markers proved difficult, as tourism supporters faced repeated obstacles in getting even meager funds for their modest programs. To overcome the continuing apathy among residents, and limited funding granted by the town governments, promoters waged ongoing campaigns to persuade the townspeople that attracting visitors helped everyone. In particular they warned townspeople that disappointed tourists hurt local business and harmed the community.

Most of the time boosters' efforts to promote tourism and benefit from the past went far beyond what their communities would support. Unlike attracting private industry, developing an effective tourist program required a strong voluntary commitment to hospitality by the chamber of commerce, business owners, and rank-and-file citizens. Often many members of the community proved unwilling to join these efforts. Few citizens knew much about their town's history or cared about it. For example, Fred Trigg, an editor of the *Kansas City Star*, knew only a handful of people living in Dodge City who could give any accurate information about events in its early history. Others rejected the lurid images of the Old West being presented to visitors. Robert Frothingham, a travel writer, observed that many Dodge City residents denied the town's Old West reputation altogether, saying that it had always been a "nice, quiet, clean town."[61] Author Charles Finger found that residents of Tombstone were "tired of being questioned" about their past. While stopped for gas, he and his companion asked a woman in a garden nearby if the town had "any history worth speaking of." She replied that as far as she could see "history was nothing but . . . crime, folly and bad luck" and the "less history people or places have the better."[62]

To overcome disinterest in promoting, boosters tried to associate community pride and its physical appearance with a town's heritage. In Dodge City the local editor bragged that the community had succeeded because "it is made up of good citizens" who are full of "ginger and pep." An editor for the *Deadwood Daily Pioneer-Times* took a more direct approach. "Your pride in Deadwood is about the best kind of pride you can have," he wrote, "it is an unselfish pride."[63] Senn, editor of the *Black Hills Weekly*, defined an ideal community as one that "is made sufficiently and abundantly fit for work, worship, play, neighborliness, home life, education, and the transaction of business." When the renovated Crystal Palace Saloon became a Tombstone theater in 1922, the *Epitaph* praised this as demonstrating community pride and an example that others should follow to "present a cleaner and more beautiful appearance" to the public.[64]

Generally the newspapers aimed their appeals to local pride at civic service clubs, the primary advocates for increased tourism. They, in turn, sought out volunteers and funds to implement their site marking

Crystal Palace Saloon, Tombstone, Arizona.
Courtesy Library of Congress Prints and Photographs Division, #HABS ARIZ,2-TOMB,1-2.

programs. Ideally the best way to start a commemorative program was to work through an established respected group that had the personnel and financial resources and a vested interest in the past. Of the three towns only Deadwood had an organized group that dedicated itself to preserving memory of the past, but it was far from ideal. Initially the Society of Black Hills Pioneers undertook the local efforts. Organized in 1889 to preserve pioneer history, the group only accepted members who had arrived in the area during the first year of Deadwood's founding. Eventually it changed the rules, accepting women and later the children of pioneer families as well. In 1920 the Deadwood Businessmen's Association prodded the historical group to begin a program to mark historic spots "which will be of interest to tourists, by the erection of stone monuments and tablets."[65] By 1925 the society had marked the site of the murder of Henry Weston "Preacher" Smith, helped construct the Roosevelt Memorial, built monuments in nearby Custer celebrating the discovery of gold, and reconstructed a frontier fort near Custer.[66]

Soon it became clear that the organization lacked the energy and funds to meet the demands that Deadwood tourism boosters placed on it, and the chamber of commerce turned elsewhere. First it hired outside speakers who emphasized that visitors wanted to experience parts of the

Old West adventure to rally more public support. One told listeners that tourists expected to have the "vicarious thrills that belong to a section of the country that just left off being a frontier." He urged the residents to "recreate the unique glamour" of their town's past by marking historic spots that placed visitors more in touch with the pioneers.[67] Doane Robinson, the South Dakota state historian, described the "pull of the historic place" for tourists and added that it was "good business to properly mark places in which the community takes pride."[68] One Deadwood newspaper tried to speed action by printing a long letter from a disappointed visitor, who called for the town to create "an intelligent and comprehensive plan of marking all important and historic scenes similar to the ways events and people had been remembered in New England."[69]

When the Society of Black Hills Pioneers failed to act quickly, a local editor demanded that markers be set out as rapidly as possible. In 1924 the society admitted that it lacked people and cash for the job and asked the Deadwood Commercial Club to take over the task. In 1930 the city hired a chamber of commerce secretary to oversee its efforts to increase tourism. For the first time a person on the town payroll worked directly on this issue. Through his office the city began to mark historic points "closely associated with the last frontier which made Deadwood famous as the outstanding mining camp which flared 'highest and brightest.'" These included places that the boosters thought offered the most authentic experience of the Wild West past. They marked the site of Saloon Number 10, where Jack McCall shot Wild Bill Hickok; the place where Indians killed Preacher Smith in 1876; the Bella Union Saloon; and the site of the old Gem Theater.[70]

Tombstone lacked a historical society and town support, so its chamber of commerce relied solely on volunteers. They had built a road to the Schieffelin Obelisk but little else. Local leaders turned to groups such as the Women's Club and the Boy Scouts to mark important places, but the community made little progress in erecting any historical markers during the 1920s. In 1927 Frank Moy became editor of the *Tombstone Epitaph* and quickly took a clear stand on historic preservation. With prior experience as publicity director for U.S. senator Ralph Cameron and on the *Phoenix Gazette* staff, he saw the feeble commemorative effort as a failure to focus the town's economic potential. Complaining that the effort to locate and mark the "many places of interest" remained undone, he worked to spur enthusiasm. Chiding the Women's Club, he wrote a column entitled "Wake Up! Girls! Wake Up!" and stressed the loss of revenue when tourists failed to stop. "Hundreds of tourists pass through this town weekly," he wrote. "It is almost a sin on our part not to stop them so that they may enjoy, without expense but probably with profit to us, our matchless wealth of historic relics." Then he asked: "Will those [historic] tablets be put up?" Two years later he took credit for having made an impact on the townsfolk. Moy reported enthusiastically that the town had united "behind this effort to Put Tombstone on the map as the most interesting 'western town' of the West."[71]

In Dodge City pioneer and businessman Hamilton Bell, a life-long resident, led the early commemorative efforts. His interest grew from his deep personal connections with the political and business life of the town. He arrived there in 1874 as a railroad worker. Then he operated a livery stable and the Varieties Dance Hall. Next he turned to law enforcement, serving six terms as a deputy U.S. marshal and then town mayor. Returning to business, he owned a car dealership, operated a ranch, and had a pet shop before retiring. During the 1920s he joined Merritt Beeson, owner of the Beeson Theater, and Dr. Oscar Simpson, a local dentist and rancher, to push efforts for historic preservation. At first they worked through the Santa Fe Trail Association. Then they turned to the chamber of commerce to refurbish existing signs and put up new ones that had "matter concerning the early history of Dodge City." Later Bell led a group of business owners who sponsored building a monument at the site of Fort Atkinson on the city's west side.[72]

In 1926 these town leaders decided to organize a historical society to preserve "old relics, landmarks and other places of fame and significance." They began by placing local markers at various places in the county. Then in 1927 they tried to get outside funding from the National Old Trails Road Committee of the Daughters of the American Revolution. Old West sites such Dodge City's old Boot Hill Cemetery site and nearby places along the Santa Fe Trail topped their list of recommendations. They also supported reserving a part of the trail where the old wagon ruts dating back nearly a century were still visible. The group had a strong interest in preserving the town's first cemetery, Boot Hill. Their efforts marked the town's first move into the Western history market and drastically changed the meaning of "roadside attraction."[73]

Through these actions to create a tourist trade during the 1920s leaders of these three communities gave increasing attention to their histories. Supported by local histories and memoirs that attempted to transform unsavory earlier moments into periods of historic distinction, the chambers of commerce came to see their pasts not as something to be hidden but as valuable untapped commodities. This new attitude affected how they selected and market buildings and places deemed important in the effort to give tourists the authenticity that they craved. Once they accepted the towns' past as an economic benefit, boosters could attach their frontier moments to an evolving historic identity. Mostly this remained a top-down activity pushed by small groups of local business owners or even single individuals rather than average citizens, few of whom showed much interest in either history or tourism. Each city developed an identifying nickname for its promotional materials. Deadwood became the "Historic City in the Black Hills," while Dodge City labeled itself the "Cowboy Capital." Tombstone tried "Arizona's Historic Shrine" before choosing the "Town Too Tough to Die."[74] Realizing that memory clearly had value encouraged a shift in basic views of each town's past. In the drive to promote tourism business leaders joined with local governments to create attractions that pushed the limits of authenticity—and taste.

5 ⟋ Boot Hills as Attractions

Roadside markers, monuments, and buildings affirmed tourists' hopes that the Wild West that they had read about or seen in early films really had existed. Marked sites offered physical proof of its reality but still left too much to the imagination. As a true Wild West shrine owed its importance to moments of community disorder and violent people, a cemetery filled with heroes and villains could give visitors one place to find support for their preexisting images. However, contemporary realities rarely met those expectations. Instead of seeing rustic graveyards with quaint or colorful epitaphs, tourists to Deadwood during the 1920s found a staid Mount Moriah Cemetery with more than 2,500 graves and a few defaced statues. In Dodge City a large school occupied what had been the frontier cemetery, and in Tombstone visitors saw only a long-abandoned burial ground covered with trash and garbage.

This neglect changed slowly, as local citizens realized that some tourists wanted to see the old burial grounds, which therefore came to have some commercial value. During the 1920s and 1930s business and government leaders acted to create local attractions. Those partnerships gradually reinvented and marketed each town's pioneer graveyard for tourists, as a clear signal of local leaders moving toward accepting the Wild West as part of the community's official memory. In their efforts to attract visitors, the three towns not only gave death a new twist but made their burial grounds or "Boot Hill"s a signature feature of Old West commemoration. These transformations served as graphic examples of the ways in which the towns expressed their newfound appreciation of their Wild West moments. They began selecting and creating historic attractions because of their market appeal.

At first Dodge City lagged behind Tombstone and Deadwood in developing a tourist trade. Without the economic needs driving the other towns, it moved slowly toward acknowledging its past. When local promoters began to do so they created and marketed a new form of attraction, clearly mixing hucksterism and reality. The effort started in 1927 when Hamilton Bell and several other business leaders persuaded the city to buy the long-abandoned potters' field (cemetery where the town buried indigent or impoverished townspeople).[1] Of the three towns only Dodge City named its first burial ground Boot Hill. Tombstone locals could not remember hearing the name. They called their graveyard the "old city cemetery." According to longtime resident John C. Hancock, "tenderfoot writers," who "started to write up the west," popularized the name "Boot Hill." His claim had some validity. Alfred Henry Lewis lived in Dodge City for a time and certainly heard the term there. He used the label in his Wolfville stories, linking it to Tombstone. A resident there echoed the idea that it had come from Dodge City because in its "heyday it was fully as wicked" as his town.[2]

Because the name apparently came from Dodge City, it was fitting that the re-creation of that town's Boot Hill to serve as a historic attraction became the pivotal event in beginning its physical commemoration of the past. Like both Tombstone and Deadwood, it followed a pattern of early neglect and abandonment to rediscovery and exploitation, as community values changed from civic progress to accepting the past as a part of tourism's economic potential. Dodge City's first public cemetery began when it needed a place to bury a dead cowboy. The town's rapid early growth transformed the site into prime real estate, and in 1878 the Dodge City Townsite Company sold it to developers who expected to build homes there. Thinking that the new homeowners might object to having their houses sitting on a graveyard, the new owners persuaded the city to move the bodies. When the coroner exhumed them, he reported the corpses "resting quietly with their boots on" but could only recognize a few because "all the headboards, if there ever were any, had long wasted away."[3] Acting to distance the town from its earlier negative reputation, the city bought a large part of Boot Hill and built a school there. The *Hays Sentinel* recognized this act as "the proudest evidence of enlightenment upon the one surviving relic of barbarism." Despite that hope, in 1890 when the town razed the school and replaced it with a larger three-story building, the citizens still called it the "Boot Hill School."[4]

In 1925, when the Dodge City Board of Education announced that it would close the outmoded school and sell the property, local boosters decided to turn Boot Hill into a national attraction. The *Dodge City Daily Globe* backed this idea. It reported that "Boot Hill is known [from] coast to coast and could be converted into one of the show places of the city" and that "there is a sentiment here that the historical value of the tract should be capitalized."[5] Representatives from all of the major social and economic clubs urged the city commission to buy the property, but their enthusiasm ran head-on into public apathy and opposition. On the April 1925 public ballot the measure lost by a two-to-one vote. At that point the Protestant Hospital Association bought the property, hoping to remodel the old school and use it as a hospital.[6]

When the association gave up its plan and decided to sell the building at public auction two years later, interest in using the site for historical purposes reemerged. Moving quickly, the Dodge City Real Estate Board sponsored a new campaign to buy the property. Within hours boosters circulated petitions among the business leaders, calling on the city to purchase Boot Hill. They delayed the auction until a $12,000 city bond election could be held and launched a major effort to get the voters' support. Linking historic preservation to community economic progress, the campaign's backers urged voters not to hold back city advancement. Buying the cemetery property, they reminded the citizens, "is an investment that will return to the taxpayers much more than it will cost," urging them to "vote to save Boot Hill." This time their efforts worked. On April 20, 1927, Boot Hill became city property with taxpayer support.[7]

Having acquired the cemetery, the boosters had to decide how to make best use of it. They faced several divisive issues: opinions differed sharply over how much of the valuable land should be devoted to historic commemoration and what should be done with the rest. After eight months of debate, the city commission decided to accept a proposal from Dr. Oscar Simpson, a retired dentist and amateur sculptor. He offered to erect a "large statue of a western cowboy" at a "commanding position" on Boot Hill at no cost to the city. When completed it would stand in front of the new city hall, to be build there in a Spanish style as a tribute to the town's earlier position on the Santa Fe Trail and its heritage as a part of the old Spanish Empire.[8] This plan clearly did not focus on what most Americans in the late 1920s thought of as the Old West, but it forecast town leaders' interest in moving toward that goal.

Simpson's contract for the Boot Hill statue came in part because of his prominent role in Dodge City's preservation efforts. A long-term resident, he arrived in 1885 and moved into politics after years in business and being active in the chamber of commerce. He retired in 1922 and turned to sculpting and town history. Believing that Dodge City was the most "historic town in the state" except for Lawrence, which had a Civil War role, he claimed that it represented a defining symbol of the American West. "Unquestionably the most typically western in habits and customs of any town that ever existed," Simpson told a reporter, "it produced more national characters and notorious gunmen than all the rest of the wild towns of the turbulent west combined."[9] His romanticizing of Dodge City's wild past had an ironic twist: as a longtime prohibitionist, he had publicly supported closing down the town's saloons during the 1880s.

By accepting Simpson's offer to build a cowboy statue, the business leaders recognized the need to commemorate at least some of the town's controversial past. They wanted the monument to honor "the cowboy, whose activities greatly influenced and colored the early day history of Dodge City." Sculpted out of reinforced concrete, and based roughly on a likeness of the chief of police Joe Sughrue, the figure was described by the local paper as a "long, gaunt, rangy cowboy" with a "trusty six shooter," which "truly described the real cowboy as he was known in the early days."[10] On November 4, 1929, the city dedicated Simpson's statue as part of a larger historical celebration that included laying the corner stone for a new Dodge City Hall. The inscription at the base of the cowboy read "on the ashes of my campfire, this city is built." Hoping to give the scene an authentic western look, preservation supporters placed rocks nearby and planted sage and cactus around the statue.[11]

Erecting the monument opened a decades-long debate over which history Dodge City should commemorate. During the discussions, the views of those wanting to create a monument devoted to preserving community memory and proponents of developing a tourist attraction blended together gradually. The preservation group became the Southwest Historical Society in 1931 and led this debate. Hamilton Bell served as its first president, and Oscar Simpson was a charter officer. Aware that Dodge City had been slow to capitalize on its history, the members of the society worked to create a Boot Hill museum that they hoped someday "would be known throughout the nation." The group expected that making Boot Hill a national tourist attraction would succeed because the Old West that it represented had a strong appeal to a new generation of Americans "which had succeeded the actual participants in episodes of those history making days." To support their argument they pointed out that the tourists' most frequently asked question was "Where is Boot Hill?"[12]

Not everyone thought that a museum offered the best way to capitalize on Boot Hill's fame, but many people agreed that it was past time to take some action. "Why should Dodge be ashamed of Boot Hill?" a local editor asked. "Have we become so goody goody that the days of the primitive, elemental west offend our fine sense of right and wrong?" C. C. Sales, a prominent local banker, echoed that idea, asking: "Why do magazine writers continue to feature Dodge City in stories which always go over big?" The answer seemed obvious. "It is because of historic old Boot Hill." Sales argued that if the city did not preserve the site these changes would make "old Dodge City" a thing of the past. He recommended that the town erect a simple granite monument "so that a stranger visiting Dodge City may know he is standing on the site of the Old Boot Hill cemetery; and so future generations may not forget [that] Boot Hill was a very important part of the stage on which was enacted that great melodrama, the Early Life of Dodge City."[13]

Another member of the preservation committee, Joe Hulpieu, proposed a far more elaborate scheme for marking the hill. His 1931 plan included a large diorama with replicas of the Santa Fe Trail and cattle trails. Along the path he envisioned metal statues of wagon trains, buffalo, Indians, and Wyatt Earp. He expected that this early Depression era proposal would offer jobs for unemployed locals and attract tourists, apparently not having thought through how people could travel to tourist sites in the bad economy. Hulpieu presented his idea to the city commission in February 1931. There it faced a competing proposal that called for the commissioners to forget about historical preservation and build tennis courts at the site. At first the officials took no action. A few weeks later, however, excavations on the hill led to rumors that the city planned to level it and build the tennis courts. That prompted an immediate "Save Boot Hill" campaign. Forty members of the Lion's Club declared that they would protest any effort to start building tennis courts on what they called "the center of historical interest in the southwest." Dodge City mayor Henry Hart met the protesters from the Lion's Club and others from the

Southwest Historical Society to assure them that the excavation work was part of an effort to clean up the hill. To avoid future misunderstandings the commissioners established a special committee to create an official plan for the site.[14]

The new committee had surprisingly wide backing. Many people seem to have accepted the idea that tourists needed something authentic to see when they arrived. In a March 1932 telephone poll the newspaper found strong public interest in preserving the site as a historic park. Boot Hill was the "greatest asset Dodge City has as a tourist attraction," one backer asserted, but he had no specific ideas about what to build there. Following Dr. Oscar Simpson's earlier cowboy theme, the Southwest Historical Society proposed erecting a cowboy boot six feet high with spurs attached, but the city took no action.[15] This time Simpson led the move to build a parody of the early graveyard at the actual site to entertain visiting Rotarians during their 1932 convention.

The effort included fifteen concrete faces and sets of boots sticking out of gravelike mounds. Hand-painted epitaphs meant to be clever sat atop each of the haphazardly scattered graves. One example read:

> Shoot em up Jake
> Ran for sheriff 1872
> Ran from sheriff 1876
> Buried 1876

Some lay open and revealed bones and skulls, and one featured a real skeleton. Simpson installed a large dead tree that towered above the graveyard with as rope dangling from one of the branches. A sign nailed to the tree read "Horse Thief Pete was hung on this tree in 1873." Although a reporter for the *Dodge City Globe* described Boot Hill's new life as "all very sad," Simpson's creation drew so much attention from visitors that it remained after the convention ended and almost overnight became the city's main tourist attraction.[16]

A month later Simpson dedicated an officially sanctioned set of longhorn steer heads put into place to coincide with a Lion's Club convention in Dodge City. Unlike his Boot Hill parody, the concrete busts became the center of an organized public celebration. It included a parade of mounted Dodge City Lion's Club members dressed in cowboy costumes, visiting Lion's Club drum and bugle corps, and local marching bands. The event marked broad

Hangman's Tree at Dodge City museum.

Courtesy Stephen Brown (sjb4photos on Flickr.com).

public acceptance of commemorating the town's frontier moment. To add authenticity, the base for the heads incorporated rocks from the old county jail and the inscription "My trails become your highways."[17] Dedication speaker C. C. Isely described the monument as recognizing the growing national interest in the Old West, as shown by the "dozens of magazines for sale in New York and Philadelphia." He reminded the audience of the need to preserve the memory of "a fragment of the Old West for our children."[18]

For the next fifteen years Simpson's statues on Boot Hill stood as the only monuments to Dodge City's past. The town lacked money to do more and had no specific plan of action. Meanwhile, Boosters and preservationists offered a long list of ideas that included a museum, the Santa Fe Trail display, a two-room sod house, redoing the old Front Street buildings, and even a brass buffalo. Hamilton Bell's museum proposal got the most attention. The city commissioners endorsed the plan, but the Dust Bowl–ravaged town had no funding for any project. While discussions continued, the town had little choice but to accept the comic version of the Boot Hill cemetery as its sole tourist attraction. In 1935 the chamber of commerce erected a sign near city hall that read: "This is Dodge City's famous Boot Hill burial ground of the six shooting bad men." As part of the same project, the city replaced Simpson's crude epitaphs with more professional-looking ones.[19]

This mixing of hucksterism and authenticity took a new turn when the town commissioners realized that they could exchange the right to sell souvenirs for a promise to maintain the site. F. W. Steele, a longtime city resident and "pioneer southwestern photographer" who had gathered a large collection of cattle industry pictures during the 1890s, became the first concessionaire. In return for permission to sell his photographs out of an old chuckwagon at the site in 1935, he agreed to register guests, oversee publicity, and display a collection of his photos at the city hall. Just a year later William B. Rhodes took his place. Another longtime resident, he had been a farmer, ranch foreman, chief of police, and cement contractor. He retired at age eighty-four and for the next ten years became the Boot Hill custodian in exchange for the right to build a souvenir stand and information booth.[20]

As the site's popularity increased, Rhodes's role as caretaker expanded. Gradually he became the graveyard's interpreter and souvenir salesman. During his decade-long stint he became a living personification of the site, dressing like a cowboy with a hat and boots, wearing a blue bandana and a heavy gold watch to show his prosperity. Over time Rhodes made the hill his private interpretive site. He built a picket fence, a souvenir stand, and an information booth and added his own exhibits to Simpson's earlier ones. If asked, he gave tourists his version of Boot Hill and Dodge City history. When he retired at age ninety-six in 1946, he held the reputation as "a showman of the highest regard."[21]

Rhodes's showmanship fit well with a campaign to make Boot Hill a major tourist attraction. A special chamber of commerce travel committee directed by Hamilton Bell and Harry Carey tried to lure increasing numbers of visitors to the town. At times their ideas appeared silly and got little support. One of Bell's 1937 proposals called for the city to dress the local police as cowboys, mount them on horses, and make them available to answer tourists' questions.[22] Later that same year Harry Carey published the first tourist promotional pamphlet, entitled *The Thrilling Story of Famous Boot Hill.* The Southwest Historical Society distributed 10,000 free copies to gas stations and information points across the state. In a marked change from earlier booster literature, *The Thrilling Story* ignored ideas about Dodge City progress. Instead it focused on the town's early history, with grainy historical photos and descriptions of buffalo hunting, cattle drives, famous law officers, and Boot Hill, limiting discussion of modern Dodge City to the last half page. The cover reinforced this split between past and present. Beneath a drawing of a cowboy hat that partly covered a pistol the subtitle "Old Dodge 'The Cowboy Capitol'" appeared. Below an illustration of a mounted cowboy shooting a rifle was the other half of the subtitle: "and modern Dodge City."[23]

As Boot Hill's popularity grew (it had 358,000 visitors in the 1946 early postwar tourist boom), some in the community continued to reject the kitschy presentation of their town's past. The older booster rationale continued to view the cattle-drive era as a milestone in the town history, just one of the steps toward progress and modernity. In a 1935 column the editor of the *Dodge City Journal* contended that Boot Hill illustrated the eternal struggle of human virtue, lofty thought, and gallantry to overcome the forces of depredation, beastliness, ignorance, greed, and sadism. "Boot Hill," he concluded, "is really not a monument to history but merely an episode."[24] Six months later a reporter for the *Dodge City Daily Globe* gave a more realistic view. In an article entitled "Boot Hill Burlesque" he observed that tourists appeared to have only a minimal interest in monuments representing authentic history, the cowboy statue, steer busts, and a bell that hung in Dodge's first church. Instead, he noted, many visitors "seem more interested in the bogus attractions" such as the hangman's tree and the cement faces. "Fakes may not be the real history," he wrote, "but the visitors certainly lap them up."[25] The reporter recognized an idea that surfaced in the nineteenth century and still operates: to be consumable the Old West only needed a pretense of authenticity.

While Dodge City created its Boot Hill stories and relics, boosters in Tombstone followed a similar path. Yet it differed by having both an authentic location and its original inhabitants. As in Dodge City, outside publicity awakened Tombstone boosters to the potential lure that their sites offered. Once that became clear they struggled to get community support to develop the buildings and locations as official attractions. Tombstone promoters had a unique motivation among the three communities for paying attention to their cemetery. They had allowed it to become a garbage dump. Unlike Dodge City's Boot Hill, which had remained in public memory because of the Boot Hill School, Tombstone's original graveyard lay forgotten and neglected before its rediscovery. Started sometime in 1879, the site became an improvised burial ground until 1884, when the town established a new one. After that people called it the "old cemetery" and forgot about it.

That changed in 1919, when Frederick Bechdolt's articles in the *Saturday Evening Post* and his 1922 book *When the West Was Young* called it "Boot Hill." His writings gave readers a romanticized picture of frontier cemeteries and what they could see in Tombstone. Looking back, Bechdolt described each frontier town as having a Boot Hill: violent potters' graveyards, which were mere vestiges of a time in their history when "there was no law save that of might." For the author Tombstone's first burial ground offered graphic testimony to the slow recession of the Old West legacy's in the face of progress. "Here straggling mesquite bushes grow on the summit of the ridge," he wrote, "cacti and ocatilla [*sic*] sprawl over the sun-baked earth hiding between their thorny stems the headboards and long narrow heaps of stones which no man could mistake." Some of the headboards, he added, still bore faint epitaphs "which tell how death came to strong men in their full flush of youth." Yet "the majority were simply cedar slabs whose penciled legends the elements have long since washed away." Bechdolt believed that the graveyard's location added to its attraction. It lay on the summit of a ridge where visitors could see "the granite ramparts of the Dragoons frown all the long day, and the bleak hill graveyard frowns back at them."[26]

Sign at entrance to Tombstone, Arizona, in 1937.
Photograph by Dorothea Lange; courtesy Library of Congress Prints and Photographs Division,
#LC-USF34-016690-C.

When tourists arrived in Tombstone expecting to visit this windswept monument, the vista that they found could only disappoint them. Frank Moy, editor of the *Tombstone Epitaph*, described the scene clearly: "Among the desert briars which cover the hill between the cairns are piles of tin cans, broken bottles, rusted pots and pans, old shoes, and all the rubbish of modern city homes."[27] As visitation increased, so did community embarrassment. In 1925 a Canadian tourist who had traveled to see the site complained that it was "the most pathetic garbage dump" he had ever seen. The *Epitaph* noted that the same visitor had been shocked to find that Dodge City's graveyard had been "obliterated" and replaced by a schoolhouse on the site. Yet the editor wrote that Dodge's treatment of its cemetery could not compare to Tombstone's "desecration of such a sacred relic."[28] Others echoed these feelings. When John Clum, the first town mayor, returned, looking for his first wife's resting place, he could not find her grave or even the cemetery. In Phoenix the *Arizona Gazette* chided the citizens for their lack of pride in the town's pioneers. Even the current mayor, Ostorius Gibson, admitted that "neglect of a burial ground is a sad enough reflection on a community, but rubbish deliberately cast on such ground is a disgrace."[29]

A garbage dump clearly hurt both civic pride and the town's fledgling tourist efforts, and Tombstone boosters moved quickly to change things. Arlington Gardiner, working with the Tombstone Commercial Club, organized and led a drive to turn the graveyard into a tourist attraction. First he persuaded supporters to begin using the name "Boot Hill." Then he enlisted Mayor Gibson as a supporter. In 1923 the boosters persuaded a Boy Scout troop to start clearing away trash from the site. Once officials realized that the task went far beyond what a handful of scouts could do, town leaders appealed to the state legislature for clean-up funds. They asserted shamelessly that the townspeople should not have to bear the costs of rehabilitating what had become a famous national burial site before making any serious effort to do that themselves. Here pioneers "went over the hill with their boots on," the petitioners wrote, "in protection of themselves and their families and for the preservation of law and order, so that we who are here today could enjoy the liberties and opportunities of this day."[30] When the state officials failed to respond, Mayor Gibson asked Frederick Bechdolt, Badger Clark, and other famous western writers for donations to match cash pledged by John Clum. He proposed using the money to build a fence around the cemetery and to identify the graves. When that effort collapsed, the city returned to urging voluntary organizations and the Boy Scouts to continue picking up cans and gathering refuse.[31]

Disappointed but not ready to quit, Gardiner and Gibson joined editor Frank Moy in a renewed effort to move beyond building a fence and clearing trash. Through the *Tombstone Epitaph* the editor urged locals to become aware of the site's potential to attract tourists and appealed to their pride in the town's past. "No remnant of the good old, bad hectic days of Tombstone is more intriguing to the imagination than this place of mystery," he wrote. "Who were these people buried on the hill whose slopes face the rising sun? Were they the two-gun men; the stage robbers; the feudists; the cattle rustlers; the gamblers; the cowmen, young and reckless of life? Or were they the common, quiet householders, the fathers of little children, the ranchers, the miners?" Moy lamented that no one knew because most of the graves lacked headstones or any other markers.[32]

While this challenge brought the issue to the townspeople, it took the completion of U.S. Highway 80, the "Broadway of America," to persuade leaders that they needed to transform Boot Hill from a town dump to a tourist attraction. In 1932 the city chose the chamber of commerce as the official custodian of Boot Hill and directed it to prepare the site for the thousands of expected visitors who would travel the new road. At least part of the motivation for promoting the cemetery came from Arlington Gardiner's visit to Dodge City's Boot Hill. He reported what Dodge leaders had done and pointed out that Tombstone's graveyard had real bodies, so he recommended focusing on what could be done with the existing graves. Because almost none of the plots had any markers, he enlisted Henry Macia, a former mine manager and local restaurant and lodge owner, to begin the difficult process of identifying and marking the graves.[33]

Looking forward to visiting tourists, they made the reinstallation of the headboards of the town's most famous incidents—the gunfight at the OK Corral and the four Bisbee robbers hanged legally in 1884—the top priorities. The chamber of commerce asked the townspeople to share any information about others buried there so that authentic information could be posted on a signboard at the cemetery site. Frank Vaughn, the former Tombstone resident who helped bury the Clantons and McLaurys, joined the hunt for their burial places and assisted in reproducing the headboard texts.[34] To help clean the area and find other graves the city hired six workers. At the site they drove crowbars into the ground to find coffins or bones, filled and rounded plots with dirt, and cleared the spaces between the graves to make the cemetery what the *Epitaph* called "a credit to our little town."[35] Then in late 1932 the town leaders persuaded the Arizona Highway Department of the new tourist attraction's importance. The department granted permission for the community to build a byway to the "showplace of old Tombstone" along with a six-foot by twelve-foot black-and-white sign that could be seen and photographed easily by passing motorists.[36]

By January 1933 incoming motorists could read a new sign: "Welcome to Tombstone and Boot Hill Graveyard." Its simple message merged the town's identification with its past. One observer called it the "very essence of Tombstone history," as "the stories the board tells, of gun battles, hangings, murders, [and] lynchings, are the stories of Tombstone at the height of its wild and extravagant glory." When the numbers of curious travelers increased, Boot Hill gained more outside attention. The *San Antonio*

Evening Herald called it a "paying graveyard and evidence that people like reminders of a rip-roaring past."[37] The chamber of commerce boasted that it is "now being considered by many writers and touring directors as one of the great drawing cards of the southwest" and asked the state highway commission for money to erect a black manganese monument shaped like an Indian teepee with a copper plaque dedicated to the unknown soldiers buried there. By 1937 the city handed out flyers proclaiming that Boot Hill had been "voted the outstanding attraction for tourists along the Broadway of America."[38]

As with many promotions, publicity about the cemetery raised expectations far beyond what the site could deliver. As late as 1936 only 15 of an estimated 180 graves had any positive identification. At first the absence of marked graves added to the image of a fading Wild West that so many popular writers had helped to develop. To some the lack of identification for each grave demonstrated the violent nature of people buried there. Editor Moy speculated that "whoever they were, they died with their boots on, as was befitting a regular western guy." This description went back to at least 1925, when a Tucson paper had referred to Boot Hill as the "outlaw cemetery" where unknown men were shot and buried without ceremony in "a lonely grave just six by three."[39]

A 1930 radio broadcast described the graveyard as a "desolate, windswept cemetery" where the inscriptions were "worn away long ago and whatever grass there may have been has yielded to the desert." It was "not much of a cemetery, but appropriate, somehow, for men who died with their boots on."[40] A local reporter had little positive to say either. He referred to it as a place where few could "claim distinction for their good deeds—for many were murderers." An account in the *Arizona Daily Star* in 1929 said that "180 pioneers, miners, gamblers and two-gun men" lay buried there. "Some of those died natural deaths, but many were shot or hung. . . . How many thrilling stories of Indian raids, saloon fights, and mine claim jumping lie buried" there! National papers made similar comments. The *New York Times Magazine* called it a "gray, barren promontory. . . . Under its slabs those old days of violence lie buried, along with their victims."[41]

As long as Boot Hill had a few headstones or other markers to certify its violent past (those of the OK Corral victims and hanged criminals) visitors could imagine it as what one called a "monument to the swashbuckling men and women who settled the frontier." Yet eventually the lack of grave markers and visitors' insistence on authenticity became a liability. The image of a wind-swept knoll populated by the remains of violent criminals came to an abrupt end in 1937 when Mrs. F. D. Smith came from Missouri to find her mother's grave. Flora Stumph, the woman in question, had died in 1884 from the effects of anesthesia while sitting in a dentist's chair. Locals showed Mrs. Smith an iron-fenced plot in Boot Hill that fit with her late father's description of the site. The idea that a plain housewife lay buried in Boot Hill aroused a storm of controversy. Some questioned the identification of the location. One former resident argued that because fences had been used to mark the graves of the "righteous" at the time, upstanding citizens must have been buried in another cemetery. After all, everyone knew that "Boot Hill was reserved" for men and women who died in "debauchery or lawlessness." Some weeks later Stumph's niece Bertha Strinker came to town and verified the grave as that of her aunt. Embarrassed by the negative publicity that the episode created, the Tombstone City Council ordered markers for the graves that could be identified.[42]

The Stumph affair ended any doubts that Boot Hill included more than just victims of violence. Less than a year later a new group, the Boothill Boosters, used the death of Quong Kee, a former Tombstone restaurant operator, to get positive attention. They raised money to have him buried on Boot Hill. Obtaining support for this venture proved easy, as many saw the 97-year-old Kee as a link with the old days. With the funds in hand, they sponsored a statewide radio broadcast and an Easter sundown service to dedicate a monument to him. The service marked a shift from the outlaw emphasis a decade earlier. Kee's identification as a restaurant owner affirmed the memory of many locals that the gunfighter hyperbole obscured the actions of real community builders, the true town pioneers. At the service one of the speakers lauded Kee as a man "never accustomed to the handle of a six-shooter, but rather the handle of a frying plan." Another longtime resident, Ethel Macia, framed the ceremony as a regular event but with a frontier slant. She described Boot Hill as a place where "many of Tombstone's finest people were laid to rest: the wife of the mayor, the baby son of a physician, the young daughter of a businessman . . . as well as those who helped to make the glamorous blood and thunder history." To distance the burial ground even more from its outlaw reputation, Macia reminded her listeners that at one time the cemetery included both Chinese and Jewish sections.[43]

The Stumph and Kee incidents marked a basic change in how the town promoted its cemetery. Its brochures from the late 1930s admitted that the "famous Boot Hill grave yard" contained "180 graves of persons in all walks of life." A later pamphlet depicted it as a "last resting place for pioneers of the Old West," where "outlaws and peaceful citizens alike are buried."[44] Despite this effort outside writers continued to emphasize the outlaw side of the story. For example, Joseph Miller's 1938 article "Here Lie the Bodies" focused its description specifically on the graves of the Clantons, the McLaurys, and the four Bisbee bank robbers hanged in Tombstone. Writing for that same magazine a decade later, Lenora Brimmer took a more even-handed approach. She said that a visit to Boot Hill helped "to recapture the pioneering spirit of the frontier." While she acknowledged the "good people who made up the background," she devoted most of her article to "the outlaw section" of the cemetery.[45]

Boot Hill publicity brought more visitors but also more vandalism and souvenir hunting. Locals and tourists alike wanted to take something from the cemetery home with them as they did when touring Deadwood's Mount Moriah Cemetery. Just a year after Quong Kee's monument had been completed, the city built a fence of sharp-needled ocotillo to limit the damage, but this failed completely. By 1944 vandals had chiseled the monument down to its concrete base and had stolen the protective fence. Elsewhere only four graffiti-covered wooden headboards erected by the chamber of commerce remained. Attacking what it called pillaging of the "Shrine of America," the *Tombstone Epitaph* accused the townspeople of failing to do their "duty to posterity" by ignoring the repeated damage to the Boot Hill markers. Surely this would hurt the tourist trade, the reporter wrote. He urged city officials to hire a guard for the site and to begin charging admission that would fund some restoration work at the cemetery.[46]

A year later in 1945 Tombstone followed Dodge City's lead, granting Emmitt Nunnelly, a Wild West aficionado, permission to operate a souvenir stand for one year in exchange for daily upkeep of the cemetery. For the next year he and his wife cleaned the site, worked to identify more of the graves, and marked them with metal signs set in concrete to prevent any more thefts. In late 1946 Nunnelly died in his Boot Hill office. In thanks for his work there, the city allowed him to be buried in the old cemetery. After her husband's death Lela Nunnelly expanded the souvenir stand, added restrooms, and in 1952 published an official guide to the cemetery. Of the 250 graves listed in the guide, 101 of the occupants supposedly had died from hanging, stabbing, or shooting or at the hands of the Apaches.[47] Tombstone's Boot Hill, like its Dodge City counterpart, had its own version of exaggerating authenticity to earn a profit.

While Deadwood, the third of the three towns, did not have to invent a "Boot Hill" to meet tourist expectations as the others did, it too used the existing cemetery to attract tourists. The major difference was that it still used the historic Mount Moriah Cemetery as its regular graveyard. By the 1930s it contained over 2,500 graves, and the limits of taste curbed some of the exaggerated commercialism that occurred in Dodge City and Tombstone. Rather than focusing on outlaw graveyards based largely on fiction, Deadwood depended on the fame of characters already established as Old West icons. Initially the town had buried its deceased in an improvised graveyard called Ingleside, on level ground near its growing main street. When the land became more valuable, in 1878 city council members decided to add it to the existing fourth ward and move the cemetery. They chose a higher and less desirable spot and over the next few years moved the remains to the new site, now called Mount Moriah. Because many of the original graves lacked any identification, the town placed fifty of the corpses in a potters' field. Opening a new graveyard brought some reorganization: organizations and ethnic groups including the Chinese, Jews, Masons, firefighters, soldiers, and members of the Society of Black Hills Pioneers all had their own sections. Citizens organized the Deadwood Cemetery Association in 1892 to oversee the planning and maintenance at the site.[48]

The movement of the bodies would probably have attracted little attention (as had happened in Dodge City) except that it involved the town's most famous dead citizen, Wild Bill Hickok. Beginning soon after his burial, a parade of gawkers came to see the gunman's Ingleside grave and take souvenirs. In the first three years after his death they stole three headboards from his plot. In 1879 Mount Moriah inherited Hickok's notoriety with his reinterment there. Much of the attention stemmed from the obsession of Louis Shoenfield, a Deadwood resident and one of the four men who exhumed the corpse. He clearly wanted public attention and made wild accusations. Even before the body was moved, he claimed that grave robbers were about to steal it and urged Wild Bill's brother Lorenzo to have it moved. Shoenfield also spread rumors that bombs had been placed around the grave to deter looting. Charlie Utter, one of Hickok's friends, accused Shoenfield of being a "bilk" who wanted personal notoriety.[49]

Shoenfield seems to have been the source for the claim that when disinterred Hickok's body appeared to be completely preserved. The *Black Hills Daily Times* repeated the story quickly, proclaiming "Wild Bill Petrified" and attributing this to his godlike status. A heated debate followed, as Henry Robinson, the undertaker who supervised this event, denied seeing anything unusual about the corpse. Others disagreed. John McClintock, author of *Pioneer Days in the Black Hills* and one of the four men who witnessed the casket opening, recalled that Hickok's "body, to our great astonishment, appeared to be in a perfect state of preservation." He reported tapping the body with a stick the size of a cane: "The sound from the tapping was much the same as would result from the tapping of a wall, and not of solid stone." McClintock commented that the "body of the great gunman, one of the greatest man-killers that the world had ever known," was reburied. The argument about it being petrified faded soon after.[50]

If Deadwood residents could honor Hickok by allowing him to become a deity through petrification, they could also enshrine a martyred servant of God in the Old West by giving him a proper burial in Mount Moriah. Less than a year after reburying the gunfighter, the local paper urged Methodists to find and reinter the body of Henry Weston "Preacher" Smith, a minister allegedly killed in 1876 by the Indians. The Reverend M. Cummings, new pastor of the Methodist church, ultimately took up the challenge. Working with the local undertaker, Henry Robinson, in 1883 he found the unmarked grave in the old Ingleside graveyard. Cummings staged an elaborate funeral for the minister. Eight years later Smith's remains were moved yet again to a plot nearer to the center of the cemetery and much closer to Hickok's resting spot.[51]

As the two main tourist attractions at Mount Moriah, the Hickok and Smith graves became repeated targets for souvenir hunters. They destroyed Hickok's 1879 wooden headboard, whittling off chunks of it. Apparently the town had no funds to spend protecting the graves, so in 1891 a citizens' committee raised money and hired a New York sculptor, J. B. Riordan, to create a red sandstone monument of the gunman nine feet tall. When finished it bore the epitaph "Custer was lonely without him." The sculptor also erected a full-sized statue of Smith. The locals hoped that the new memorials would end vandals' attacks on the grave markers. Unfortunately, the new statues only gave them more possibilities. While they continued to pick away at local hero Smith, they turned most of their attention on the nationally famous Hickok. Within a decade he lost his mustache, long hair, shoulders, and nose.[52] This continuing defacement embarrassed promoters, who believed that it would cast the town in a bad light and worried that they might lose their main tourist attraction. In 1893 the *Deadwood Daily Times* raised the fear that some enterprising capitalist might "resurrect the body and take it east for exhibition." It urged the townspeople to watch the cemetery and catch vandals in the act in the hope that this would stop the desecration.[53]

The repeated damage to both monuments embarrassed town boosters, who were concerned that it hurt the town's image. After someone broke off what remained of Hickok's head the *Daily Pioneer-Times* declared the "well-known landmark, that has been visited by so many," is beyond repair. It warned that outsiders would lose interest in the community unless the town renewed or replaced the grave markers, as "a visit to Deadwood is not complete without an inspection of Wild Bill's monument."[54] Within a year the town began raising funds to commission a life-sized statue to be protected by a wire fence. The campaign used the familiar tourist-centered rhetoric to gain public support. A new monument would attract easterners "who have read of the man in life, whose deeds, with those of others of his stripe, made Deadwood so famous that the tenderfoot feels shaky even yet when he steps upon the soil," one local paper reminded its readers.[55]

When Calamity Jane died on August 1, 1903, in nearby Terry, South Dakota, her funeral brought a third historic character's body to Mount Moriah. The corpse's return from Terry to Deadwood produced varying stories, as had her life. Tied to an upright chair and carried by wagon, her remains reached Deadwood. The mortuary workers had to protect it from people trying to cut snippets of hair. Rumors at the time said that Calamity Jane had asked to be buried next to Hickok's grave, where she had posed for an earlier picture, but there is no evidence that the Society of Black Hills Pioneers took that into account when locating her grave. In any case, they had her remains buried next to Hickok's newly refurbished grave. Her burial site had a large urn decorated with cherubs, rather than another statue. With her interment Deadwood's cemetery could boast of having both Wild Bill Hickok and Calamity Jane, a "double attraction to exhibit to visitors from the east."[56]

By the 1920s Deadwood's graveyard trinity had become the centerpiece of its historical commemorations. As tourism grew during that decade, Mount Moriah and its three famous characters played a large role in carefully designed promotions. The chamber of commerce and the Black Hills tourist associations focused almost all of their efforts on Deadwood's Old West period. This illustrated the major shift that had begun several decades earlier after the editor of the *Deadwood Daily Pioneer-Times* had urged citizens not to emphasize their Old West Past. If they continued to do so, he warned, eastern visitors who "expect to find Deadwood's romance of twenty-five years ago" will miss seeing its modern progress.[57] By the 1920s and 1930s boosters ignored his advice. Instead new tourist guides of the era included short biographies of Calamity Jane, Hickok, and Smith, often written in dime-novel prose. One described the town as a place where it was "not so long ago that a quick finger and a nimble eye meant life or death." Another called it the "Sodom and Gomorrah of modern ages" and the "wild west capital of the world" but a place where only a few traces of "its fabled wickedness survive." Among those remaining, it pointed out, were the graves of the "two famous characters it has given history," Calamity Jane and Hickok.[58]

Advertisers in the Black Hills hurried to use tourists' hopes to find connections between Mount Moriah's notorious residents and the town's history for their businesses. Clearly, some visitors fully accepted the frontier images that they had seen in popular books and magazines. After visiting, one tourist wrote: "What a train of thought that name [Deadwood] arouses; what scenes of wild border life these majestic hills" have seen. "Up there on Mt. Moriah, 'Wild Bill' and 'Calamity Jane' lie in the hills they loved, and the youthful reader still thrills as he pores over their exploits." The editor of the *Kimball (South Dakota) Graphic* agreed, noting that the town still "carries all the charm and adventure of the wild days of gold dust, easy living and quick clean up fortunes." He added that Hickok died there and his memorial stands on the "brow of the hill in Mt. Moriah Cemetery."[59]

Although biographies such as Duncan Aikman's *Calamity Jane and the Lady Wildcats* depicted both characters unfavorably at the time, local tourist materials continued to portray them as heroes. This allowed the towns to ignore their criminal or antisocial actions and give them positive virtues instead. Hickok appeared as a fearsome and chivalrous police officer, unjustly murdered. One guide called him "Deadwood's idol" and a "refined enforcer of law and order." Another described him as "absolutely fearless," as a hero who died before he had time to establish order in Deadwood. Similarly, S. Goodale Price blamed Hickok's death on the fact that his "war on bad men on the frontier made him a marked man." The author of the *Beautiful Black Hills* said that Hickok "was simply a gentlemanly gunman; one who shot only in self-defense, or else to uphold the dignity of the law."[60] The official information distributed by the chamber of commerce echoed much of this, describing Hickok as a gunman to whom "the majesty of the law was everything" and "not a bad man in any sense." It added the myth that the town had decided to appoint him sheriff when he died.[61]

The same booster literature presented Calamity Jane as a boisterous but kind-hearted frontier woman and gave no hint of her reputation as an alcoholic sometime prostitute. In *Black Hills, Land of Legend* S. Goodale Price called her a woman who "beneath that rough exterior" had "a heart of gold." Another tourist handout pointed out that "old timers around Deadwood are still eager to testify in chorus to her good traits and to the service she rendered to the Black Hills Pioneers." According to several other visitors' guide materials, this reputation came from Calamity Jane's efforts at nursing sick pioneers back to health and her generous spirit. One wrote that "she was always ready to share her money and provisions with those who needed it."[62] Deadwood boosters clearly felt that once they had raised their local heroes to icons they had a responsibility to protect their images.

Calamity Jane presented a special challenge because she lived far beyond the frontier era from which her fame resulted and many stories about her could not be authenticated. For example, rumors about her life and actions including one that she and Hickok had been buried in the same grave had circulated widely.[63] In 1937 Federal Writers' Project researchers working on a biography of her for their South Dakota guide disputed Deadwood's version of her story, setting off a storm of controversy. First they questioned the vague data about her life and found evidence suggesting that she might have lived until 1911 and been buried in Montana. That raised doubts about whether her remains had been buried at Mount Moriah. The researchers accepted that she was buried there in a plot near Hickok, but only after having been moved there from an earlier grave. Their conclusion described her as practicing the "life-long trade of prostitute" and as a woman who eventually "sank lower in the social scale."[64]

This questioning of the authenticity of Calamity Jane's character and burial came as a major shock to chamber members. To resolve their differences the Works Progress Administration (WPA) and Deadwood Chamber of Commerce searched for a death certificate and for any living relatives to verify facts about her burial. Nell Perrigoue, secretary of the chamber, defended the authenticity of Deadwood's version of the story. She noted the difficulty in getting official birth or death records and argued that using testimony from living pioneers offered the best means for settling disputed facts. After extensive questioning of local witnesses, she concluded that "the real and only Calamity Jane ever known in this section of the west, died in 1903 and was buried on August 4, in Mt. Moriah Cemetery." Defending her character, Perrigoue stated that "she was never known to have lived the life of a prostitute in an open manner; that pioneers and other citizens accepted Calamity Jane at all times and remembered her for deeds of kindness." The chamber secretary offered to file affidavits and newspaper documentation to prove the authenticity of the data and send along a photograph showing that Calamity and Hickok never shared the same grave plot. At that point she considered the question of the "real Calamity Jane who is buried at Mt. Moriah" closed.[65]

Featuring Deadwood's famous grave sites in new publicity materials during the 1920s and 1930s came as part of an organized promotional campaign led by Black Hills tourist associations to lure increasing numbers of motor tourists and some of the growing numbers of visitors to dude ranches nearby. The fresh appeals, along with Deadwood's own tourist camp and chamber of commerce activities, fit well with growing national attention to the Old West and its characters. Hoping to transform a mere visit to a pilgrimage, promoters began describing a visit to their community in semireligious terms. One guide pointed out that "not only Deadwood, but thousands of visitors climb this hill to visit the shrine of these three early idols." A reporter for the *Minneapolis Journal* used the same imagery, recalling that when he visited the graves the ground around them had been "worn bare by the tread of thousands of pilgrims who visit the spot."[66]

The increasing number of "pilgrims" raised the ever-present question of who should be responsible for the grave sites and their upkeep. From its beginning in 1892 the Deadwood Cemetery Association had done both for Mount Moriah. Because the burial ground remained in use, unlike the Boot Hills of Dodge City and Tombstone, the flood of tourists increased costs dramatically, far beyond the association's limited funds. This meant that upkeep and security suffered, raising complaints from tourists. A visitor from Minnesota expressed disappointment over the appearance of Hickok and Calamity Jane's graves on "behalf of myself and others who feel the same way." He grumbled that the "long clover growing within the enclosure of Wild Bill's tomb completely covers the inscription of the headstone" and suggested that the graves needed more regular attention. The "tourists I met," he commented, all "spoke of this lack of attention to the graves of these notables . . . feeling that this is the least that could be done by those having Deadwood's interests at heart."[67]

The *Deadwood Daily Pioneer-Times* used the criticism as it tried to rally the community to use its history as an emblem of civic pride and as a major tourist attraction. "We who live in Deadwood," the editor argued, "including nearly all of us, are prone to discount the value of our early day history . . . to tourists and visitors," and "this careless attitude is shameful." He urged his readers to focus attention on their most well publicized attraction. The story of Wild Bill and Calamity Jane known "in song and story from one end of America to the other" deserved more local attention. In fact, he wrote, "Deadwood owes it to herself and to our visitors to perpetuate whatever remains to commemorate their deeds and associations."[68] This scolding had little impact. Neither the townspeople nor the local government took any immediate action.

Despite the local criticism, vandalism continued. As souvenir hunters continued to chip off body parts at Hickok's memorial, the results drew national ridicule of Deadwood. Writing in a 1930 issue of the *Saturday Evening Post*, Courtney Cooper recalled his visit to Mount Moriah. He described the Hickok statue as "a sad representation": instead of being the "dominant figure which he was supposed to be, the statue now allows him to be as chinless as a groundhog." The article included a photograph of the defaced monument.[69] Preacher Smith's statue fared no better. Gradually it too lost its ears, nose, beard, one arm, and finally its entire head. Often tourists climbed the monument and had their picture taken with their face replacing Smith's. Calamity Jane's marker got the same treatment. In 1933 visitors hacked the floral urn that decorated her plot to pieces with crowbars. Unable to halt the repeated vandalism, the Deadwood Cemetery Association dissolved in 1938 and surrendered its function to the city at the end of that year.[70]

Soon after the town extended its control to the monuments at Mount Moriah, it asked the chamber of commerce to find new ways to market the cemetery. At first that group took little action except to propose cleaning and putting up markers in the Chinese section of the burial ground. Then in 1940 a new South Dakota State Highway Commission program designed to boost tourism offered to provide signs for historic sites to the cash-strapped authorities. Chamber of Commerce secretary Nell Perrigoue responded quickly, identifying nine sites worthy of "historic interest." Not surprisingly, they included the three graves at Mount Moriah as well as two others related to Hickok's death and the place where the citizens captured his murderer, Jack McCall. When the signs arrived, she wrote that they were "welcomed with enthusiasm by local citizens as well as visitors."[71]

While the chamber worked on new plans for marketing its past, it could not decide what to do with the historic grave sites. If tourists followed the new markers they came to Hickok's pockmarked and headless statue, standing in a completely ineffective wire mesh cage. Preacher Smith's monument looked just as bad. The *Black Hills Weekly* reported that Salvador "Dali or some other surrealist sculptors might like the way he looks now, but the ordinary person thinks he's having a nightmare." Not only had vandals stolen the head, but "somebody has balanced a round sandstone rock where his head should be, featureless, not a face . . . just a round rock."[72] In 1943, two years later, another vandal toppled the statue's remains completely. With each of the Mount Moriah monuments to its leading historical character either defaced beyond recognition or destroyed, the town had little to offer visitors. In the debate over how to commemorate their Old West heritage, some chamber members wanted to put up large photographs at the graves. Others favored having new busts installed. Unable to decide and perhaps unable to raise enough money to take any meaningful action, in 1950 the chamber asked the Boy Scouts to clean the grave sites.[73]

The unwillingness to care for the cemetery ended three years later, when a member of the Wild Bill Hickok Foundation in Abilene, Kansas, visited. He reported the lack of upkeep to the president of that group, who fired off a letter to the mayor of Deadwood. It asserted that the town had no right to Hickok's body because he had never been a citizen of Deadwood and because it had allowed his grave to be desecrated. The letter asked that the body be exhumed and returned to Kansas, where it would be given the proper care and respect it that deserved. This spurred the chamber into action. Its new plans included better fences, the removal of what remained of Hickok's statue, and placing a replica of the original headstone of "sufficient size to be photographed easily" at the grave. The city and private donations financed the project.[74]

Meanwhile Deadwood mayor Ray Ewing rejected the request from Abilene. He replied that his town was "capable of seeing to it that in the final analysis the grave will be preserved for future generations with all the glory, and the historical aura to which it is entitled." To head off any moves to disinter Hickok's remains, town authorities notified the state attorney general that they would demand that the state militia protect the grave if Abilene citizens tried to remove the body. Dakota authorities forwarded the request to the Kansas attorney general, who immediately distanced his state from the issue. He assured Dakota officials that it was illegal to disturb a grave in Kansas and assumed that South Dakota had a similar law.[75] Improvements at Mount Moriah calmed the situation briefly but failed to end the vandalism. When thieves stole the new headboard in 1956, exasperated officials tried another approach. They had simple granite markers embedded in large stone walls surrounded by a sturdy metal fence placed atop each of the three graves. It took until 1961 to complete this project.[76]

Deadwood's hesitation to become responsible for Mount Moriah and its promotion followed the pattern of local governmental involvement in the management of Tombstone's and Dodge City's Boot Hills. In each case the growing tourist industries encouraged the towns to create attractions that needed government assistance. The early lack of long-term funding forced the communities to depend on voluntary labor to support a growing but nebulous industry that many rank-and-file citizens did not entirely accept. The growing governmental support resulted from efforts by their chambers of commerce or similar groups. They acted as semiofficial agencies of the cities, setting agendas for promotion, assuming responsibilities for physical maintenance, directing voluntary involvement, and channeling local and outside funding. In large part this resulted from actions by individuals who shared membership in chambers of commerce and local governments, such as Arlington Gardiner in Tombstone and Hamilton Bell in Dodge City. Deadwood, however, had a paid city employee, Neil Perrigoue, who served as the link for the government, the chamber of commerce, and local clubs and service organizations. The creation of Boot Hills in Tombstone and Dodge City and the adoption of the Mount Moriah characters in Deadwood became business enterprises directed and supported by leaders who used their pasts to bring economic benefit to their communities.

These efforts to increase tourism repeatedly faced the temptation of creating attractions to satisfy public cravings for the Old West. That, in turn, led toward stories that overemphasized lurid events and colorful or dangerous people in each of the towns' pasts. At times this hucksterism threatened expectations of authenticity that brought many tourists to the towns in the first place. Still, as long as the visitors expected the Old West to reflect their images, the towns tried not to disappoint them. That meant selective embellishment of gunslingers, prostitutes, and outlaws and a deemphasis of some important aspects of town building. That came with a cost and divided communities, because many local citizens rejected the Wild West images of their past. Their objections ran head-on into what had become a national phenomenon, resulting from "the fact that the general public, looking to the West as the one great romantic spot of America, wants its West as raw as possible." This translated into the idea that "every mining camp must have been a lawless, brawling camp with vigilantes working overtime and every tree decorated with human fruit."[77]

Some people living in each of the three towns clearly saw their history this way. Author Charles Finger met folk in Tombstone who proved more than willing to provide him with the Wild West he wanted. One "old rap-scallion" whom he described as "a well-developed agency of information" took him on a tour of all the old sites, embellishing them with stories of his personal experiences with gunfights, gambling houses, and outlaws. Later a disappointed Finger learned that his guide with the "magnificent memory" had lived in Michigan until 1929 and came to work in Tombstone as an umbrella maker.[78] Local businesses and governments used ideas similar to those offered by Finger's guide when promoting attractions for traveling customers. In all three towns they focused on the pioneer era of the Old West, using forms of hucksterism based on images from lurid dime novels and the Wild West shows of the late nineteenth century. As the towns commodified their pasts, they moved beyond just marking specific Old West sites, repeatedly merging fact and fiction. The development of their Boot Hills shows this clearly. Dodge City had an ersatz cemetery that lacked human remains. Deadwood could boast of having real corpses but not the original graveyard. Tombstone had real graves often filled with unidentified remains.

6 🔫 Old West Celebrations

By the 1920s the growing flood of curious tourists, arriving to get a taste of the Wild West, proved its continuing market value and persuaded city and business leaders that their futures had a clear link to their famous pasts. As already discussed, they attempted to attract visitors by appealing to their desires for the romantic Old West through advertising campaigns, marking historic sites, and creating other attractions. When boosters and local chambers of commerce turned away from stories of local progress to Wild West themes, they struggled to enlist community support for tourism. Major public celebrations that began in each town in 1923 offered one of the most powerful ways to galvanize public interest. Even though these events varied, they signaled a change in how the communities defined themselves. Leaders of all sorts who had glossed over their town's colorful but violent earlier histories now used public celebrations to assert their distinctive identity as authentic western places. Through annual repetition these occasions permanently fixed that identity on these communities.

Each town's public presentations illustrated the ways in which local business and political leaders saw the role of the past. All of them had to unify the community in order to enlist wide local support. Where Dodge City's early celebrations emphasized modernism, from the start those in Deadwood and Tombstone emphasized the Old West. All of the public events had wide appeal and occurred at a time when Americans looked nervously at the changes taking place after World War I: the country's new international role, its shift from rural to urban values, the materialism of a new consumer society, continuing massive immigration, and a perceived loosening of public morality. One way in which Americans dealt with their new modern society was to look at their frontier past. By remembering the pioneering experience and the values that they thought it fostered—perseverance, individualism, opportunity, and hard work—they could face the challenges of the new corporate society. When communities used images of the Wild West, they met both local and tourism needs.[1]

Public commemorations gave cities a chance to turn their past into a positive asset. Event originators presented street violence, gambling, prostitution, drinking, and gunfighting as amusement. The switch proved relatively simple. By the time town leaders began organizing their public celebrations in the 1920s, forms of western entertainment had become well established in theaters and Wild West shows. Stage plays with western themes based on the lives of Buffalo Bill and Wild Bill Hickok had appeared since the 1870s in New York, Chicago, and elsewhere.

As western productions grew in popularity over the next twenty-five years lighting, set design, and special effects became more sophisticated. Often these included large-scale visual effects such as gunfights, train wrecks, and daring horsemanship. Displays in theaters, in turn, helped inspire Wild West and Indian medicine shows that crisscrossed the country at the end of the nineteenth century.[2]

These shows presented the spectacle of the West on a scale far larger than the stage could offer. Between 1884 and 1938 "Bill Shows" (called that because of "Buffalo Bill's Wild West") offered world audiences a blend of circus, dime-novel plots, and dramatic visual imagery, all blended with some authenticity. Cody and his promoter, Nate Salisbury, structured the Wild West performances to give patrons a general picture of the Old West punctuated with events such as the holdup of the Deadwood Stage, reenactments of famous battles with Indians, and gunfights between established heroes and villains. To add authenticity, the shows included herds of buffalo, western-style clothing, wagons, horses, and large numbers of guns. Added realism came from including well-known westerners such as Cody, Sitting Bull, Annie Oakley, and Buck Taylor in its programs. At its peak between 1894 and 1898 Cody's performance covered 30 acres, employed 467 people, and required 52 train cars when it moved.[3] Its popularity fostered a series of rivals, including Pawnee Bill, Miller Brothers 101 Ranch, Cummin's Indian Congress, and others. Although each Bill Show had some unique acts, they all included features such as an opening parade, authentic characters, western clothing, Indians, marksmanship demonstrations, and rodeo-style activities.

By the time Deadwood, Dodge City, and Tombstone began planning their events in the 1920s, the shows had represented ideas of the Old West for two generations. Each town's reputation encouraged it to include acts similar to those in the Wild West shows, because local promoters assumed that the public expected to see them. At the same time, the three communities had one advantage over stage presentations, Bill Shows, or films. They had been the physical setting for some of the West's most famous events. Real western characters had walked their streets, and historic events had occurred there. Therefore they could claim to offer a higher level of authenticity than other shows by including local relics, actual (if increasingly aging) participants, and stories of well-known heroes.

As the fifty-year anniversaries of their towns' beginnings approached, organizers in each place debated how they should deal with their controversial pasts. Some of the citizens remained sensitive about their communities' sordid reputations. They believed that promoting modernism and progress offered the key to local prosperity. In 1921 Dodge City addressed the issue first when it decided to hold a semicentennial celebration. Local businessman J. P. McCullum proposed that the town combine its fiftieth birthday celebration with the hundredth anniversary of the opening of the Santa Fe Trail. Chamber of commerce members Hamilton Bell, Merritt Beeson, and Heinie Schmidt, the same men who later worked to preserve Boot Hill, joined this effort.[4] They tried to bypass concerns about giving the negative events in Dodge City's past too much attention by labeling them as the first steps in town growth from a frontier outpost to a modern community. To focus on that idea, the leaders combined the anniversary activities with the Southwest Fair, the region's annual three-day showcase of commercial, agricultural, and industrial development.

What they called the "Pageant of Progress" became the largest public celebration to date in the town, tracing the history of southwestern Kansas from pioneer days to the arrival of automobiles and airplanes. Although the planners called it a pageant, Dodge City's semicentennial focused mostly on a parade. By stressing solid families, sound local government, churches, schools, strong businesses, and modern technology, it distinguished the modern town from its frontier beginnings. At the same time, it tried to include pioneer values such as piety, hard work, entrepreneurship, and community loyalty. Attempting to combine past and present, the parade organizers had floats for the early cattle drives, a sod hut, and a modern house and family activities. For authenticity it included horse-drawn wagons, buggies, and even a live buffalo to remind viewers of the homesteading days.[5] Technological progress was the focus of the parade, which featured showing new model cars to represent the town and modern farm equipment for the country side. With over fifty floats and three thousand participants, the pageant stretched for a mile and a half and had an estimated twenty thousand viewers.[6] The clear message of the procession was that harmony and prosperity had grown from the pioneer values and that the town welcomed all who shared them.

Wanting to stress their image as a western town with strong frontier roots, Dodge City planners encouraged people to wear vintage clothing and asked town businesses to decorate storefront windows with historical artifacts and antique furniture. They also encouraged aging pioneers to walk or ride in the parade.[7] The display of old-timers, quaint relics, and costumed cowboys in the age of jazz, prohibition, and flappers showed viewers how far the community had progressed. The commemorative souvenir booklet reinforced this idea, contrasting old yellowed photographs of the town with 120 views showing modern schools, churches, and businesses. Local newspapers echoed the organizers' theme. Watching the pioneers and old wagons move "over paved streets, through a prosperous business section," one noted the stark "contrast to days gone by." The reporter concluded that "the wild days of Dodge City, the 'hell hole' of the west are indeed distant memory." The modern city "stands as their monument."[8] Another wrote that pioneers who were still alive had "lived in two ages": "many is the time they have boasted of their good fortunes at seeing telephones, cars, electricity, and paved streets that were not even a dream on the barren waste known on the map as southwestern Kansas."[9]

Many observers rejected the parade's message, finding it neither unique nor interesting, only disappointing. In fact to them the past appeared far more attractive than the present. When the parade ended, Chester Leasure, editor of the nearby *Hutchinson Gazette*, commented that the distinct contrast between old and new Dodge brought more attention to its famous history than town promoters had intended. To him the celebration gave solid evidence that Dodge City had "put aside such childish [frontier] things." However, he had no interest in the modern town, whose "streets paved with red brick and not slippery with red gore" offered him nothing distinctive or unusual. Instead the editor looked back to a time when "Dodge's Front Street was known from coast to coast as hell with the lid blown off." Ignoring the boosters' wishes, he gave his readers a long description of Dodge as a "twelve o'clock" town inhabited by the "sons of Belial" where hard but stalwart sheriffs such as Bat Masterson and Pat Sughrue had enforced the law.[10]

The semicentennial materials avoided any such descriptions of Dodge City's history. Instead the organizers presented a safe past that featured cowboys as builders of the modern livestock industry and sod-house homesteaders as people who laid the groundwork for civilization and agricultural triumph. Aside from the brief appearance of a single outlaw, the Pageant of Progress ignored all unsavory aspects of the town's past. There were no references to gambling dens, saloons, street violence, or famous gunfighters in the parade. By stressing cowboys, pioneers, and standard western entertainments such as horse racing, the city showed that it accepted selected forms of frontier identity while refusing to make its violent reputation part of the official memory.

When the observance ended, Dodge City newspapers hailed the Pageant of Progress as an unqualified success. It brought many visitors and solid profits to the town, yet the celebration did not become an annual event until the end of the decade.[11] In 1922 the city returned to hosting the annual Southwest Fair, with its focus clearly on modern business developments, livestock, machinery, new car models, and agriculture. The confident leaders of the prosperous and growing city saw no economic need that might persuade them to capitalize on their famous past. Yet the Pageant of Progress had elevated awareness of the town's history among its organizers and many of the citizens. For the next few years leaders such as Hamilton Bell, Merritt Beeson, and Heinie Schmidt turned their attention back to less ambitious efforts such as preserving and marking historic sites. In 1929 they helped organize the city's next big public celebration of its past, "The Last Round-Up."

Although Dodge City's semicentennial concentrated on its prosperity and strong local institutions, similar observances in Deadwood and Tombstone took a different path. They grew from efforts to stimulate town business and boost community unity at a time of economic slippage. In both cases the impetus came from having to sooth wounded civic pride as well as celebrating their fifty-years as communities. Deadwood's decision to establish an annual event began two years before its fifty-year birthday and grew out of a 1923 dispute with its sister city, Lead. Two years earlier the towns had decided to host joint Fourth of July celebrations in alternate years and agreed to help each other pay for the costs. In 1923 Lead broke the agreement, deciding to hold its own celebration. That left Deadwood as the only town in the Black Hills Area without any holiday festivities. The Deadwood Business Club announced that it would host its own event but not that year, because no funds had been set aside for it. Each of the other Black Hills communities held events that emphasized a historic event or other special activity, but Deadwood's novel past rested on its frontier moment. Some local leaders gradually realized that the town's past might become a distinctive celebration. In the summer of 1924 the *Black Hills Pioneer* asked: "Why Not Let Deadwood Have Its 'Days of '76' Homecoming Celebration?"[12]

By then the members of the Deadwood Business Club had conceived the first "Days of '76." Unlike Dodge City leaders, they had no qualms about basing their festival on the town's notorious history. They decided to capitalize on it and moved to create "one of the greatest events in the history of the Hills." Their proposal recommended that the celebration become an annual event, modeled on "the days of '76, when the town and the Hills were in their infancy, and 'dour, delightful, devilish Deadwood' was an alliteration every adjective of which was deserved." The organizers hoped to create a pageant that gave a true-to-life picture of past events and colorful people. They made their intentions clear from the start. "Deadwood will be the lure which will draw hundreds within her limits," the *Deadwood Daily Pioneer-Times* reported.[13]

As a largely commercial proposition, the Deadwood Business Club took over sponsorship. Even though the idea to have the event came from the club, some of its more conservative members hesitated to back the venture unless the group got community support. In their campaign to persuade the uncommitted, the members surveyed retail operators, prohibition supporters, and local civic groups before moving ahead. They organized an executive committee that included town leaders and appointed Earl Morford, publisher of the *Deadwood Daily Pioneer-Times*, to manage the planning.[14] When the celebration unfolded, the Days of '76 became a local version of a Bill Show. It included an introductory parade, reenactments of historic events, appearances of famous characters, and other western activities, all with an emphasis on authenticity. The organizers designed

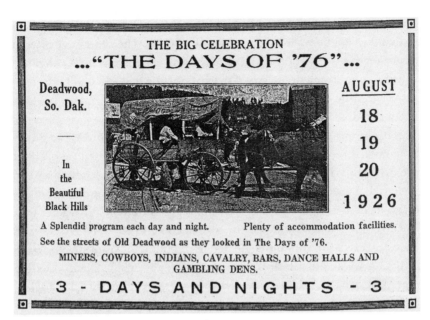

"The Days of '76" advertisement, 1926.
Courtesy South Dakota Historical Society State Archives Collection.

the event to entertain visitors with images and activities that matched their expectations of a real Old West experience, like a Wild West show. Yet the distinctive community flavor of the floats and activities of town businesses and organizations made the event different from generic Bill Shows.

The organizers realized that success depended on getting the solid involvement of the townspeople. Publisher Morford wrote that "community cooperation and the instilling of the spirit of the occasion into every person in the city" were crucial "for the staging of the event." Otherwise, he warned, the festival "might just as well be abandoned." Planners asked organizations such as the Women's Club, the Girls' Club, and other women's groups to volunteer to help and held public meetings to provide information, get participants, and assign tasks. At the same time, Morford reminded town merchants of the potential for advertising, sales, and profits, which he hoped would encourage business leaders and citizens alike "to lend a helping hand."[15]

Deadwood's planners tried to have the townspeople participate in advertising the festival by urging them to change their appearances. They asked the men to stop shaving and join a newly formed More Whiskers Club so that they might resemble the early gold seekers. The committee offered prizes for the most impressive beards and threatened to hold kangaroo courts to fine any men who dared shave. Equating membership in the club with civic pride, town leaders used the slogan "Be loyal to your town—help make the More Whiskers Club and the Days of '76 celebration a success." This effort brought immediate results: at least 150 men joined the group in its first three or four days. The local papers highlighted news about the growing Whisker Club, asked women to wear old-style clothing and men to don western-style hats with Days of '76 hatbands, and encouraged everyone to hang signs about the celebration on the bumpers of their cars.[16]

Having persuaded many of the townspeople to change their appearance, the executive committee turned its attention to businesses and store owners. It wanted to transform downtown Deadwood into a period setting and suggested that retailers cover the front of their stores with tree bark or other materials to create a frontier atmosphere. To be certain that business owners understood, they showed copies of an old photograph depicting a "wild and untamed" Deadwood with a "jumble of log buildings" and men "dressed in top boots, flannel shirts, heavy trousers, with hats and six shooters." They oversaw delivery of the timbers and assured reluctant store owners that "those who have used them are glad they have done so."[17] As the celebration neared, many townspeople got into the spirit. Some merchants put historical artifacts in their store windows, while others hung old-time signs in front. One grocery store had a replica of an 1876 banner that read "Gold Dust Taken Here for Groceries."[18] Each time merchants joined the effort the *Deadwood Daily Pioneer-Times* used their action as an example to prod others into action.

Despite the flood of publicity and continuing public meetings, not everyone welcomed the upcoming festival. Some feared that its Old West orientation would damage the town's already tarnished reputation. Edward Senn, publisher of the *Deadwood Telegram* and a staunch prohibitionist, claimed to write on behalf of "some who have regard primarily for the moral influence of such affairs." Although he never identified them, he asserted that many were worried that the celebration would be "largely a reproduction of the underworld life of Deadwood in 76 with its saloons, gambling and other forms of vice and carousel [*sic*]." These, in turn, would release present restraints and return the town to the "spirit of revelry and

debauchery which formerly held too prominent a place in Deadwood."
He warned that the result might be its being "blacklisted as something
inimical to the moral welfare of young people." Rather than having a
program that focused on "the red light, night life of the gold camps and
their lawlessness," he suggested a series of reenactments of events like the
murder of Wild Bill Hickok, "faithfully reproduced in a way that would
be thrilling and instructive."[19]

As the celebration approached, Senn's attacks became more strident.
When he learned of the organizers' plan to have reenactments of saloons,
dance halls, and gambling dens, he complained that people with high
moral views had been misled and now would be supporting "something
which they will have to regret and condemn." Pointing out that "it has been
difficult for Deadwood to live down the evil repute inherited from the days
of '76 even after it has been cleaned of cesspools," he demanded that the
negative elements of the celebration be dropped from the program lest they
"drive away from the city, the class of citizens most needed."[20] To support
his arguments, he claimed that "some good people" were boycotting the
event because they feared that it signaled "letting down the bars." His
carping irked many town leaders, who assured him that the advertisements
were all figurative. The female dancers would dress modestly, the saloons
would serve only soft drinks, and the gambling would be done with play
money. Nevertheless, Senn warned that the Days of '76 put Deadwood
on public trial. The celebration could offer something "instructive and
commendable" about the town's past or it could glory "in the evils of the
early days." In any case, he nagged that the public officials and celebration
organizers held the responsibility for upholding public morality.[21]

Few business leaders shared the editor's worries. They saw the celebration as a way to benefit from their local history and worked to help make
it authentic. For example, the Homestake Mining Company in nearby
Lead sponsored an exhibit of old mining equipment and processes from
panning and rockers to stamp machines and an early air drill. Some of
the promoters arranged for Cavalry Troop C from Fort Meade to appear
fully equipped in the parade. Others got permission to hire Indians from
the Pine Ridge Agency to take part in the parade and perform traditional
dances afterward. The organizers believed that the presence of Sioux
"would attract great attention, but also prove most interesting and novel
to the visitors from outside the state."[22]

Days of '76 planners imitated the Dodge City efforts to get townspeople involved, asking them to take out old clothes and other items that could be used in the parade or shown in the "hall of relics." Citizens responded, finding items that fit the Old West theme, including a copy of the town's first newspaper, 1877 wanted posters for stage robbers and murderers, vintage firearms, Indian beadwork, and historic photographs. Two "Deadwood Stage Coaches" made famous in the Deadwood Dick novels and as a regular feature in Buffalo Bill's Wild West show drew the most attention. An enthusiastic reporter described the Concord stage as "one of the pioneers of the west." He noted that when it is "drawn by six prancing horses and loaded down with fearless and aggressive men of the old frontier and supported by outriders [it] is going to attract attention."[23]

On August 15, 1924, after months of intensive preparation, the first Days of '76 began. Unlike Dodge City's effort to highlight its progress away from its pioneer roots, Deadwood proudly showcased them. It created an annual western event mixing authenticity and entertainment. A mile-long parade with floats and marchers with an Old West theme opened each of the two days. Miners, soldiers, Indians, and impersonators of the first city officials rode or marched among floats that carried the sons, daughters, and grandchildren of local pioneers. Floats aimed at tourists included one from the state highway commission showing Black Hills scenery, another from the game commission with animals from state parks, and a reproduction of the monument to Theodore Roosevelt. While the overall focus remained on the pioneer past, some elements of town progress such as the Campfire Girls, Elks, and car dealers completed the show.[24]

When the parade ended, activities shifted to Deadwood's amusement park. Wild West action became central. Indian dances, shooting contests, bronco riding, horse and pony racing, mining demonstrations, and trick roping completed the standard rodeo fare. The planners copied Wild West show offerings with reenactments of Indians attacking an emigrant train and bandits holding up a stagecoach. In the evenings the town offered public dances, band concerts, and opened its faux gambling hall, with faro, roulette, dice, and card games to amuse the visitors. Airplane rides were the only concession to modern times.[25]

Unlike Dodge City, Deadwood played up its famous historic characters. Reenactors playing the roles of Wild Bill Hickok, Calamity Jane, Deadwood Dick, and Preacher Smith had central roles in the so-called historic scenes presented as minidramas. On the first day local performers reenacted Hickok's murder and a wedding by Preacher Smith, while a Baptist minister gave Smith's undelivered last sermon. The next day handbills announced the second act of Hickok's story, "The Trial of Jack McCall." The play strayed from much of the central story. It hinted that Hickok's assassination resulted from corrupt officials' fear that the gunfighter was about to become city marshal. Then the local actors put Calamity Jane at the center of events and implied that she and the gunman had a romantic relationship, while adding dime-novel character Alkali Ike to the story.[26]

Days of '76 organizers and regional newspapers described the celebration as an "unqualified success" and almost immediately began planning to make it annual. They estimated that between five thousand and eight thousand people had attended some of the events. Even Edward Senn, its most vocal opponent, dropped his objections and became a strong supporter. The editor thought that the commemoration offered a model for building community strength, an "object lesson to the people of Deadwood [of] what they can do if they pull together." He reported that even though the town's population had shrunk to only one-third the size of its boomtown days, "Deadwood is yet very much alive and can come back." For him the Days of '76 success proved the marketability of the town's history. It showed visitors' desire to recapture the days of the Old West, something that Deadwood could deliver. "No other city has such a glamour of romance thrown around it by the writers of fiction," the editor wrote. Visitors reasoned that "here and here alone, they can find the nearest return to the scenes of the tales that enthralled them in youth." Tying the celebration's success to the rapidly growing automobile-based tourism, Senn thought that in a few years thousands of visitors would choke the city and nearby forests with their cars and campers.[27]

The editor told his readers that Days of '76, if "pushed and directed" as it should be, would become "one of the biggest drawing cards of the entire west." He urged that it should be incorporated and have professional management and promotion and gave a list of suggestions on how to improve the event. He called for more historical authenticity and suggested that the town needed a permanent Hall of Relics or historical museum. Next he proposed redoing the buildings in the downtown business district to make them look as they had during the celebration. The show itself should have fewer rodeo acts and place more emphasis on pioneer activities, because those would "be the biggest drawing cards" for tourists. Even though he supported developing the pioneer elements of the town history, the editor worried about placing too much emphasis on the Wild West parts of the story. "Why confine reproduction of the night life of Deadwood to its seamy side as was done in this year's celebration?" he asked. Instead the event needed more focus on "notable social" functions such as high-class parties and dances of those days, in order to "have a sobering influence on some of the youth today."[28]

While Senn's wishful thinking about using the Days of '76 celebration as morality lessons clouded his assessment of its market qualities, town leaders implemented some of his ideas. In the next few years more professional management directed the event, placing stronger emphasis on historical accuracy and using more sophisticated promotion. At the same time, the basic elements of the 1924 event—community involvement, focus on the Old West, reenactments, relics, historic characters, and western-style events, interspersed with community progress—remain the basic structure today. More significantly, the Days of '76 organizers marked a major change in the way community leaders had come to terms with Deadwood's reputation. Now endorsed by the city and defined as a business enterprise, controversial frontier events and people became exciting entertainment. This expression of community memory, given legitimacy by citizens who endorsed it through public performance, exhibition of relics, wearing costumes, sporting beards, and changing the town's appearance, gradually replaced the earlier mixed feelings about the town's past. That involvement did not mean a rejection of the modern. Rather it signaled that town leaders accepted what they saw as the town's special place in American history and its role in the great frontier epic.

Tombstone, the last of the three towns to commemorate its past, began its effort in 1929 with the Helldorado celebration. That event shared Deadwood's goal of bolstering community morale and helping the town's economy. Local circumstances allowed its organizers to go a step beyond those in either Deadwood or Dodge City. Tombstone's advantage came from having vintage buildings still standing that could serve as the perfect backdrop for an authentic historic presentation. This persuaded leaders that they could turn their town into a total Wild West spectacle with reenactments, relic displays, and aging pioneers as participants. "The show will be Tombstone," the local paper proclaimed, "the scene will be

Tombstone and the entire town will live once more in the scenes and atmosphere of 1879."[29]

Officially, the event marked the fiftieth anniversary of the town's founding. But part of its motivation came from William H. Kelly's effort to restart the local economy and stop any further population loss. Son of the former owner of the *Tombstone Epitaph*, he became its editor and publisher in 1928. From the start he used the paper to develop the town's tourism potential. In fact one critic accused him of being more interested in "sensational ballyhoo on behalf of Tombstone" than in journalism.[30] Kelly took over the *Epitaph* the year the town became fifty and did everything he could to rouse community support for the anniversary. He expected it to include a small parade and a few speeches that would give him a chance to publish a fifty-year special edition of the newspaper. At first his enthusiasm attracted few followers, but he pushed ahead with plans for a special anniversary edition. At that point William Breakenridge's book *Helldorado* came out, focusing renewed attention on Tombstone. Kelly decided that the town should take advantage of the publicity.[31]

By the spring of 1929 Kelly envisioned starting a public celebration based on the town's storied past and using the buildings that had survived from pioneer days to attract tourists. Given the number of visitors already coming to see the Bird Cage Theatre and Boot Hill, Kelly hoped to lure even more by transforming part of the town to its 1880s appearance. Rather than having the western events held at a show grounds as at Deadwood's Days of '76, he wanted the town streets and buildings to give visitors an authentic Old West experience. To rally community support, he assured his readers that thousands would travel to "see Tombstone rehabilitated as it was fifty years ago." That scene would include the usual collection of cowboys, stagecoaches, and Indians, all "thundering through the streets of the most romantic and historic town left in the West." He predicted that people from all over the country "would want to witness that kind of show if Tombstone would give it to them."[32]

Ironically, the first support came from a rival editor in Bisbee, who asked: "Why not start immediately to lay plans for the greatest celebration ever attempted in the West?" The muted response in Tombstone persuaded Kelly that building interest in his scheme might take a while. In early June 1929 he met with the city council, offering to organize and manage the celebration, and pledged to back the event in return for 60 percent of the profits and a salary of $150 a month. The council accepted his proposal. It pledged to help create an early mining camp atmosphere in the town and agreed to give visitors "as near a picture of Tombstone as it appeared in the 80s as possible."[33]

With the *Epitaph* as collateral, Kelly borrowed between five thousand and six thousand dollars, gambling that he could profit from printing jobs and the special edition of the *Epitaph* that he planned for the celebration. Later the mayor also contributed $1,000 to help meet expenses.[34]

Kelly moved quickly and in a few weeks announced his plans. First he wanted to repair and reopen the Bird Cage Theatre and the Crystal Palace Bar and block off the streets in the business district. Then he proposed transforming some vacant buildings into old-time saloons and dance halls and others into minimuseums. As Deadwood had done, he suggested that stores and businesses be remodeled to look like the early 1880s whenever possible. Next he called for a program featuring the "entertainments of the early days," with cowboys and miners showing off their skills. Except for an "old time show given in the same manner that characterized the old variety," Kelly's ideas duplicated those used in both Deadwood and Dodge City. The parade would have marchers wearing 1880s clothes and floats showing transportation and important local characters from the era. Although he wanted some items showing the town's progress and its status as a modern community, Kelly could not resist its Wild West heritage and the gunfighters and lawmen from its violent past.[35]

Kelly realized that chances for success depended on effective promotion. He accepted the city's demand that he work with an experienced promoter and hired George Pound, who had a background in event marketing. Pound advised him to cover the entire state with general news of the show. The ads should highlight frontier-era law and order events and be as accurate as possible in presenting the 1880s era. The promoter stressed having authenticity in every presentation or exhibit. "The twist of the sign, the size and shape of the lettering, the position of the beer keg, and the shape of some man's hat is going to make or break this thing," he insisted.[36] A publicity specialist from Dallas urged Kelly to "get completely away from the idea of Rodeo, Barbeque, or any of the other time-worn free amusements. . . . People want to be thrilled and are ever looking for something different and something out-of-the-ordinary." John Clum,

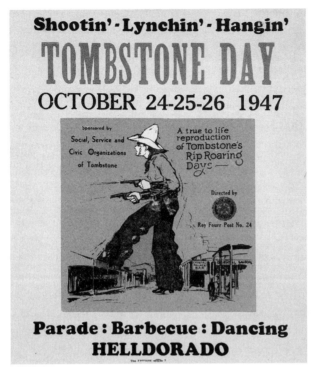

Helldorado advertisement, 1947.

Tombstone's first mayor, reminded Kelly that the purposes of fairs and expositions were both publicity and entertainment.[37]

Based on these ideas, advertising for the event presented Tombstone as a town frozen in time that would soon come back to life. Flyers assured readers that "Helldorado" was no rodeo or carnival. Instead it was a "true-to-life reproduction" of the historic city. "A person standing in the streets of Tombstone today could easily visualize the town in Ed Schieffelin's time," Kelly wrote. One press release stated that while "many years have gone by since the Earp brothers and Doc Holliday shot it out with the Clantons and the McLowrys [sic] yet the fight might well have taken place yesterday," because "progress has left undisturbed the historic scenes of that day." It encouraged Tombstone citizens "to live again for a few short days the episodes of fifty years ago."[38] Writing to the Southern Pacific Railroad for help with publicity, he bragged that this would be the "first time in the history of the West" that an entire town was transformed back in time. The railroad agreed to help with publicity and to run special trains from Tucson and California to carry visitors.[39]

Hoping to get the widest coverage possible, Kelly tailored the publicity to meet other newspapers' interests in the Wild West. The press releases promised that Helldorado would depict the days of "quick riches from mines and gambling tables," when "cattle rustlers, stage robbers, and other desperadoes played poker and drank bad whiskey until the complexion of Tombstone would change."[40] In an article for *Progressive Arizona and the Great Southwest*, Kelly promised that the celebration would describe the town's founding and its "many notorious characters." Kelly got national attention for the celebration with articles on Helldorado that focused on Earp, Holliday, and other historic figures in papers such as the *Los Angeles Times Sunday Magazine* and the *New York Herald Tribune*, among others.[41]

To give their event some aura of historical authenticity, the planners enlisted historians and pioneers who had lived in Tombstone during the 1880s as consultants. The editor hoped that they would advise the Helldorado planning committee on how to make the reproduction of early-day scenes as accurate as possible. He persuaded Walter Noble Burns, author of *Tombstone*, and William Breakenridge, author of *Helldorado*, to help and named the celebration after Breakenridge's book. He added state historian George H. Kelly, Edith Kitt (secretary of the Arizona Historical Society), and James H. McClintock (author of a multivolume Arizona history) to the advisory group. Several other well-known Arizona figures including Governor John C. Phillips and John Clum, Tombstone's first mayor and founder of the *Epitaph*, joined the planning committee. Whether or not these people offered useful information or ideas, boosters apparently thought that their names looked good on the promotional material.

Like his counterparts in Deadwood and Dodge City, Kelly hoped that the event would become a reunion of surviving pioneers. He thought that having a group of past residents attend would give further historical legitimacy and make it a once-in-a-lifetime event. The publicity that he sent out affirmed this intention. Chamber of commerce president Arlington Gardiner stressed that a gathering of "old timers" was a unique historical event and should be documented. He worried that "the pioneers are passing away more rapidly each year, and there will never be such an opportunity to meet so many and obtain photographs of those who made history here." As word of the celebration spread, Kelly's efforts succeeded in attracting a number of well-known people who agreed to attend. These included George Parsons, a close associate of the Earps and John Clum, and also a niece of town founder Ed Schieffelin. Anton Mazzanovich, author of *Trailing Geronimo*, offered to come dressed "gun and all," sing songs, deal faro, and imitate "characters of the old days." The organizers established a California Helldorado Committee and asked John Clum to help get former residents in California back to town for the celebration, using a special Southern Pacific train that the railroad had promised.[42]

Town leaders gradually increased the pressure on local citizens to help create an authentic 1880s town. Helldorado planners' assurances to visitors that they would see a "true to life picture of the famous mining camp as it appeared 50 years ago" translated into the hard work of removing garbage and trash as well as cleaning, painting, and repairing dilapidated buildings. During the summer workers removed forty years of accumulated rubbish from the Bird Cage Theatre and repaired its rotting floor, while carpenters renovated the Crystal Palace. The people installed hitching posts, covered the main street with dirt, built two arches over it, constructed two performance stages, and set up an elaborate system of electric lights for evening performances in the downtown area. Organizers soon realized that the repair and restoration effort took more time and money than they had expected. As the time for the opening drew near Kelly sent out for carpenters with experience in building movie sets to finish the work. On the eve of the celebration he pleaded with citizens to pick up trash and weeds to present an improved picture so that guests to Tombstone would get the "full benefits" of their visit.[43]

As in Deadwood and Dodge City, Helldorado promoters urged citizens to loan artifacts that lent historical integrity to the event. The organizers realized that they needed old objects to enhance the period setting of the newly restored downtown buildings. Mayor Ray Krebs and the city council called for saloon pictures, mining equipment, old guns, and other items. The historical exhibits committee asked people to loan period cooking utensils and other household items, promising to keep them safe and display them in "an elaborate" exhibit. During the last several weeks before the even opened William Kelly negotiated the loan of an old Modoc stage from the Prescott-based Arizona's Frontier Days Association to use in the parade.[44]

The organizers wanted townspeople to do more than volunteer time and lend personal items for the displays, asking them to wear period clothing too. "Although every effort will be made to make the Helldorado area as nearly accurate as historically possible," the *Epitaph* told its readers, that effort would lose much of its value unless the local citizens appeared in costume. The editor requested that all of the townspeople take part and printed guidelines for the styles of period clothing that he thought fit the image that Helldorado promoters wanted to portray. "Local men can dress as cowboys, freighters, miners, gamblers, troopers, or prospectors," he suggested, while women could vary their dress from the clothing worn on the covered wagons to the "more elaborate costume of the ball room and theater." As in Deadwood, the organizers formed a whisker club, the Tombstone Helldorados. Its members agreed to "grow beards, mustaches, and sideburns to help advertise" the upcoming celebration.[45]

During the summer and fall of 1929 town leaders struggled to inspire the Tombstone public to take part in the celebration, but low morale and a dismal economy challenged their efforts. Apparently the officials' calls for townspeople to clean the streets and paint or repair shabby buildings failed to stir many people to action. Those activities took time, energy, and money, and some citizens may have seen the celebration as just another desperate effort to attract new customers for the failing town merchants. Others may well have objected to seeing hundreds of strangers overrun their community and having to answer questions about a past that they wanted to ignore or forget. Decades later Kelly recalled that "Tombstone in those days was a sad old town. The depression had started, business places were few and their intake scarce. Barely hanging on, building owners hoped that someone would come along, rent a store and actually go into business."[46] At the time Kelly thought that Helldorado offered an economic turning point that might offset the community depression. Tombstone's history, he wrote, "has inspired the publication of four books, and perhaps thousands of newspaper stories and magazine articles" and the publicity about this event "would undoubtedly attract both the visitor and investor. A new hotel, new homes, possible a sanitarium would inevitably follow. The time is ripe, the opportunity is present and the task is not beyond our capabilities."[47]

Local political leaders agreed. The city council expected that the event would be a turning point in their efforts to capitalize on the "historic and climactic attractions of this place." The mayor and Arlington Gardiner saw the event as a means of advertising that might attract investors "to remain in Tombstone and make their homes here."[48] As preparations entered their final stage, outside events spurred efforts to make the event successful. The possibility that Tombstone would lose its position as county seat loomed in the background. Often during the 1920s the nearby towns Douglas and Bisbee both had called for a special election to move the county seat out of Tombstone. Talk turned to action in the summer of 1929, when Douglas donated a site for a new county building and $100,000 to help pay for its construction. Because the Cochise County government offered solid jobs in a community with few other options, the possible move would hurt Tombstone severely. "Tombstone would be a ghost city," the *Epitaph* predicted. "Douglas has so many advantages and Tombstone so few that it would be regrettable to take the one remaining lease on life away from the colorful town."[49]

Facing this uncertain future, the planners hoped desperately that their event might sway voters. "Whether the celebration will influence the situation is unknown," the *Arizona Star* remarked, "but it will turn all southwest eyes to Tombstone and should make many to hesitate to take from the silver camp its greatest claim to modern day popularity." The *Graham County Guardian* noted that "the loss of the court house will sound the death knell of Tombstone, this fact stands alone out about everything else and many voters, not actuated by selfish interest, will pause at the ballot box before he casts a vote against the old pioneer town."[50] Facing this possible financial disaster, editor Kelly responded that Helldorado would not be "a death wake, but rather a revival for the city that once dominated southern Arizona." Local citizens apparently agreed, because they rallied to support the event.[51]

With the county seat election in the background, Helldorado opened on October 29, 1929, in wretched weather. A cold, driving rainstorm caused the town electric plant to fail, leaving the celebration in the dark and delaying the festivities until the next day. That evening late visitors arrived to find the entire town totally dark, hotels filled to capacity, and only cots with a single blanket available for that night. Undaunted, the executive committee members brought out kerosene lamps and candles, giving the first evening an accidental detail of historic accuracy.[52]

Other than transforming its downtown business area into a living stage, the format of the show resembled the first Days of '76 celebration in Deadwood. Tombstone's effort to erase all signs of modernity in order to create a Wild West atmosphere marked the biggest difference between the two events, which otherwise shared many components. Each opened with an Old West parade and featured aging pioneers on some of the floats. John Clum, the first mayor, and the honorary sheriff, author Billy Breakenridge, led the parade. It included historic horse-drawn vehicles, costumed cowboys, floats carrying women, and children dressed in pioneer clothing followed by others with bewhiskered men dressed as prospectors. When the procession ended, visitors could dance, gamble with fake money, and enjoy soft drinks in the newly opened saloons.[53]

As in Deadwood and Dodge City, the planners recruited Indians to give their event more authenticity. Kelly persuaded the nearby agency officials to provide "six Apache men who can ride horseback and who will be willing to wear appropriate costumes" and take part in the parade and in reenactments. Then, in an act completely at odds with his efforts at historical accuracy, he hired a Yuma Indian band that agreed to "do a reasonable amount of Ballyhooing for the different attractions." Even though the Apaches appeared in their traditional clothing, the Yumas marched in red shirts and dark slacks, wearing feathered war bonnets. Completing their totally unauthentic look, the drum major waved a pistol rather than a baton or staff. John Clum later recalled enjoying the band immensely but noted wryly that neither he nor his friends could "remember ever having seen or heard anything like it during those 'early days' of the camp."[54]

The marching band proved to be the only exception to Kelly's definition of 1880s authenticity. Striving to make Helldorado a unique Old West reenactment, he rejected most acts that did not fit into that theme. Yet the university of arizona Cowboy Quartet was allowed to perform on street corners, but only if it acted as if the singers were just a few cowboys in town for a good time. Other acts included mining drilling contests, a medicine show, trick shooters and ropers, and a cowboy clown. The organizers persuaded Annie Duncan, the former Tombstone Nightingale, to perform. Backed by a troupe of younger can-can dancers, she sang 1880s tunes that she had performed at the Bird Cage Theatre decades earlier.[55] As in both Deadwood and Dodge City, the nearly four hundred early settlers who returned received special attention. On day two, "pioneers' day," the town honored those who had lived in the Southwest forty or fifty years earlier with a banquet and gave the extra recognition at a ceremony honoring the memory of Ed Schieffelin, the town's founder.[56]

Despite the effort to authenticate Helldorado by using peaceful events, the program included reenactments of the more famous violent ones too. Kelly later recalled that he had tried to focus on entertainment available in the early mining camp and on the excitement and romance of early western life. Those goals disappeared when dozens of suggestions for acts reached his desk. Some of the most graphic called for restaging the OK Corral gunfight, the lynching of John Heath, cowboys shooting up the town, and Apaches attacking a buckboard filled with terrified pioneers. Sifting through the ideas, the planners decided to use the gunfight at the OK Corral, a lynching, and the robbery of the Modoc stage as the major events. Of those, only the OK Corral fight got much careful planning and was a carefully documented reenactment. Mayor Ray Krebs told a Bisbee Rotary Club audience that the OK Corral reenactors would use three of the original weapons and that two eyewitnesses would help to direct the scene.[57]

When the dust cleared and the crowds had left, the organizers proclaimed the event a major success. By their count more than six thousand visitors had witnessed it. Although it had brought the town some national publicity, the celebration netted only a few hundred dollars and did little to help its economy. Some regional newspapers praised the event planners for their effort to make it historically authentic, but other observers rejected that claim. In a review for the *Epitaph*, John Clum, the town's first mayor, complained that the program aimed more at luring tourists rather than giving an accurate picture of past days. Neither he nor his longtime friend rancher Billy Fourr recognized anything about Tombstone from the days they lived in the town. "We mutually assured ourselves that we were not as desperate and devilish and depraved fifty years ago as the 'Helldorado' publicity literature and press dispatches had painted us." He labeled the OK Corral reenactment "repulsive and distressing," thinking it "inconceivable that any normal spectator derived either pleasure or benefit from viewing the mock battle."[58] He clearly misjudged what tourists would expect and enjoy.

Other commentators had different reactions to Helldorado. As the election for the county seat loomed, it became a bittersweet symbol of the town's past glory. The *Arizona Daily Star* reported that that the community "may be a Tombstone" and added that celebration was the new "'Epitaph' added to the slowly growing lists of inscriptions that mark the final resting place of Tombstone's great and glorious" past. As the event ended, "stark reality came back to rule in Tombstone, a tomb of memories." Telling its readers that Helldorado would never be repeated, the *Phoenix Gazette* opined that it seemed likely that "the final curtain has dropped in the Bird Cage and the last lights have gone out in the Crystal Palace."[59] In the November 20 election county residents chose to move the county seat from Tombstone to Bisbee by a two-to-one vote. Combined with the national stock market crash in late October 1929, that appeared to signal the town's final collapse. William Kelly, Helldorado's most active single promoter, became one of the first casualties. Lacking revenue from publishing legal notices for the county government, the value of the *Epitaph* fell from nearly $16,000 to only $4,000, so he sold the paper to Walter Cole and left town.[60]

Even more than Deadwood, Tombstone had tried to transform the entire town into an image of the Old West, inspired in large part by the books by Bechdolt, Burns, and Breakenridge about the town. This Wild West spectacle of Helldorado backed by the city government came to have broad community support and gradually offered a powerful new identity for the town, at least partly filling the void left by losing its role as county administrator. From that point on, many residents defined their community as a living historic spectacle, a kind of time-machine that could bring people back to the Old West.

Just two weeks after Helldorado ended, Dodge City held what it called "The Last Round-Up" to mark the dedication of the city's famous cowboy statue on Boot Hill. The new event marked a major change in how the town dealt with its early past. Instead of treating it as a means of celebrating modernity, Dodge now joined the other two towns by accepting its position as an emblem of the Old West and an inheritor of pioneer values. In the years after its semicentennial, momentum built gradually for a new commemoration of its past. The annual Great Southwest Fair included some attention to regional history. In 1925 a professional director, working with a 400-person ensemble, presented "The Story of the Southwest." It traced local settlement, beginning with the Indians and moving to the 1870s when the pioneers arrived. In 1927 a new pageant, "Pioneer Days in Western Kansas," had a Wild West focus that included an "epic battle" between Indians and settlers. The event used large-scale outdoor action, with mounted cowboys and Cheyenne Indians brought in from Oklahoma for authenticity. Because of the regional emphasis, Dodge City had little specific role in the program. It appeared as part of the setting, as one of "scattered border towns . . . inhabited by hard-bitten saloon keepers, dance hall sybarites and gamblers, lawless men driven from the boundaries of the law."[61]

This pageant served as a prelude to "The Last Round-Up" celebration held two years later. During the summer of 1929 Hamilton Bell, Oscar Simpson, Heinie Schmidt, and Merritt Beeson began organizing an event to commemorate the unveiling of Simpson's cowboy statue on Boot Hill and the laying of the cornerstone of the new city courthouse there. Mayor W. Otis Thompson proclaimed the day a school and business holiday and pledged full community cooperation. As in the other towns, promoters wanted to get as many people as possible involved, so they organized a number of committees and asked local business and civic organizations such as the Rotary Club and the Dodge City Women's Club to help.[62] The Last Round-Up began the town's cautious shift toward recognizing its Wild West past, although not as extremely as Helldorado and Days of '76 had done.

Envisioned as a salute to the community's still-living pioneers, the celebration echoed events in both Deadwood and Tombstone and reflected a growing awareness of the need to honor the aging pioneers as the last link to the heroic past. Event organizers promised old residents of Dodge City and the area a place of honor in the "monster parade" and a formal public reception afterward.[63] The city intended this recognition of the pioneers as more than a way of honoring their achievements. The planners saw their lives as proof of the community's important place in history. Jess Denious, a member of the organizing committee and editor of the *Dodge City Daily Globe*, expressed this idea clearly. He wrote about the "sterling worth of the folks who pioneered this country" and hoped that the memories of the pioneers' hardships would be enshrined as part of the city's history on Boot Hill.[64]

Local publicists recognized the strong marketing appeal of the title "Last Round-Up." To them it seemed to mark the last chapter of events in the Old West for a national audience still intrigued by stories of the frontier. Heinie Schmidt told a *Globe* reporter that many people "sense something different and they are correct. This probably will be the last gathering of early notables in the Southwest." Outsiders clearly shared this view. Newspapers from New York City, Kansas City, Oklahoma City, and Omaha as well as the *Christian Science Monitor* all asked for stories of the event. Stuart Lake, then writing articles about Dodge City as a prelude to his book on Wyatt Earp, agreed to cover the celebration for the *Saturday Evening Post*.[65]

In addition to the pioneer reunion, the Last Round-Up promoters used many now-familiar practices to authenticate the event and to bolster community pride. At first, like their counterparts in South Dakota and Arizona, the boosters found it hard to rally local interest or support. For example, when the pioneer relic committee asked merchants to display artifacts in their store-front windows, few bothered. Frustrated committee members tried using pressure through the pages of the *Globe*. "It looks as if we'd have The Last Round-Up with the streets reflecting the twenties instead of the seventies," one editorial grumbled. "That is no way to cooperate." About a week later the paper trumpeted its own pioneer window display as an example for other merchants to follow. The organizers had more success with commemorative publications. They tied a reissue of Robert Wright's 1913 book on Dodge City and a new souvenir booklet entitled *The Last Round-Up* into event publicity. The booklet outlined the events and offered a pictorial history of the community from "sod house to city" as it traced the town's progress.[66]

The celebration included most of the same elements that other pageants had used or would use. Its Wild West theme offered a tribute "in honor of its six shooting founders." The Last Round Up had a large parade with four sections: historic, patriotic, pioneer, and civic. Its historic section featured a cowboy band, thirty Cheyenne Indians, a float with a settler's sod house, and old wagons and stagecoaches. Despite this historic overlay, examples of modern progress appeared throughout the program. The parade lacked the large number of commercial floats and heavy civic boosterism so evident in the earlier semicentennial. The procession ended at Boot Hill, where viewers watched the unveiling of the cowboy statue and heard an address. After the speech people went to the fairgrounds to see a "Western Thriller" that reenacted an Indian attack on a stagecoach and a battle between soldiers and Indians.[67]

As in the case of the celebrations in Deadwood and Tombstone, town leaders depicted the Last Round-Up as an overwhelming success. They estimated attendance at the event as between 20,000 and 25,000 spectators, far more than in either of the other communities. The event signaled a willingness to shift the community's identity beyond being a modern progressive city. By 1929 it had recognized the monuments on Boot Hill as tourist attractions, accepted Robert Wright's 1913 book on early Dodge City as its official history, and developed a historically conscious group of long-term residents. These acts signaled the beginning of the town's gradual movement to embrace its western heritage and to celebrate its public identification as a special place in the history of the Old West as defined by public images from popular literature and film.

Unlike Dodge City promoters, commemoration organizers in Deadwood and Tombstone created their events as both civic promotions and commercial enterprises. To compete in the marketplace successfully they gave the events formal financial and organizational structures. The first effort to do this led to incorporation in Deadwood when the leaders established the Days of '76 Amusement Corporation under direct control of the chamber of commerce. A few years later Tombstone followed suit by forming Helldorado, Inc., with a loose connection to the chamber of commerce there. With business and political leaders such as Fred Gramlich in Deadwood and Ray Krebs in Tombstone working as leaders in their events, few doubted the economic goals in each community. These people understood that their events needed both familiarity and novelty to succeed commercially and helped shape their celebrations to do just that. At first they drew heavily on the proven attractions of Wild West shows and popular literature. Later they struggled to keep their attractions fresh while claiming both novelty and authenticity. Talking to an audience at the Deadwood Commercial Club, one speaker reminded them of the need for a program that offered typical elements. Eastern visitors, he said, "don't come to the Black Hills to dance or play bridge—they can do that at home. . . . They are fascinated by Indians, by accounts of early day characters, by historic spots."[68]

Both Deadwood and Tombstone struggled to continue their celebrations after the first few years. Keeping them novel and vital enough to attract visitors each year led them to borrow such things as rodeo acts and pageants as well as expanding successful formats. Deadwood held its celebration every year after 1924, and it quickly became a local tradition. More importantly, the town benefited from its location in the Black Hills, then becoming a major tourist attraction. Both state and local marketing efforts tied to the carvings on Mount Rushmore brought increasing outside interest from 1927 to 1937. Deadwood's economy remained stable during the Depression because of the continuing operations of the Homestake Gold Mine in nearby Lead. Tombstone's Helldorado, in contrast, lapsed only three years after it began. Its promoters failed to get essential outside funding, the local economy collapsed, and the population declined sharply when the town lost its position as county seat.

Promoters in both Deadwood and Tombstone tried theatrical pageants as one popular form of entertainment. At first both groups called their parades and other acts pageants, but neither actually tried a large-scale theatrical production until the year after their first event. In 1925 Deadwood promoters offered a program entitled "The Spirit of Deadwood," using dancers and spirits to depict aspects of the town's history. After two years the organizers decided that they needed to change the format, however, so they hired an outside professional firm. The new format relied heavily on more traditional western elements, including a stage holdup, the assassination of Hickok, and some two hundred Sioux Indians from Pine Ridge. From that point on Indians played central roles in Days of '76 celebrations. They set up teepees inside the town to allow "easterners and tenderfeet" a chance to see "children paying around their temporary homes and the bucks and squaws in all their savage finery parading the streets."[69] During the Depression other tribes sought employment in the Days of '76 events, proclaiming their own authenticity. In 1938 J. E. Hihawk offered to replace the "bunch from Pine Ridge" with performers from the Cheyenne River Reservation. His group of fifty people included "five professional fancy war-dancers, four old veterans or warriors who took part in the Battle of Little Big Horn Mountains, and one prominent figure, a nephew of the famous Chief Sitting Bull." As late as 1972 local reservation promoters still assured Days of '76 organizers that the Indian section in the event would "be colorful and authentic as possible in every way."[70]

The Deadwood promoters also added a rodeo component to strengthen the western authenticity of their event. Rodeos were a standard form of western entertainment showing ranching skills such as roping, horsemanship, and bronco riding. Decades earlier William Cody and other Wild West show operators had popularized these activities. By the 1920s many western communities had begun to host rodeo competitions. Professional circuits developed, transforming informal events into an official sport with cash prizes and regional championships. In 1928 Deadwood added a rodeo, but the large purses needed to attract top competitors reduced profits and split the organizers. Those who objected feared that the rodeo expenses coupled with the effects of the Depression might wreck the Days of '76 event. After several years of debate and program changes, in 1933 the chamber of commerce canceled the entire celebration. The Women's Auxiliary of the Chamber of Commerce stepped in and reinstated the rodeo, which became a permanent part of the program.[71]

After the success of the first Days of '76, some of the organizers decided that Wild West elements might be used as tourist attractions for longer parts of the year. The trial of Jack McCall, Hickok's murderer, became a regular summer event and featured the grandson of the man who had built the original scaffold for his hanging in Yankton. Chamber of commerce secretary Nell Perrigoue used the show for civic promotion at other times. During World War II she staged it in Yankton to help raise money for the Red Cross and routinely performed it for visitors such as travel editors and state officials. Although the event was advertised as "an authentic play based on actual proceedings of the miners' court," she modified it to fit advertising opportunities. A good example occurred in 1944, when Jack Paige of WNAX in Yankton invited her to find a "tie-in" with an appearance of the Lone Ranger and his horse Silver at that city's Midwest Farmer Day. "A great many of his shows" told the story of Deadwood, so she agreed and offered to do the skit and suggested having the Lone Ranger capture Jack McCall and bring him to justice.[72]

Because Deadwood's central attraction rested on the stories about Hickok and Calamity Jane, town publicists selected people from among the Days of '76 performers to represent its storied history. Skillfully they transformed three local figures into town celebrities meant to give living proof of Deadwood's claim to historical legitimacy. Each person represented some aspect of the figure whose name they took. "Poker" Alice Tubbs, a cigar-smoking former madam and longtime resident of nearby Sturgis, suited the role of Calamity Jane. She had gained attention because of her colorful mannerisms while dealing faro during the first Days of '76, and because of rumors that she had once been accused of murdering two soldiers from Fort Meade.[73]

"Deadwood Dick" Clarke played the role of a frontier scout and swash-buckler, as had his namesake of the dime-novel era. As in the case of Tubbs, his pioneer status grew out of his longtime residence. A retired railroad worker, he lacked any real pedigree as a western hero but had played the fictional Deadwood Dick during the first Days of '76 event and enjoyed it. Soon after that he began bragging about having been an Indian fighter, Pony Express rider, and stagecoach driver. Playing the role well, he wore his hair long, dressed in buckskin high boots, and wore a western hat. In 1927 he pitched a tent at the Pine Crest Tourist Park and began telling stories to visitors. Recognizing his value to the town, the chamber of commerce built him a cabin, where he entertained large numbers of tourists. One reporter thought that they considered him "the mecca of their visit to the Black Hills."[74]

The chamber of commerce used both Tubbs and Richard Clarke to represent the community whenever it needed Wild West representatives. After both of them died in 1930, Nell Perrigoue chose a new personality: "Potato Creek" Johnny Perrett was the town's next historical celebrity. A Deadwood resident since 1883, he eked out a living panning for gold. In 1929 he gained instant local fame by finding one of the largest gold nuggets ever taken in the Black Hills. Still living in a prospector's shack, the tiny man (four feet eight inches tall) sported a long flowing gray beard, wore gold-rimmed glasses, and had extensive knowledge of placer mining. Perrigoue realized that Perrett could help market the town nationally and took him to participate at Chicago's 1941 International Travel Show. According to the *Black Hills Weekly*, he was the "hit of the show." She soon got him an interview on the CBS show *We the People*, depicting him as a "genuine old-time prospector." When he died in 1943, Deadwood honored him with a massive funeral and buried his remains in Mount Moriah near the graves of Hickok and Calamity Jane.[75]

Perrigoue's elevation of Perrett into a local hero and her use of reenactments drawn from the Days of '76 celebration into traditional fixtures outside that event served as a means of weaving historic commemoration of the Wild West deeply into Deadwood's social fabric. Through repetition, historic skits, and colorful personalities the event gradually became part of local tradition and of the town's identity. The Days of '76 celebration grew into an integral part of Deadwood's seasonal routine and has survived uninterrupted since 1924 because its administrators allowed it to develop by using a traditional western cultural identity.

Tombstone lacked location, timing, and the strength of tradition to sustain its Helldorado in subsequent years. Like their Black Hills counterparts, its organizers struggled to keep it a vital affair by adding a pageant, experimenting with new styles of presentation, and later adding a rodeo. Depression conditions in Tombstone closed the early celebration era. After the town lost its position as the county seat and editor Kelly, its chief promoter, left, the remaining leaders needed to regroup. They joined Walter Cole, new owner of the *Epitaph*, to plan for the 1930 event. This resulted in a stronger emphasis on early violence and the men involved in it to attract visitors interested in the Wild West. The new show offered "additional gunplay in accord with the spirit of the scenes being portrayed." Cole announced that these shifts would make Helldorado "more virile than any other show" while keeping it authentic. "Not a lurid feature of the rip-roaring 80s will be deficient in any detail," he wrote, assuring readers that "there'll be plenty of action."[76]

"Action" translated into what the *Epitaph* labeled as a "gun and fun" festival with a large number of historical skits. Instead of the actions taking place in the town streets, the planners moved them to a stage set up at the high school as a formal pageant. Unlike the professionally written productions in Dodge City and Deadwood, a local minister wrote the script for Tombstone. His production focused exclusively on violent episodes that supposedly illustrated the frontier era. It had an Apache massacre, a fight between cowboys and miners, an elaborate stagecoach holdup, a claim-jumping scene, a vigilante lynching, and the climactic gunfight at the OK Corral.[77] Promoters tried to make their sensational show more credible by claiming some authenticity. Such "thrilling features," Cole wrote, would be "reminiscent and historically truthful to the days when Judges Colt and Lynch ruled the roost." When the 1930 celebration ended, editor Cole described the Helldorado pageant as an "American Oberammergau": it should be staged in the natural amphitheater around the city because it raised Tombstone to national importance.[78]

Unfortunately, Depression-wracked Tombstone could not sustain the celebration. Desperate to keep their town alive, its promoters turned to marketing the health benefits that the local climate offered. At the same time, their history remained central in all of the community-sponsored publicity. After attending a Tombstone booster meeting, a *Los Angeles Times* reporter remarked that it was the first discussion that he had ever heard "where the subject of the debate was how to cash in on a bad reputation."[79] Much of the discussion centered on how to spend an $8,000 state appropriation to the city for basic costs of Helldorado for the next two years. With cash on hand the event organizers expanded the celebration to four days and added more violence, including "ten outstanding episodes in the camp's bloody history on each of the four days."[80]

Despite their efforts, violence alone could not sustain the event. In 1931 the town's economy collapsed as the last elements of the county government left. The next year's organizers added a rodeo despite their earlier claims that it had no place in their celebration. Even with the new addition community support faded. When the state appropriation ended in 1932, the city ended Helldorado. The next year it staged a "super rodeo" instead. Efforts to organize a Frontier Days Rodeo continued intermittently during the 1930s but never brought an event with community-wide support.[81] Despite its brief life, the tradition remained firmly planted in the community. After its successful revival in 1946 the public celebration in the town replicated many of its earlier features. At the same time, it had a more solid economic footing and benefited from widespread publicity generated by movies during the 1930s and 1940s.

By the end of the 1930s public commemorations in Deadwood, Tombstone, and to a lesser extent Dodge City had established their collective pasts as a separate world from the present. City and social leaders elected to ignore modernism as they recast their identity in terms of the Old West to make their communities more economically stable. They worked to make the Wild West authentic by using costumed participants, historic reenactments, pageants, rodeos, Indian encampments, and old artifacts. Together local officials and chambers of commerce supported a new civic identity based on the idea that their towns held a heroic and monumental place in American history. Some business and political leaders still hesitated to abandon the values of progress and modernity that they believed held the keys to future prosperity. Their hesitation remained central until a series of films about all three towns during the 1930s and the impact of television after World War II brought an unprecedented wave of tourists west and new chances to capitalize on the past. Until that happened few of the business and political leaders could anticipate the full power that these media had to elevate western imagery to new heights and the major effects that this would have on each of their communities.

7 ☞ Movies, Television, and Tourism

Entertainment and profits stood at the center of all forms of western tourism from the skiing industry in Colorado to casinos in Las Vegas. Efforts to use Old West history as varied as ersatz Boot Hills, historic sites, books, and community celebrations clearly fit this pattern.[1] When tourists arrived in Deadwood, Dodge City, and Tombstone, they wanted entertainment. The Wild West succeeded across all media because it offered people a chance to escape the pressures of modern life. It let them engage, however briefly, in the fantasy of a simple time and place that they perceived to be real. Publishers, theaters, Wild West Show producers, and town boosters all accepted this and made their western presentations as thrilling as possible. All of them blended familiar images, dramatic reenactments, and famous heroes in ways that they hoped would seem accurate. In the twentieth century motion pictures and television became the most powerful forms of entertainment and highly successful image makers of the West. Films and television clearly had a decided advantage over other types of popular recreation. They required little more than an hour or two in front of a screen and could be seen in virtually every town in America and abroad and later in every living room.

Movies and television were godsends to publicity-hungry towns, eager for any kind of attention that could be used as promotion. The new media helped attract tourists and heighten community prestige, as the towns became movie locations and developed association with famous stars. Celebration organizers saw films and television, as kindred spirits in the world of entertainment and repeatedly used Hollywood glamour to draw attention to their events. Nor was this a one-sided relationship. Film and television producers inherited the need to authenticate their productions and associated themselves with the towns that they depicted to enhance their credibility. By the 1960s this relationship grew to the point that tourism promoters and event organizers sought to capitalize on their town's movie and television notoriety by shaping local commemorations and actions to match the expectations that Hollywood created among tourists.

Movies popularized ideas about the West more than any other entertainment form, and western stories offered early filmmakers great plots. Thomas Edison filmed scenes of western life as early as 1894 and in 1903 produced his classic *The Great Train Robbery*. Its sweeping success inspired so many sequels by the Edison Company and its rivals that by 1914 some film reviewers had already proclaimed the western a tired genre. Much of the early success of Edison and his competitors lay in the new technology's ability to take viewers beyond Wild West shows, pageants, and stage productions. Movies could transport viewers to actual or perceived western landscapes and towns, an advantage that expanded rapidly with the use of sound and later color.[2]

Early filmmakers drew freely on western subjects presented in other media. From the start they transferred famous western characters, plot lines, settings, and stories from dime novels, slicks, pulps, and popular history to the screen. Given their characters' fame and their reputations as violent places, Hollywood producers often sought out Deadwood, Dodge City, and Tombstone. Throughout the twentieth century each town benefited from the industry's interest, providing a location, a setting, or a character or story closely associated with it. The effects often accumulated over time as studios remade popular subjects such as the gunfight at the OK Corral and the Hickok assassination over successive generations, giving those events the power of tradition for American audiences.

Deadwood benefited primarily from a long series of films and serials featuring its two official characters, Wild Bill Hickok and Calamity Jane. These expanded their long-established fame, gave them heroic roles, and often focused on the mythical romance between them. As long as the two remained in the spotlight, curious tourists continued visiting Mount Moriah Cemetery to see their graves. At one point Nell Perrigoue, Deadwood's chamber of commerce secretary, asked Universal Studios to "consider erecting statues at the graves" because so "many pictures that originate in Hollywood are built around the lives of the frontier characters Wild Bill Hickok and Calamity and centered in the Deadwood gold camp."[3] As early as 1915 a locally produced Nebraska movie, *In the Days of '75 and 76*, featured the pair. Hickok also appeared as a major character in the 1923 film *The Last Frontier* and as the main subject in William S. Hart's *Wild Bill Hickok* that same year (although the film was set in Dodge City). One of the most famous portrayals of the pair was Gary Cooper's Hickok and Jean Arthur's Calamity Jane in Cecil B. DeMille's 1936 epic *The Plainsman*. Calamity Jane, often Hickok's paramour in films, achieved Hollywood stardom in her own right in *Calamity Jane and Sam Bass* (Universal, 1949) and more notably in Warner's 1953 musical extravaganza *Calamity Jane*, where Doris Day played her part.[4] Even Deadwood Dick resurfaced in a fifteen-chapter serial by Columbia in 1940, in which the ubiquitous Hickok helped him.

Dodge City appeared in movies that focused on cowboys and cattle drives. The first indication of its potential came in 1916, when an eastern studio expressed an interest in making a movie version of Robert Wright's book *Dodge City: The Cowboy Capital*, calling the "woolly days of the town" a "fine subject for the screen." The first film to depict Dodge as the main setting, however, was William S. Hart's *Wild Bill Hickok* in 1923, followed seventeen years later by the most famous portrait of the town, Warner Brothers' production *Dodge City* in 1939, starring Errol Flynn and Olivia de Havilland.[5]

Dodge City and Tombstone both gained a permanent connection to Wyatt Earp, who became a favored Hollywood topic after Stuart Lake's publication of his book about the gunman in 1931. The Earp story offered filmmakers all the elements of a successful western: a hero seeking to bring order to a corrupt and immoral frontier town, dangerous opponents, and an epic battle between good and evil at its climax. The first film rendition of Earp came in 1932 with the adaptation of William R. Burnett's 1930 novel about Tombstone, *Saint Johnson*, for the film *Law and Order*. A long series of movie versions of Lake's Wyatt Earp biography followed, beginning with *Frontier Marshal* (Twentieth Century Fox, 1934; refilmed in 1939). In 1942 Paramount adapted Walter Noble Burns's book *Tombstone* into *Tombstone: The Town Too Tough to Die*. In 1946 John Ford retold story of the OK Corral in Fox's *My Darling Clementine*, with Henry Fonda as Wyatt Earp. Director John Sturges offered his version of the epic battle with Burt Lancaster and Kirk Douglas in *Gunfight at the O.K. Corral* (Paramount, 1957).[6]

Filmmakers, like their Wild West show predecessors, understood that they should use public ideas about authenticity in their presentations of

Poster for *Tombstone: The Town Too Tough to Die*
(1942), Paramount Pictures.

the West. In his memoir actor and producer William S. Hart recalled being inspired to make realistic western movies after seeing an "awful" western picture and coming to the conclusion that "here were reproductions of the Old West being seriously presented to the public—in almost a burlesque manner." Another Western movie star of the 1920s, Ken Maynard, told the *Tombstone Epitaph* in 1927 that his "interest in the history of the West was being put to practical use by him in giving the public as nearly as possible a true impression of the places and the spirit that prevailed in the old days." Maynard added that "it was his aim not only to be interesting in his acting but also to be historically accurate." Director Cecil B. DeMille told readers in his memoir that he so insisted on authenticity in filming *The Plainsman* that he made Jean Arthur, the actor playing Calamity Jane, learn to manipulate a ten-foot bullwhip. He also boasted that he shrugged off executives who asked him not to kill off Hickok, telling them he "could not remake history to that extent."[7] Presenting former outlaws like Frank James and Emmett Dalton or ex-sheriffs such as Bill Tilghman in film roles became another way of adding historic credibility to early films. Even Wyatt Earp himself appeared in a bit role in Alan Dwain's silent film *The Half Breed* (1915). Studios also recruited frontier participants as historic advisors. Hart was acquainted with both Bat Masterson and Wyatt Earp and used some of their ideas in his film *Wild Bill Hickok*. The ubiquitous Earp also developed close associations with actor Tom Mix and director Raoul Walsh. Director John Ford later told film historian Peter Bogdanovich that he based his version of the OK Corral gunfight in his movie *My Darling Clementine* on a conversation with the former marshal.[8]

As they tried to gain historic credibility, studios moved beyond talking to individuals and develop ties with the towns where many of the events in their films took place. Before making his 1923 *Wild Bill Hickok*, Hart stopped in Dodge City, where he claimed to have met the "entire population and that of the surrounding country." To his surprise "every citizen who owned one had a forty-five belt full of lead on his hip," in an obvious effort to impress their visitor. While there the star received a gun from the last man killed by Sheriff Chalkley Beeson and a tour to Boot Hill. Hart also made a point to visit the city soon after the Last Round-Up in 1929 and sent a telegram to Beeson praising its heritage: "The streets of Dodge City may be paved down deep with concrete but the spirits of Wyatt Earp, Bat Masterson and all those other great frontiersmen will not be buried up."[9]

Small towns like Dodge City, Deadwood, and Tombstone welcomed the studios' interest. Leaders in each town viewed a celebrity's visit or film made about it or one of its historic personages as recognition of its significance and a means for advertising. As early as 1921 Tombstone had appeared in a Border Film Company movie entitled *Only Girl*, which the local papers called an "inestimable value for publicity." The *Deadwood Daily Pioneer-Times* called *The Overland Stage*, filmed nearby in 1927, a "credit to the community." Its "worth as an advertising medium to Deadwood and the Black Hills cannot be estimated," the paper noted, because the film would "instill in the minds of those who see it a desire to visit here and see for themselves the country that has played so vital a part in the development of western history." Following the release of Hart's *Wild Bill Hickok* in 1923, the *Dodge City Daily Globe* reported that "never before has Dodge City received more widespread publicity than she is now receiving, and will continue to receive for the next 18 months or two years." Boosters saw that the "tale of Dodge City and the Great Southwest, a region whose early history is unsurpassed in richness is being given to millions on the screen."[10]

The reciprocal needs of filmmakers and boosters translated into a strong mutual relationship between them. Towns regularly took an active hand in reinforcing the Hollywood connection. Almost from the start, film stars joined commemorative celebrations. The organizers generally welcomed any type of celebrity as a way of attracting publicity. Deadwood's Days of '76 scored a major coup in 1927 when local organizers arranged for President Calvin Coolidge, then vacationing in the Black Hills, to attend the event. While there he posed for pictures wearing a Sioux headdress and looking most uncomfortable. Aside from President Coolidge, so many politicians participated in these local celebrations that they rarely received much attention. Townspeople held western movie stars in special regard, however, because they established an immediate connection to the larger-than-life world of Hollywood and its glamour. When film star Ken Maynard announced that he would participate in the 1926 Days of '76 celebration, one Deadwood newspaper reported that "it is certain the presence here of these celebrities of the movie world will enhance the interest which visitors will take in the celebration."[11]

The studios also benefited from the publicity that the towns created. Film producers had a strong interest in community celebrations, where they got more press attention and became identified with a newsworthy historical commemoration. In both 1924 and 1925 Jack Hoxie, a western movie star and former Wild West showman, rode in the first two Days of '76 parades and emceed its programs at the amusement park. The next year the First National film production company came to town and filmed the movie *The Overland Stage* after the celebration ended. This depicted Deadwood's 1876 gold rush period and used costumed and bewhiskered townsfolk as extras in the production. To help publicize the film, the studio's leading man Ken Maynard and his horse Tarzan arrived in Deadwood on a special train with an entourage of twenty people, to join the celebration and remain in town while filming sequences around the Black Hills and Lead.[12]

Hollywood associations also became part of early planning for the 1929 Helldorado in Tombstone. In keeping with his effort to make the event a spectacle, William Kelly tried to persuade a studio to film Tombstone during the celebration, describing it as a unique chance to get economical

footage for future movies, because the town was a natural "lot" with historically accurate architecture local people in costume and a large number
of horse-drawn vehicles. The tactic worked; Pathé Sound News agreed
to cover the event in a film short, saying that it "would be an excellent
medium of municipal propaganda." It also aroused the interest of Ken
Maynard, now with Ken Maynard Productions (Universal Studios). He
offered to suspend production on his current picture in order to bring
an entire company to Tombstone to film the events and historic spots if
the organizers would announce the star's coverage. That would "secure
national publicity at no cost whatsoever."[13] Maynard's offer met immediate
resistance from William Breakenridge, whose attorney informed him that
copyright laws covered many Helldorado scenes reenacted from his book.
Breakenridge saw Maynard as an interloper who was "trying to bust in and
get a picture worth at least $50,000 for nothing. And I as the author of
the book shall surely protest." Rather than risking the danger of a public
fight between the celebration's namesake and the film star, the city council
telegraphed Maynard that they would grant him permission to film for
$3,000, but he refused the offer.[14]

Local boosters took every opportunity to remind movie producers
of their town's history, hoping to have the community picked as a film
location. In 1927 Heinie Schmidt and Merritt Beeson of Dodge City met
a special train carrying Hollywood executives and producers and gave
them historic literature and pledges of support in the hope that a studio
would pick the town as the subject for a future movie. When appealing to
Hollywood executives, boosters stressed their celebrations as sources of
historic authenticity. After learning that Paramount Studios intended to
base an epic movie on Hickok's life (DeMille's *The Plainsman*), Bert Bell,
president of the Deadwood Chamber of Commerce, and his successor, Nell
Perrigoue, reminded executives that the Days of '76 featured Hickok as a
central character and that the event itself "had more local color displayed
on the streets of Deadwood during the three days of this show than can be
found anywhere in the United States." The town offered facilities complete
with "characters of all descriptions, nationalities, and numbers, local color
galore, together with the cooperation and support which truly typifies this
community as purely WESTERN." In 1939 Tombstone went to the extent of
advertising itself for sale as a movie set in the *New York Times*. Often these
efforts paid off. The Black Hills became the setting for *The Deadwood Stage*

with Tom Mix (1926), *Men of Daring* with Jack Hoxie (1927), and *Sitting Bull* with Boris Karloff (1954). Not surprisingly, sometimes the movies filmed on location failed to achieve what the promoters expected. Tombstone was the site of a 1936 horror film entitled *The Crime of Dr. Forbes,* and in 1959 Deadwood allowed filmmaker Roger Corman to shoot *The Creature from the Cave* (aka *Beast from Haunted Cave*) there.[15]

Towns sought to get direct benefits from Hollywood by hosting film premiers of movies about the community in a local theater. Studios also saw those debuts as way to gain additional credibility by association with the towns that they depicted. Authenticity, however, could be easily redefined. At times communities became so eager for the prestige of a Hollywood opening that they accepted major fictionalization of the film with few questions. In 1923 William S. Hart arranged to have an advanced premiere of his movie *Wild Bill Hickok* at the Beeson Theater in Dodge City. Even though Hart bragged of historical accuracy in his memoir, his film took major liberties with actual locations and events. He set the movie in Dodge City even though Hickok never spent time there (he served as marshal in Abilene, Kansas). Hart also associated the gunfighter with a pantheon of historic characters, including Abraham Lincoln, Calamity Jane, George Armstrong Custer, Bat Masterson, and, for the first time, Wyatt Earp. Reveling in the attention that Dodge City received from the film, town leaders ignored these obvious breaches in truth. In a review of the film the *Dodge City Daily Globe* expressed the view that Hart "truly depicted the life of the tough town in the West."[16] Newspapers in Deadwood, which believed their town had the proprietary rights to Hickok and Calamity Jane, had a different opinion. After learning of the film, the *Deadwood Daily Pioneer-Times* complained that the scenes were "faked" in California and lacked "correct historical settings." Neither did it have good things to say about the lead actor. "Old Bill Hart in the character of Wild Bill Hickok cannot very well be other than a travesty and his efforts must create disgust in the minds of those who knew the real Wild Bill in life," the paper concluded.[17]

When the musical *Calamity Jane* premiered in Deadwood in 1953, that city had its turn to bend authenticity while meeting community desires. After an aggressive public relations campaign by Nell Perrigoue in 1952, Warner Brothers agreed to include Deadwood and Lead in the list of communities debuting the movie. To get extra publicity, the city organized a parade and other activities surrounding the initial showing. What had seemed to be a normal civic celebration suddenly turned sour when the governor of South Dakota, Sigurd Anderson, proclaimed that he would not attend the premiere. He objected to the film because it "did not present a true portrayal of the frontier characters Calamity Jane or Wild Bill Hickok, nor did it present an accurate account of early South Dakota history."[18] A week later Heinz A. Grabia, a Baptist minister in Rapid City, joined the attack. The movie "was not of high caliber," and its title "signified nothing but degradation and disgrace," he said. Blaming the film for contributing to juvenile delinquency, Grabia slammed the Deadwood Chamber of Commerce for promoting a "picture that does not represent the high standards and morals of our people." Facing these criticisms, Deadwood mayor Ray L. Ewing issued a proclamation declaring Calamity Jane Week, with the disclaimer that the picture was made to "furnish entertainment only and carries with it certain features which are of more than usual interest to the people of this community, as a publicity medium."[19]

The clearest example of the unwritten partnership between moviemakers and community leaders occurred in 1939 when Warner Brothers announced that it would stage the world premiere of its new epic *Dodge City* in Dodge. Hosting this film marked a major turning point in the way the town identified with its past. The unprecedented level of attention that the event attracted proved a dramatic reminder of the town's marketability as a Wild West icon. As a result, city and social leaders' heightened interest grew out of Hollywood's version of Dodge City history, not one grounded in reality. The town's residents had already shown a willingness to overlook facts that contradicted the benefits of publicity, as shown in their earlier reaction to Hart's *Wild Bill Hickok*. Now, dazzled by the presence and glamour of Hollywood's largest stars and the attention of one of its most powerful studios, many Dodge City promoters embraced its Hollywood reflection.

The premiere developed because of a carefully orchestrated plan by Dodge City business leaders and Warner Brothers to stage a publicity stunt that would overshadow the opening of the epic *Gone with the Wind* from rival studio Metro-Goldwyn-Mayer (MGM). In the winter of 1938 Warner Brothers publicity department executives told members of the Dodge City Chamber of Commerce that the studio intended to film a historic epic based on early Dodge City events and might be willing to hold a premiere of the film in their city. Warner Brothers confirmed the rumor after the studio had gathered information on the town's history, claiming that the studio and the city shared the goal of directing public interest to Dodge City.[20] In response Frank Dunkley, the secretary of the chamber of commerce, sent the studio a five-page synopsis of Dodge City's history. Then he held a meeting to rally local support and organize a planning committee. At the meeting Jack Wooten, representing Warner Brothers, confirmed the studio's hope to make the Dodge City opening "one of the greatest premiers [sic] the world has ever known." He assured citizens that the company had "gone to every effort to produce as nearly as possible a picture that will be a credit to this community and Warner Brothers."[21]

Wooten informed the citizens that the company intended to bring the entire cast to Dodge City dressed in their movie costumes. The studio wanted to make it look as if the idea for holding the premiere in Dodge City came from the town, so it asked the city to circulate a petition requesting that it hold the premiere there, signed by "every leading person in Dodge City and the state of Kansas." Warner Brothers asked for a joint resolution from both houses of the state legislature supporting the petition. Wooten, the studio representative, told chamber members that the studio expected the community to stage a Wild West celebration to complement the film premiere. As a central feature he wanted a rodeo, furnished with trick riders from Warner brothers, where the stars could be highlighted as official rodeo guests. The studio even prepared a complete plan of how the stars would be officially greeted. When the Atchison, Topeka, and Santa Fe train used in the picture brought them to the city, the town would hold a stagecoach race to the depot and meet the arriving stars. Then the visitors would give a short program from the theater stage, covered nationally by radio. Finally, Warner Brothers asked that the film be shown concurrently in all three Dodge City theaters. As the meeting ended, the chamber elected Jess Denious, the publisher of the *Dodge City Daily Globe* and a state senator, to be president of the committee, giving it official sanction.[22]

The executives assumed that a small town like Dodge City would be thrilled to host a premiere, and the chamber members agreed. The city would get lots of national publicity as well as economic benefits from visitors coming to see the event and from the studio itself. Yet the thrill of seeing many of Hollywood's major stars in person seems to have prompted Dodge

City's enthusiasm for the premiere. In letters to studio officials, chamber of commerce spokesman Dunkley assured them that the populace was behind the "program one hundred per cent," with the observation "it appears that the success of the entire program hinges on one feature, and that is the appearance of the Stars of this picture at Dodge City, Kansas." He indicated that the only thing needed to make the celebration a real success would be an official confirmation from Warner Brothers of the extent of its actual involvement.[23]

The studio decided not to make its plans public until it received the petitions from Dodge City and the state of Kansas. In the meantime local organizers signed a contract with the Butler Brothers Rodeo of Elk City, Oklahoma, for a full-scale rodeo in May of that year. No sooner had they recruited the rodeo than rumors began circulating that the premiere would move to Kansas City instead of Dodge City.[24] These fears disappeared after the official Kansas delegation including Senator Denious, lieutenant governor Carl Friend, chamber of commerce president Harry Stark, Jack Wooten, and officials from the Atchison, Topeka, and Santa Fe Railroad rushed to Hollywood with their petition. On February 20, 1939, before rolling studio cameras, the delegation presented Jack Warner, the head of Warner Brothers Studios, with a official scroll made of buffalo hide, requesting that Dodge City be the premiere site, along with a list of 15,000 signatures from Dodge City and other Kansas cities plus the legislative resolutions that the studio had originally requested. Warner accepted the invitation quickly and promised that stars Errol Flynn and Olivia de Havilland as well as other main cast members, along with a host of other available actors, would arrive in Dodge City aboard a special Santa Fe glamour train. Some of the company executives, photographers, camera crews, members of the national press corps, trained horses, trick ropers, and stuntmen would arrive at the same time.[25]

On March 9, 1939, Warner Brothers stunned town planners when it moved the premiere's date ahead to April 1, to upstage the anticipated opening in Atlanta of MGM's *Gone with the Wind*. This left the Dodge City officials with a month or more between the premiere and the rodeo. They had signed a rodeo contract for May, so they changed its name to the "Boot Hill Round Up." Responding to the local organizers' complaints, Jack Warner agreed to finance the rodeo as well as to equip the rodeo grounds if the town would have a parade, street dance, and other activities.

Warner's solution did not solve the problem of the Boot Hill Round Up. After repeated discussions, organizers decided to keep the May rodeo and use the film premiere to open their six-week inaugural Boot Hill Round Up celebration.[26] With planning having to move ahead quickly, committee members patterned the event along familiar lines and added activities associated with western celebrations. Mayor Arthur Nevins urged male citizens to grow whiskers and asked locals to dress in period garb and display relics in store windows. The committee organized an old-timers' reception along with a western-style parade featuring cowboys and bands. To meet the demand for western clothing, merchants stocked up on boots, cowboy hats, and kerchiefs. Following the dictates of Warner Brothers, organizers kept the parade completely western and requested that businesses use horse-drawn vehicles rather than cars and trucks to pull their floats.[27]

For its part Warner Brothers launched a massive publicity campaign to focus the national spotlight on Dodge City. Expecting large crowds, government officials directed state troopers, national guardsmen, and police from neighboring communities to help keep order in the town. The studio assumed that tourists would strain local housing in Dodge City, so it assigned the stars to sleeping quarters in the "glamour train." As it converged on Kansas from California, a similar special train left New York City filled with members of the press corps, including Ed Sullivan, then an entertainment columnist with the *New York Daily News*. The two trains met just outside of town and together made a carefully staged entrance into the city while the Santa Fe Railroad band played "Oh, Susannah" to some 20,000 people waiting to see the film stars. Dignitaries at the scene included Kansas governor Payne Raiser, Franklin Roosevelt Jr., and the governors of Colorado and New Mexico. Jack Warner kept his promise to deliver the studio's top stars. Humphrey Bogart, Rose Marie, Jean Parker, Gilbert Roland, Ann Sheridan, Jean Parker, Eddie Foy Jr., John Garfield, Bruce Cabot, Leo Carrillo, Buck Jones, Jane Wyman, Alan Hale, John Payne, Hoot Gibson, and others emerged one by one to greet the crowd. Errol Flynn, the film's star, dressed in buckskin, emerged last and accepted the key to the city on behalf of the studios.[28]

Following their arrival, the actors in western costumes from the movie took prominent roles in the parade, either riding horses or sitting aboard wagons. At parade's end they joined the public at the Warner Wild West

Crowds at the Dodge City depot preparing to meet the stars of the movie *Dodge City*, 1939. *Courtesy Kansas Heritage Center.*

show in the newly completed Dodge City arena. A live NBC radio broadcast and street dance followed the rodeo. *Dodge City* ran continuously in the town's three theaters throughout the night, highlighted by surprise visits by film stars. All told, an estimated 100,000 visitors swelled the town. During the entire premiere Warner Brothers controlled much of the publicity. Neither the celebration notices nor the film advertising mentioned anything about Wyatt Earp's experiences in Dodge City. apparently the studio feared that any attention given to Earp would be free publicity for Twentieth Century Fox's film *Frontier Marshal*, which featured Earp as its central figure. So Warner Brothers press releases describing Dodge City focused on its other hero, Bat Masterson.[29]

The celebration's success reawakened interest in the town's history. After the premiere a *Dodge City Globe* reporter observed that "almost every conversation" included "the suggestion that the community should permanently capitalize the Old West glamour which it disclosed in surprisingly large quantities" during the event. Heinie Schmidt, one of Dodge's main boosters, expressed this idea repeatedly. Unlike the reporter, he complained that many people failed to appreciate that the town had a major "publicity and entertainment resource." "Dodge City can be made to symbolize the Frontier West and become a popular visitation point for thousands of visitors," he predicted. The new enthusiasm and the swell of publicity following Premiere Day carried into the first Boot Hill Round Up rodeo six weeks later. Dodge City rodeo organizers took full advantage of the chutes, corrals, and bleachers hurriedly constructed by Warner Brothers as well as Jack Warner's pledge to have studio's stars attend the Round-Up rodeo. It barely eked out a profit of $186. Still, the large attendance—6,000 people on the last day—persuaded the organizers to call it a success and to talk about making the Boot Hill Round Up rodeo an annual event.[30]

The Boot Hill Fiesta and Dodge City Days shared many elements with the celebrations in Deadwood and Tombstone. Each included a parade, western-style activities, a relic display, and a whisker club. Dodge City celebration organizers, however, kept the link forged with Hollywood during the *Dodge City* premiere. Building on the euphoria of having stars in town, each successive Boot Hill Fiesta and Dodge City Days attempted to feature a major western celebrity from either the movies or later television. The *New York Times* reported that the event had "accrued more publicity for Dodge City than any production of a similar caliber." Hollywood also saw the advantage of the publicity that it received from the local celebrations. Years later Harry Friedman, the national services editor for Warner Brothers–Seven Artists, recalled the premiere as legendary "among Hollywood press agents." Hoping to maintain the successful association with the Old West town, studios eagerly provided celebrities dressed in western costume as "stars of the show" every year to Dodge City celebrations until well into the 1960s, including Rex Allen, Roy Rogers, Smiley Burnette, Tim Holt, Michael Ansara, Tex Ritter, Eddie Dean, and members of the *Gunsmoke* television show cast.[31]

World War II and its aftermath brought an economic upturn in Tombstone, Dodge City, and Deadwood. This created a newfound confidence and helped to revive interest in local historic commemoration. Deadwood's Days of '76 continued to be performed but in a reduced version. That reflected a loss of population after a 1942 wartime order to close down all the working gold mines. Dramatic change came in Tombstone, the most depressed of the three. In April 1945 local leaders reached their goal of becoming a health resort when Father Roger Aull, a Catholic priest from

New Mexico, decided to start a clinic for the treatment of arthritis there. He developed the facility around the belief that chlorine gas in specific doses broke down calcium deposits in patients' arthritic joints. Tombstone city officials, desperate for a new health facility, converted the jail into a community center to accommodate health seekers. It is unclear what they used for a jail at that point. The plan worked. Health seekers filled all of the available housing, along with two new tourist courts. The *Arizona Daily Star* reported that the restaurants ran out of food by 4:00 P.M. because so many people had arrived in town. Patients drawn to the clinic helped reverse Tombstone's downward population trend. By 1950 the number of residents had climbed to 910, up from 822 ten years earlier. Over the next decade the population rose to 1,283, strengthened in part by the growth of nearby Sierra Vista. Fort Huachuca, which had expanded during World War II, closed and then reopened during the Korean War.[32]

Deadwood also saw its economy recover as it built on its position as the county seat. Once the war ended, the Homestake Mine in Lead and nearby Bald Mountain reopened gold operations, bringing a surge of population into the Black Hills. That, in turn, increased demand for building materials, spurred lumber production by several nearby firms, and boosted the local economy. Despite this modest recovery, disastrous fires swept through Deadwood in 1948, 1951, 1952, 1954, and 1955. These destroyed many of the city hall and municipal records.[33] Dodge City also profited from the booming postwar economy. Beginning in 1946, it reversed earlier population losses as agricultural and livestock conditions rebounded and the city strengthened its role as southwestern Kansas's leading commercial and shipping center. Its population grew from 8,333 in 1940 to 11,332 in 1950.[34]

After World War II a new interest in western tourism helped all three towns recover. Once gas rationing ended, Americans used many of their accumulated savings for travel and leisure-time activities. Resorts that had lain dormant during the war reopened as roadside commerce flourished. At the same time, local and national campaigns to improve road quality resulted in a radical increase in paved roads and completions of sections of the interstate highway system by 1960. As more Americans purchased cars, many vacationed in the West, camping in national parks and visiting places of regional interest. In 1945 an estimated 5 to 7 million tourists visited the West. The number had grown to 20 million ten years later and had reached 50 million by 1960.[35] To deal with this flood of visitors,

Deadwood and other Black Hills Chambers offered a tourist school for its business community in 1947. Dodge City officials held meetings with the Kansas Industrial Commission in 1953 to explore new ways of appealing to tourists and improve amenities.[36]

Increasing western tourism dovetailed with strong patriotism after the war and sharply increasing interest in western films and literature, as Americans responded to feelings of national exceptionalism.[37] A flood of western movies and historical literature focused new attention on old stories and heroes from Deadwood, Dodge City, and Tombstone. Biographies of Wyatt Earp, Doc Holliday, Wild Bill Hickok, Calamity Jane, Luke Short, Bat Masterson, and others appeared. At the same time, the towns themselves became major historic subjects. Between 1949 and 1952 nonfiction accounts by Stanley Vestal, John Myers Myers, Robert Casey, and Roderick Peattie narrated the histories of all three communities.[38] These books and articles in magazines such as *Frontier Times* and *True West* provided an overlay of authenticity that helped local commemorations use and counter the fictionalized accounts in films and later television.

This growing national interest sparked new efforts to hold historical commemorations in each of the three cities immediately after the war. The rebirth of Tombstone's Helldorado proved the most dramatic. In 1946 the local American Legion chapter organized what it called Tombstone Day, combining a parade, public barbecue, a reenactment of the Earp-Clanton gunfight, and a lynching, all parts of the earlier celebration, with a dramatic play entitled *The Drunkard*. The legion sponsored the event the following year then in 1948 turned it over to the chamber of commerce, which returned to the old name Helldorado and got financial support from local bars and restaurants. Organizers of the new program focused on reenactments, quadrupling the number of street "episodes" and added a narrator to describe the killings.[39] Not all of the observers thought that the new program had succeeded. Tucson's *Arizona Daily Star* termed the expanded program "a pageant of death," which resembled "guerrilla warfare." After the "bloodletting," the paper continued, "the spectators, now either gun-happy or completely subdued, turn to barbecue, dancing or a perusal of the carnival."[40]

Western Ways, the Tucson promotional agency contracted by event promoters, made dramatic episodes the celebration's focus after 1948. Each year, a company press release stated, "Tombstone puts on the 'standard' entertainments for civic celebrations out West—parades, rodeo, football games, whiskerino contest, crowning of the Helldorado queen . . . but what makes Tombstone's Helldorado the 'biggest show in the West' are its street-scene reenactments of historic incidents from its colorful past." The event's success—10,000 people viewed it in 1949—showed the popularity of street violence.[41] The next year *Epitaph* publisher Clayton Smith led a group of interested citizens that reactivated Helldorado, Inc. They hoped that having a formal organization could end squabbling over sponsorship among civic groups and make event organizing a year-long activity rather than a seasonal event. To gain support Smith proclaimed it to be the "duty of all citizens to take some active part" in the now permanent ongoing celebration preparation.[42]

Helldorado's revival in the 1940s paralleled renewals of local celebrations in Deadwood and Dodge City. Deadwood's Days of '76 had survived during the war and afterward expanded with a high-quality professional rodeo, theme days, and a longer parade. In 1950 Dodge City's Junior Jaycees and chamber of commerce began a new annual two-part celebration. The first part, the Boot Hill Fiesta, included a city parade each spring. It combined elements of the earlier semicentennial: floats boosting businesses, marching bands, civic groups, military elements, and city services—given a western twist with wagons, Indians, and groups of cowboys. Whisker groups appeared alongside costumed spectators and business sponsors. The second part, the Boot Hill Round Up, held in early summer, featured an amateur rodeo and a carnival. In 1957 the Dodge City Saddle Club, sponsors of the rodeo, split from the fiesta and incorporated as the "Dodge City Roundup." After two years of financial problems, the two groups merged in 1960 to form a week-long celebration called Dodge City Days, which billed itself as a top professional rodeo endorsed by the Rodeo Cowboys' Association.[43]

By the 1950s television had become central in expanding national interest in the Old West. Deadwood, Dodge City, and Tombstone all benefited. From its emergence as a hybrid mix of radio and movies in the late 1940s, television quickly became a powerful medium in its own right and within a decade and a half was an integral part of American life. Its power lay in an ability to penetrate deeply into American family life. The new outlet gave moving visual images to viewers in their homes. At first television was a social affair, with a few neighbors gathering around the small screen to watch favorite programs. Soon more families purchased sets. TV viewing stopped being a neighborhood event and became an impersonal form of communion. Television had a decided advantage over films because it allowed viewers greater control over what they watched through program variety and competitive networks.

TV offered viewers the chance to watch favorite programs at regular times over an extended period—as long as they remained on the air. Early producers adapted the serial format pioneered by movies and radio: short episodes that appeared weekly, connected by characters and formulaic plots. Like movies, television's initial programs drew on the existing popularity of westerns. *Hopalong Cassidy* and *The Lone Ranger* premiered in 1949, followed by *The Cisco Kid* and *The Gene Autry Show* in 1950, and *The Roy Rogers Show* in 1951 (westerns later predominated on American television, with thirty-two series in 1959), exploring all avenues of characterization and situations: never-ending migration (*Wagon Train*), a perpetual cattle drive (*Rawhide*), family ranches (*Bonanza, The Big Valley, The High Chaparral*), secret agents (*The Wild Wild West*), mercenaries (*Maverick, Have Gun Will Travel, The Rebel, The Rifleman, Fastest Gun Alive*), Indians (*Broken Arrow*), and enforcers (*Lawman, Wanted Dead or Alive, Laramie, The Deputy*).[44]

Given their established association with the Wild West through movies and literature, Deadwood, Dodge City, and Tombstone soon became settings for television programs. The new medium borrowed many existing images of the towns and their characters from movies, but with greater effect. Patrons attended movies only periodically; television programs appeared weekly and sometimes remained on the air for years, which radically expanded the number of viewers. The repetition of visual images and plots intensified viewers' expectations about the nature of the three communities. Over time these images gained enough power to be incorporated into the identity of the towns themselves.

Deadwood became the first of the three to have a television program focused on its past. Not surprisingly, when producers inaugurated program series, they turned to the western hero with the longest history of marketing success: Wild Bill Hickok. The half-hour program *Adventures of Wild Bill Hickok*, starring Guy Madison as Hickok and Andy Devine as his sidekick Jingle B. Jones, began in 1951 and ran through 1958 (syndicated, 1952 to 1954; CBS, 1954 to 1957; ABC, 1957 to 1958). The same characters reprised their roles from 1951 to 1956 on a radio version of the series.

Although the series was not set in Deadwood, it kept the town's hero before the public eye for nearly a decade.

Tombstone became so closely associated with its television versions that at one point an *Arizona Daily Star* columnist wrote: "If there were no real Tombstone, TV would have been forced to invent this symbol of the Wild West at its wildest and woolliest. TV daily embroiders and enlarges the legend of the town too tough to die." Arizona governor Paul Fannin reinforced the intimate connection between the medium and the town when he asked: "What civilized portion of the world today, having been exposed to the many news media from small county newspapers to the electronic marvel of television, has not heard the name Tombstone and its cast of colorful characters that literally created the myths and legends now accepted as fact throughout much of the world?"[45]

The town's television fame rested on two major series. *Tombstone Territory* (syndicated 1957 to 1959) based itself on the actual files from the *Tombstone Epitaph* and featured the newspaper's founder and mayor, John Clum, as a central character. To ensure accuracy, producers hired Wallace Clayton, who had purchased the *Epitaph* in 1938, to serve as a technical advisor for the series.[46] The long-running ABC series *The Life and Legend of Wyatt Earp*, which premiered in 1955 and starred Hugh O'Brian, had an even greater impact. Along with *Gunsmoke* and *Cheyenne*, it marked the beginning of television's late 1950s so-called prime-time adult westerns. The six-year series depicted Earp as a roving white knight who moved from town to town establishing order but gave him a general residence in Dodge City for the first three years then moved him to Tombstone for the final three. Ending in 1961, the series concluded with a five-part sequence focusing on the gunfight at the OK Corral. Stuart Lake, author of the wildly inaccurate *Wyatt Earp: Frontier Marshal*, originated the Earp series, wrote a large number of its scripts, and served as a consultant to the program.[47]

Of the three towns, Dodge City experienced the most impact from television, perhaps as much as the other two towns combined. From 1955 through 1975—a complete generation—three series made the town their center of attention. In addition to *Wyatt Earp*, television featured two more of its noteworthy figures. NBC's *Bat Masterson* starring Gene Barry ran from 1958 through 1961. *Gunsmoke*, the most influential program by far, became the most popular television western program of all time. Following a successful radio show begun in 1952, it premiered on CBS in 1955 and

James Arness as Matt Dillon in *Gunsmoke*, 1956.
Courtesy Wikimedia Commons.

ran continuously for twenty years. Both on radio and television the series depicted the adventures of a fictional sheriff, Matt Dillon, played on radio by William Conrad and on television by James Arness. Set in Dodge City during the 1870s and 1880s, the show rapidly gained popularity, becoming the number one program in its third season, and remained in the top position for the next four years.[48]

At first some Dodge City leaders considered both the radio and television versions of *Gunsmoke* to be threats to their town's reputation. Unlike Tombstone and Deadwood, which now fully embraced their Wild West identity, many of Dodge's business and political elite remained hesitant about identifying their community with violence, saloons, and prostitutes.

At least some of this nervousness stemmed from confusion over the authenticity of the leading characters. When the radio series began in 1952, requests for history and information about the character Matt Dillon almost buried the city's chamber of commerce. Given Hollywood's long history of using fictional versions of real western characters, many listeners logically assumed that Matt Dillon was based on an actual person. Even some locals wondered. Facing the hundreds of requests for information on the sheriff, George Weeks, manager of the chamber of commerce, wrote to CBS, asking for documentation on the character. He clearly knew little more than the fans besieging his office did, because he wrote: "As near as we can determine, Matt lived here at one time, but other than that, our information is extremely meager."[49]

The volume of interest upset members of local business leaders, who worried that the show's depiction of a lawless Dodge City would give readers the wrong impression about the modern city. In 1953 Ellis Cave, the president of the Dodge City Chamber of Commerce, voiced the ideas of some business leaders who objected to the "wild and woolly publicity" that their town received. In a letter to CBS radio expressing their dismay that the series was "perhaps too well produced," as evidenced from the flood of mail addressed to Matt Dillon that the chamber received "from those who sympathize with his trying ordeal." Cave objected that "this was carrying the thing too far." He wrote that "between the newspapers, radio, movies, and the historical novel, *Dodge City* has received more publicity than any other place in this region and now comes 'Gun Smoke' [*sic*]. This means we will have to fight it all over again to let America know this is the Dodge City that was, not is." He petitioned CBS to inform viewers that the program was "merely a realistic mirror of Dodge City and Western Kansas in the course of their creation" and pointed out that the communities of western Kansas merited recognition "as cities which lead, not lag, in American progress."[50] After the television show premiered in 1955, the city offered to send economic literature to CBS for the network to send out in response to inquiries about Matt Dillon to prove Dodge City was "modern in all respects."[51] Ironically, Dodge City viewers could not even watch the show until 1960, when their town got access to CBS television.

Despite these early objections to being depicted as a Wild West boomtown, local opinion had changed dramatically by the time *Gunsmoke* became the nation's most popular show in 1959. Local business leaders realized, as had those in Deadwood and Tombstone, that television programs translated directly into profits from increased tourism. In 1958 the *Kansas City Times* noted that with the "tremendous assist from television" Dodge City was "cashing in on its riotous past," adding that "as long as westerns top the ratings, Dodge City promises to be the greatest tourist attraction of all."[52] Robert Pearman, writing about the town's newfound television fame in the *New York Times Magazine,* reported that 60 million *Gunsmoke* weekly viewers plus an additional 20 to 30 million *Wyatt Earp* watchers translated into an estimated annual tourist income of a million dollars. A year later Mayor N. O. Reese told leaders in the *Dodge City Daily Globe* that no other city had received the amount of free advertising and underscored a national study that showed tourism was the third largest business in the county. With the profits from a million visitors each year, Reese argued, 750 new jobs and 1,000 homes would be created. By 1960 local leaders accepted the fame that television series brought. Ike Bassett, speaking for the local chamber of commerce, estimated that TV could take credit for 150,000 visitors a year.[53]

Leaders in Tombstone credited the *Tombstone Territory* series with increasing the tourist business by 100 percent during its first year on the air. In 1961 the *Epitaph* observed that "TV shows still head the list of reasons why most people want to visit the old camp. *Tombstone Territory* and *Wyatt Earp* are credited with bringing lots of folks here" and that "the influx has created a new interest in further development of Tombstone as a tourist center."[54] One method that locals revived to exploit the television connection was to work actors into public celebrations just as they had done earlier with movie stars. In Tombstone Helldorado organizers enlisted Pat Conroy and Richard Eastman, the stars of *Tombstone Territory,* to be official guests of the event and appear on horseback in the 1959 parade.[55]

Similarly, in 1951 Deadwood tried to exploit the new television and radio programs *Wild Bill Hickok* by enlisting its stars, Guy Madison and Andy Devine, to serve as celebrity guests for the 75th Anniversary Celebration of the gold rush and Hickok's death. Tying their planned events to the new show, the organizers focused on Hickok as the center of the celebration and scheduled the unveiling of a granite bust of Wild Bill in downtown Deadwood as the featured attraction. When Nell Perrigoue asked the producers of *Wild Bill Hickok* to allow Madison and Devine to participate in the event, they responded with a list of demands: that local organizers hold a parade, have a best western costume competition, transport the stars into town in a stagecoach that would be part of a reenacted holdup, and provide "two guitar slinging singers" to accompany the actors when they sang. The studio understood that these requests were "reaching for the stars" but assured Deadwood organizers that this was the only way to "assure coverage by the publicity outlets that count."[56]

Perrigoue and her colleagues agreed and added several items to the studio's wish list: they promised to reenact Hickok's murder and the trial of Jack McCall and to provide elements of authenticity to the celebration. Almost no pioneers from the frontier period remained alive, so event organizers invited relatives or descendants of former townspeople. These included Judge Lee Wyman, the son of the man who built the scaffold upon which Jack McCall was hanged, the grandson of Deadwood's first sheriff, and two of Hickok's cousins. For a touch of historical accuracy they included 98-year-old P. A. Gushurst, supposedly the only living witness to the gunfighter's death. As the day-long event unfolded, a crowd of 5,000 witnessed a standard mix of authenticity and entertainment, starting with parade with "many Wild Bills, Preacher Smiths, Calamity Janes, Poker Alices, prospectors, and Calico Club members," followed by a series of reenactments and the dedication of the Hickok bust.[57]

Dodge City organizers, well seasoned in aligning events with celebrities, outclassed both the other towns with a series of publicity events in conjunction with ABC. In January 1958 the city honored its most famous lawman by celebrating a Wyatt Earp Day that featured Hugh O'Brian, television's Wyatt Earp, as its main attraction. Dressed in his television costume, the actor laid the cornerstone for a new replica of the town's original Front Street and watched as the city renamed its Chestnut Street to Wyatt Earp Boulevard. Not to be upstaged, the next fall CBS announced plans in the late 1940s to "publicize their line of adult westerns" by bringing their top television celebrities to Dodge City for an event called "Return to the Santa Fe Trail." Their list of stars for the event included *Gunsmoke*'s James Arness, Amanda Blake, and Milburn Stone; *Zane Grey Theater*'s David Janssen; *Trackdown*'s Robert Culp; *Wanted Dead or Alive*'s Steve McQueen; *Have Gun Will Travel*'s Johnny Western; and *The Texan*'s Chill Wills.[58]

To get extra publicity the network asked Dodge City leaders to plan a western celebration with a parade, fast-draw contest, Spanish fiesta, and Indian dance. Two weeks before the stars arrived, twenty-eight Dodge City retail firms and hotels on Walnut Street in the downtown business district petitioned the city commission to rename the street Gunsmoke Avenue. Some residents objected to the television producers' rewriting of the town's history and circulated a counterpetition opposing the move. While presenting their request to city leaders, L. Ralph Miller, a longtime resident, told them that "it is not essential to rename one of our streets every time a movie celebrity visits our city." Responding to this opposition, the commission voted to change the name of only one section of Walnut Street.[59]

By the 1960s *Gunsmoke* had become a central part of Dodge City's identity. A twenty-foot fiberglass statue of a cowboy affectionately known as "Big Matt" (Dillon) greeted visitors as they came into town until a windstorm blew it down. When CBS decided to cancel the program in 1967, the city commission begged the network to reconsider and launched a letter-writing campaign and an open appeal to CBS. It expressed disappointment and noted the program's "decisive influence upon the economic development of our city." *Gunsmoke,* the letter continued, was "synonymous with the individualism and courage which have formed the bulwark of this country" as well as conveying "a sense of pride, courage, and philosophy of life which could be utilized in facing the frontiers of the 20th century."[60] Kansas legislators supported the city with a unanimous resolution calling for the reinstatement of the program. In March CBS reversed its decision. The program continued until 1975, as the longest-running prime-time series to that date. In a final attempt to capitalize on the program when CBS ended the show, Boot Hill Museum director George Heinrichs tried to have the program set brought to Dodge City, but the staging was too massive to be moved.[61]

Over several decades television and movies had built up tourists' expectations that they could find the places they saw on the screen or in their living room by visiting the West. With potential revenue from tourism at stake, the ongoing question of how to satisfy visitors' desires without destroying each town's history clashed with some residents' hopes to present their communities as modern places to live. "Movies and TV paint a picture of Tombstone for thousands of people every year," the *Epitaph* observed. It went on to ask: "How do we come close to fulfilling this dream of Western glory?"[62]

For years leaders in all three communities had urged local citizens to act like westerners. In Deadwood they encouraged residents not to lose their "personality or individuality—the western hat, the picturesque garb of the cowboy, which the Easterner expects as much when he comes west as he does the formal dress of eastern functions." As early as 1949 the Deadwood Chamber of Commerce members had discussed the possibility of having "all local people wearing western attire during the summer months" and encouraged its own members to choose between wearing western clothes or becoming active members of the Days of '76 Whisker Club.[63] In 1961 Dodge City conformed to the popular interest in sheriffs Matt Dillon and Wyatt Earp by making Stetsons the official headgear of its municipal police force.[64] Clayton Smith, editor of the *Tombstone Epitaph*, asked his readers to take advantage of the town's "free advertising" by wearing western boots and hats, Mexican costumes, or Navajo blouses. Earlier he had asked that "businessmen in particular might wisely consider the effect a little western dress would have on people who stop to see Tombstone." In 1961 the Tombstone Chamber of Commerce went a step further by instructing residents to practice western mannerisms as a supplement to their western wardrobes. It is good business, the *Epitaph* reported, to "speak to all persons with a friendly good morning or 'howdy partner' particularly if you happen to have on your best western boots, plaid shirt and cowboy hat."[65]

Some Tombstone residents formed local clubs to keep the memory of the Old West alive not only by dressing the part but by acting it as well. The first of these, the Vigilantes, wanted to provide "a bit of western color throughout the year" by dressing the part and performing in reenactments during Helldorado. According to the *Epitaph*, the club included "civic minded men" who "go to church by stage coach, wear impressive .45s strapped to their middles," and give "visitors exactly what they want to see."[66] The group made its debut during the 1947 Tombstone Days Celebration and sponsored the event from 1949 through 1951 then turned it over to the American Legion and chamber of commerce, preferring to direct and organize the reenactments during the annual celebration.

Incorporated in 1954, the Vigilantes announced that their goal was the promotion of the "western frontier mode of living." During the year its members dressed in western clothing, staged shootouts and skits for public events, and "lynched" prominent visitors, throwing a noose around their neck and photographing them for the *Tombstone Epitaph*. They and other reenactors strove to relive what they thought of as life in the Old

West. Jan Olsson, a Swedish writer who spent a number of months in Tombstone in 1956, recalled his thrill at being allowed to participate in one of the reenactments. "I was quite excited at being allowed to play at Wild West in earnest: a game it was of course, but still as serious as could be."[67] For Olsson and other Vigilante members the shining moment came during the annual Helldorado, with its large number of skits ending with the climactic gunfight at the OK Corral.

The Vigilantes reflected local impulses to control the media images and turn their role-playing into a community service. Most reenactment groups wanted to keep their presentations authentic, and some argued heatedly about what was historically accurate and how to keep their acts that way. Disagreements over the role of women as reenactors eventually led to a major controversy that split the Vigilantes in 1955. A number of members' wives wanted to have active parts in the reenactments, but some of the men objected. After a series of bitter internal debates failed to resolve the issue, Morgan Livingston, a major supporter of female inclusion, and a number of other Vigilantes left the organization and formed a new one with their wives, the Ghosts of Old Tombstone.[68] Two years later some of the women organized their own exclusive female group, the Vigilettes, giving the town three separate organizations: one male, one female, and one mixed.

The deepest tension existed between the Vigilantes and the rebel club, the Ghosts of Old Tombstone, while the Vigilettes apparently remained outside this fight. For almost a decade the two rivals competed for time in Helldorado and the honor of hanging visiting dignitaries. In 1962 their bitter dispute over which group should control the celebration led to an emergency city council meeting. It also brought a series of editorials in the *Tombstone Epitaph* calling for the reenactors to recognize that the event was "bigger than the Ghosts, bigger than the Vigilantes." Angered by what he saw as moves away from the event's doctrine of authenticity, Clayton Smith reminded both groups that Helldorado, Inc., must refrain from entanglements with any specific organization and that it reserved the right to "control and exercise scouting over reenactments which will be staged for public consumption." He added that Tombstone had enough true stories and that the event did not necessitate getting the "Hollywood treatment."[69]

Organizers equated authenticity with local volunteer efforts. "No one is getting paid one cent for services," the *Epitaph* reminded readers, and "every member of Helldorado is a resident of Tombstone who take [*sic*] part because they want to." Editor Smith reassured his readers that benefits from the celebration helped support civic groups such as the Girl Scouts, Little League, the municipal swimming pool, and the fire department. The 1964 program noted that the reenactors were "dedicated to the preservation of memories and incidents of Tombstone's uproarious and exciting past, are hard working, serious minded, fun loving people who sole pay is the enjoyment derived from helping put on an important community project."[70] When talk of hiring a paid director and paying cast members surfaced in 1963, the *Epitaph* argued that it would change the traditional integrity of the show based on amateurism and authenticity. The celebration would "lose its meaning and appeal to visitors if supervised by an outsider," Smith wrote. He reminded readers that "Helldorado is a Tombstone show . . . better to drop it than see it disintegrate into a show that loses its meaning."[71] The board compromised by hiring a local director for the reenactments.

The question of "good taste" divided local civic promoters when some wanted to emphasize the violence to match what the movies and television offered. In 1956 national public concern about television violence as a possible cause for growing juvenile delinquency led U.S. senator Estes Kefauver to conduct a series of congressional hearings into the matter. Following the premiere and popularity of *The Untouchables*, considered a particularly violent series in 1959, and an escalation of violence in other programs, Senator Thomas Dodd began agitating for restrictions on television programming in 1961.[72] When the *Epitaph* used headlines such as "Frontier Violence to Greet Visitors" and "Violence to Reign" in promoting Helldorado and Vigilante events, some community members complained that the depictions of mayhem had gone too far.[73] Outside opinions seemed to affirm their fears. At one point the *Arizona Daily Star* reported that "the reenactments are performed in as good taste as violent murders can be." Earlier Inez Robb, a columnist for the same paper, had found the town's emphasis on violence repulsive. "Via tourism," she wrote, "Tombstone today lives on the senseless violence and bloodshed that distinguished it 80 years ago." She called the town's Boot Hill "one of the country's most depressing monuments to the lawlessness and wholesale violence that accompanied the winning of the west" and was convinced that "almost as much [real] blood was shed here as daily flows from home screen."[74]

Accounts of Helldorado's reenacted violence reached as far as *Soviet Woman Magazine*, which described the event for its Russian readers as a killing school for youth. "Although it is a mock manhunt and the blood that is not spilt is not real, one need not all be surprised when the youthful participants in 'galas' of this kind begin to shoot and kill in earnest," the writer noted. "It throws light on the means by which the imperialists seek to corrupt the rising generation, to cultivate animal instincts and contempt for human life in children." Responding to outsiders' attacks, the *Epitaph* defended "Helldorado [as] symbolic of the winning of the West, an honor to good citizens of early Tombstone and a product of a free community."[75] Still, even some locals had reservations about the show's contents. In 1954 church groups in Tombstone criticized the event's depictions of drinking and gambling and asked the city council not to stage it on Sunday. One city council member remarked that if the petitioners were participants in the planning they "could have produced a show to suit their ideas" but agreed to help make some of the requested changes.[76]

To reduce criticism the organizers stressed the educational value and historical accuracy of their reenactments. The Vigilantes prided themselves on documenting their costumes and performances, "spending long hours digging through old files, books, papers, and personal stories to get as nearly as possible a complete and true story of frontier life in the town too tough to die." The Vigilettes called themselves "a history club," organized "authentic" costume shows for Helldorado, and staged melodramas such as *Bertha: The Beautiful Typewriter Girl*, which from its title seemed out of place alongside stories of gunfighters. As part of its historical outreach, the group funded guest speakers and sponsored history paper contests in Tombstone schools. In 1957 celebration organizers sought to capitalize on Wyatt Earp's performance by hiring Hobart Earp, alleged to be lawman's fourth cousin, to play the gunman's part. Earp, a California lapidary and fast-draw artist, returned each year until the mid-1960s to act the role.[77]

Besides dressing and acting out western roles, businesses that catered to tourists also played a key role in creating a western atmosphere. In addition to constructing motels—Dodge City alone built fourteen to accommodate tourists—each town had souvenir stands, cafes, and garages that catered to the new influx of travelers. By the 1950s many of them had distinctive Old West names related to their town's historic identity. Dodge City's 1954 *Howdy* book listed the Boot Hill Oil Company, the Trail Inn Hotel, the Boothill Grill, the Western Cafe, and the Lariat Cafe. A 1961 tourist guide for Deadwood recommended such businesses as the Wild

Bill Bar, '76 Bar, Buffalo Bar, Gold Bar, Calamity Jane Motel, Lariat Motel, Tomahawk Tent Camp, and Gold Run Inn. Tombstone businesses blended revitalized original names along with newer ones. Promotional brochures in the 1940s through the 1960s featured the Crystal Palace Cafe, Wagon Wheel Inn, Boothill Motel, Crystal Theater, Boothill Hardware, OK Cafe, Wells Fargo Trailer Court, Can Can Variety Store, Purple Hogan, Mason's Corral Bar, Wyatt Earp Cafe, Lucky Cuss Restaurant, Johnny Ringo Bar, and Iron Chinaman Laundry.[78]

The chambers of commerce often helped construct attractions designed specifically for tourists looking for an Old West experience. "Enterprising people are giving Tombstone something with authenticity that the traveling public wants to see," the *Epitaph* wrote. The effort to satisfy visitors' desires often blended community hucksterism and history. Dodge City offered stagecoach rides in the late 1950s, and Tombstone opened some of its abandoned mines for tours. Deadwood acted more aggressively. In 1953 Charlie Waters of the Deadwood Chamber of Commerce formed a nonprofit corporation and purchased an abandoned pyrite mine, which he renamed the "Broken Boot Mine" and opened for public tours. Six years later Nell Perrigoue, Pat Wood, and James Shea opened a wax museum called the Ghosts of Deadwood Gulch, with eighty figures representing the daily life of early Deadwood. Its proprietors announced that the new exhibit was "educational in scope" and downplayed "the scenes of violence which are sometimes more dramatic."[79] A few years later they added daily performances of the trial of Jack McCall to the attraction.

Despite merging entertainment and profit, authenticity continued to be a driving principle of both official and private historic commemorations. Tombstone leaders, whose economy depended heavily on tourism by the early 1960s, remained determined to present an image based on historical integrity. "Authenticity has been the key to success," Clayton Smith reminded townspeople in 1962, adding that the community has "always operated on the premise that there's enough glamour in Tombstone's history just the way it is without adding a Hollywood touch." He urged readers to "be watchful and diligent if we are to maintain authenticity, lest we take the easy road to commercialism."[80] Many western writers supported his dedication to historical accuracy, because they objected to what they perceived as the formularized Hollywood versions of the West aimed at young people.

Frank Robertson, the president of the Western Writers of America, believed that Hollywood's "young hot-shot writers" gave a false picture of the West on television because they faced limits set by producers. "Dammit, I love Dodge City," he wrote to Ike Bassett, the secretary-manager of the Dodge City Chamber of Commerce in 1960, "and I don't like to see it being slandered. Such shows as *Gunsmoke* I like, but in most of the others there's a terrible lack of originality." Robertson thought that the situation would improve considerably if writers like his good friends Homer Croy and Harry Drago wrote the scripts. Part of the problem was that authors of articles on the West found it hard to be considered serious researchers because "society takes western history to be something for the younger set, or for Television actors," he complained. Responding directly to this idea, Frank Waters, in his introduction to *The Earp Brothers of Tombstone*, proclaimed that his intention was to expose the "'Great American Myth' of the western bad-man painted by pulps, slicks and paperbacks, one-reel Westerns, super-colossals, and the TV."[81] In the quest for the truth, writers argued among themselves over the real nature of characters. Whether the public knew much about it or not, Wyatt Earp's fame from both movies and television made him the center of a firestorm of debate between his supporters like Stuart Lake and critics including Grace McCool, Ed Bartholomew, and Frank Waters.

The differing versions of the West given by writers and Hollywood posed a dilemma for towns banking on authenticity. Clayton Smith believed that the ongoing arguments damaged Tombstone's tourist industry. "Wyatt Earp can't be a hero in one end of town and a bum in another," he wrote, "and have the visiting public impressed enough to come back or tell friends they should see Tombstone." Hoping to settle the arguments over the town's most noted figure, he recommended creating a "history school" directed by a "recognized historian" for those dealing with the public so everyone would have the same version of the past. At the same time, Deadwood residents were urged to brush up on points of interest so that they could give adequate and reliable information to visitors.[82] Both Dodge City and Deadwood issued "official" versions of their history sanctioned by their chambers of commerce. In 1954 Dodge City began providing visitors with official *Howdy* books. These described the town's history as well as its retail and municipal services. Tourists inquiring about Deadwood's past could buy an official souvenir booklet that gave a short history and stories about its leading characters at information booths set up and operated by the chamber of commerce.

Was Wyatt Earp a hero or a murderer? How many men did Wild Bill Hickok actually kill? Was Matt Dillon based on a real person? By the 1960s those questions, once discussed in informal circles, had become matters of public policy. Dodge City, Tombstone, and Deadwood all welcomed movies and television as forms of advertising. Yet what did the media advertise? No film or television program showed any interest in community progress or development. Such stories were routine in hundreds of towns across the country. Movies and television were only interested in their Wild West pasts—which, ironically, presented images that the media helped to create and perpetuate. By repeating stories about colorful heroes and lurid events, set against the backdrops of saloons, gambling dens, street violence, and prostitution, popular literature, movies, and later television made these images central in the process of defining the Old West. Lured by the economic benefits and the sense of historic importance that such attention brought, Deadwood, Tombstone, and later Dodge City accepted these images as integral parts of their identity. They adopted western clothing and mannerisms, reenacted the past, tailored public celebrations, and created business and attractions to meet tourist expectations. Was the history that these towns commemorated their own or some Hollywood version? By the 1960s entertainment and authenticity had become so deeply intertwined that it became nearly impossible to tell where one ended and the other began. Once the golden age of television westerns ended in the 1970s, the towns moved in separate directions as they worked to gain national recognition of their legitimate place in history.

8 ☛ Museums and Preservation

In each decade since the mid-nineteenth century some form of popular entertainment from dime novels to television tied Tombstone, Deadwood, and Dodge City's place in history to the Old West. These communities reinforced this through the Days of '76, Helldorado, and the Boot Hill Fiesta public celebrations. Efforts by chambers of commerce and community leaders to make the Wild West period the official town identity by using slogans, public celebrations, monuments, and historic markers led to discussions about how to preserve memory and serve the interests of posterity and local economies. Each town's need to have its claims of historic importance recognized and validated on a national level proved central to this dialogue. Achieving this goal proved difficult. Preservation of memory through museums, building restoration, or replication meant having to balance public and private agendas among the needs of tourists, local businesses, and the desire for national attention and credibility.

Each town offered the tangible elements of the past—people, objects, documents, photographs, or buildings—as proof of its historical legitimacy. These things became historically important when exhibited at annual celebrations or in town museums or discussed by local historians. In Tombstone, Deadwood, and Dodge City officials considered any object or person representing the Old West to be historically valuable. This allowed anyone, regardless of social standing, to contribute to the town's collective memory by loaning or donating a relic. Architecture and landscapes like Dodge City's Boot Hill offered even more dramatic affirmations of the past by providing the physical evidence and the imagined experience of a historic environment. Unlike individual relics, buildings and grounds changed over time through remodeling, weathering, demolition, and use by private owners. These changes raised concerns over how much of a building should be restored and questions about the meaning of "original." Of the three towns only Tombstone had many buildings standing after World War II when preservation efforts began in earnest. Deadwood and Dodge City faced a larger challenge, seeking to validate their frontier moment because fires and modernization had swept away all but a few vintage buildings. Yet the absence of historic structures did not mean losing architecture as evidence. If no buildings existed to provide the correct historic atmosphere they could be replicated, as happened in Dodge City.

Museums provided one of the most direct methods of validating the past. As institutions, they offered a way for individuals to help create their community's history. They could do this by donating, loaning, or selling objects, photographs, or clothing for public display during the annual celebrations. Instead of using the modern term "artifact," museums of the early half of the twentieth century called their items "relics." For many townspeople the objects represented the truth of a historic event or person in much the same way that certain religions preserved sacred objects that offered physical proof of their faith. Exhibit styles reflected the sacred connotation for historic relics. As in a reliquary, curators assembled and displayed objects topically, not in terms of illustrating an interpretive story but as assemblies of material evidence about an earlier time. They could be associated with a famous person, a major event, a prosperous family, or an occupational history such as ranching, homesteading, or mining. Private and public museum administrators collected and displayed relics according to what they saw as important in their community's past. In Deadwood, Dodge City, and Tombstone both private and public museums supported their community's claims of historic importance as well as functioning as roadside attractions for the tourist.

Fred Gramlich, one of the original organizers of the Days of '76 celebration in Deadwood, opened the Adams Museum as the first effort to preserve community memory. A Deadwood resident since 1898, he had developed a strong interest in museums during the 1920s after collecting relics for the event and displaying them in his stores in Deadwood and Rapid City. Gramlich had formed the Black Hills Pioneer Memorial Museum Association in the mid-1920s and opened a Hall of Relics in a vacant store in downtown Deadwood in 1926. A year later he presented a plan for a museum to be financed through public subscription to friends in the

Deadwood Business Club. The proposal received unanimous endorsement and the promise of committee support by its president, local architect Ray L. Ewing. Soon after the plans became public they caught the attention of William E. Adams, a wealthy Deadwood citizen.[1] He agreed to purchase a site for the city, pay for museum construction, and provide an operating endowment, as long as the public had free admission.

With both immediate and long-term financial support assured, the museum committee started planning for the building. They hired Ray Ewing to design the new downtown structure. His plan featured spaces to house relics as well as a meeting space for the Society of Black Hills Pioneers. Atop the structure, he designed a tower for a set of electronic chimes that could play fifty selections. The Adams Museum opened in October 1930 as the official center of Deadwood's community memory. The supporters expected it to commemorate Deadwood's role in the Old West. The *Black Hills Weekly* proclaimed that the museum would be a place where the "Wild days of America's last Frontier will be lodged, imperishably in brick and stone, to last for future generations." At the opening ceremonies Adams was a little more humble, calling it a memorial erected to early pioneers "who have gone to the great beyond."[2] To oversee and expand the museum's relic collections toward these ends, the city hired Irish-born longtime Deadwood resident D. M. Gahey in April 1931.

As curator, Gahey collected relics and photographs that he believed documented the everyday lives of early Deadwood residents, major events in town history, and objects from the local area. A sampling of the collection during the 1930s showed that he took the meaning of "relic" quite seriously. The museum displayed items reflecting local businesses and everyday community life as well as artifacts from Deadwood's Wild West era. They included the first steam engine to reach the Black Hills in 1879, a post from Custer's stockade there, a leather trunk brought to the Black Hills in 1876, the original wooden headboard from Wild Bill Hickok's grave, Hickok's marriage license and gun, objects from Deadwood's Chinatown, Indian beadworks, a bullet-ridden lithograph of the battle of the Little Bighorn from a saloon, a weather-beaten sign warning off claim-jumpers, a rifle used in Indian battles, numerous geological and mounted animal specimens, and even a miniature hand-carved nudist ranch. Decades later the Thoen Stone, a sandstone slab inscribed with a message allegedly left by seven prospectors searching for gold in the Black Hills in 1834 just before they were killed by Indians, became one of the museum's prized items.[3]

Gahey worked to keep the museum focused on Adams's original intention to celebrate early pioneers, but gradually the chamber of commerce applied pressure for a stronger Wild West focus. Tourists often assumed that a museum in Deadwood would feature the town's most famous characters, Hickok, Calamity Jane, and Deadwood Dick. Apparently many of them expected to find more relics related to their stories than the museum had on display. This fascination irked the staid curator, who once confided to a *Rapid City Journal* reporter that "too much emphasis has been placed on Deadwood's notorious characters." He wanted to emphasize the town's community builders and have "due credit and reverence placed on the unsung heroes who settled this roaring gold camp and saw it through its many privations to the modern town it was today."[4]

Despite Gahey's personal feelings, the chamber of commerce expected the museum to become a tourist attraction. Speaking for the group, Nell Perrigoue marketed it as an Old West memorial. One of the brochures described it as "chock full of mementos of Deadwood's mad early days— from Wild Bill's marriage certificate to big, raw gold nuggets." Another flyer stressed the authenticity of the collections, bragging that it "offers one of the most unique and valuable collections of any museum in the entire west." "The historic displays in the Hall could not be reproduced at any cost, many of them being brought into the Black Hills during the gold rush of 1876." The early internal layout of the museum also catered to the Old West. On the first floor the displays related mostly to Hickok, Deadwood Dick, Calamity Jane, and later Potato Creek Johnny along with exhibits on local Indians, while the upper balcony featured an extensive gun collection and some Little Bighorn relics. Objects such as clothing, tools, and mining equipment relating to early-day pioneer life remained in the basement.[5]

In spite of Deadwood's claim of historic importance, the Adams Museum, the graves at Mount Moriah Cemetery, and its other attractions all failed to give any sense of Deadwood's legitimate place in western history. This began to change in 1935, when Congress passed the Historic Sites Act. Shortly after it became law, federal surveyors began gathering data about potential sites, including early mining camps like Deadwood and Tombstone, to nominate for the new historic landmark designation. During the World War II period the project stalled for over a decade until the 1957 Historic Sites Act revived it. Then a new committee reviewed the list of eligible sites and made its recommendations to the National Parks, Historic Sites, Buildings and Monuments Board. On July 4, 1961, Deadwood became a National Historic Landmark. The Park Service report focused on the town's reputation and famous characters. "As well as most, perhaps better than any other, Deadwood has come to typify the wide-open lawlessness of the frontier mining camp," it wrote. "Much of Deadwood's present renown stems from the exploits of such notorious individuals, Wild Bill Hickok, Calamity Jane, Poker Alice, California Jack, and the legendary Deadwood Dick."[6] Deadwood's 1966 application for listing on the National Register of Historic Places continued to emphasize its Wild West identity. According to the authors, the town retained its atmosphere because many of the old buildings still survived, including Saloon Number 10, the site of Hickok's assassination.[7]

A few years later Deadwood city officers and the chamber of commerce decided that they needed to restore the historic integrity of the business district. In 1971 the city office of Housing and Redevelopment began trying to preserve the few remaining vintage downtown buildings. When it made little progress, it gave way to a Historic Preservation Advisory Commission, which by 1975 was struggling to ignite local interest in city-wide preservation, hoping that refurbished buildings would boost tourism.[8] The movement ebbed during the 1970s recession, which slowed any wide-scale voluntary restoration. Preservation interest resurfaced in the 1980s then took an unusual turn after a disastrous fire in 1987 gutted three historic buildings. In its aftermath a number of business leaders and members of the chamber of commerce proposed legalizing gambling in Deadwood. Supporters of this initiative called themselves the Deadwood You Bet committee and organized a state campaign to persuade legislators and voters that a large portion of the revenues would be used to finance the historic restoration of Deadwood.

In 1989 the gambling and preservation movements united. At the same time when the Deadwood You Bet committee began its lobbying campaign, the city government passed an ordinance taking over the Deadwood Preservation Commission. In January 1989 it gave the commission review power over buildings in the downtown district. Meanwhile the gambling arm of the preservation movement gained the endorsement of the State Historic Preservation Center and the Black Hills, Badlands and Lakes

Deadwood renovations, ca. 2006. *Photograph by Carol M. Highsmith; courtesy Library of Congress Prints and Photographs Division, #LC-HS503-6191.*

Association, the major sources of tourist promotion in the region. Given the rising support, the state legislature placed a proposed constitutional amendment to allow gambling before state voters. On November 8, 1988, they approved the measure: legalized gambling returned to Deadwood.[9] By 1990 the town had reached two major goals: the federal government had officially recognized its past and financial support for preservation seemed assured.

As in Deadwood, Dodge City's movement to keep the memory of its Old West heritage alive resulted from a mix of local efforts at historic preservation and actions to increase tourism. The 1929 Last Round-Up celebration and Stuart Lake's biography of Wyatt Earp two years later persuaded newspaper editors that modernization threatened the town's pioneer legacy. During the late 1920s and early 1930s Dodge City newspapers reported concerns about the passing of elderly pioneers and the end of an era. "The survivors of those turbulent days are being reduced rapidly," the *Dodge City Daily Globe* wrote. "They have seen the thundering herds give way to the pfut-pfuting combines which symbolize the transition of the Southwest." When a gas station replaced a former a livery stable several months later, the newspaper returned to the same theme. "The press of civilization and the speed of commerce are obliterating the evidences of the frontiersman's day." It called for help preserving some of the past, "before those prairies are covered with paved highways and the famous groves and landmarks are swept away by the inevitable march of progress."[10]

After 1929 Last Round-Up and its displays of relics heightened awareness, discussions about how to preserve the town's history shifted toward building a museum. The *Globe* reported "plenty of conversation" about the need to house the "hundreds of relics of frontier days which in time will be beyond value." It pointed out that the new city hall recently constructed at old Boot Hill had space set aside for just that purpose and claimed that a museum there would offer "a combination of frontier interest that should attract strangers. Dodge City owes it to the heritage handed down to it to preserve properly those articles of an earlier day." Despite those feelings, the town's first museum was not on Boot Hill as so many desired but in Hamilton Bell's downtown pet store. In 1932 Bell, then president of the Southwest Historical Society, offered the group a room in his building to showcase relics and other items loaned from the private collections of its members.[11]

While Bell and the Southwest Historical Society members waited fruit-lessly for city action, Merritt Beeson, one of Bell's close colleagues in the group, founded what became a larger museum. Like his associates Hamilton Bell and Doc Simpson, Beeson had a strong commitment toward the preservation of its early history fostered by his lifelong association with the town. Beeson remembered entering the museum business in 1932 by accident. When author Stuart Lake published his book *Wyatt Earp: Frontier Marshal,* he asked Beeson to ship him some historic relics relating to Dodge City for a California exhibit to promote his book. Beeson recalled that he "gathered up quite a display" and sent them to Lake. When the author returned the material almost a year later, townspeople besieged Beeson to see the relics made famous by the California exhibition. In response, Beeson and his wife arranged the items in their basement and then began collecting more historic objects from neighbors and community members and friends who wanted to have them exhibited. By the end of 1932 Beeson had gathered over 500 objects and another 2,000 photographs.

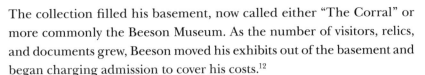

The collection filled his basement, now called either "The Corral" or more commonly the Beeson Museum. As the number of visitors, relics, and documents grew, Beeson moved his exhibits out of the basement and began charging admission to cover his costs.[12]

Through his museum Beeson became the self-proclaimed custodian of the town's history. He wanted the artifacts, photographs, and documents to show the city's true story. Interested primarily in its early period, he collected many items related to its historic characters and "glamorous days." He appealed to Wyatt Earp's widow for Earp material and to friends and acquaintances for gambling items. By 1935 his collection had grown large enough that he hoped it would create "an authentic documented history of Dodge City that could not be found anywhere else."[13] He expected to use the material to overcome the media-created fiction about his city with carefully documented history—a stance that he believed tourists shared. "Thousands of visitors have been through the museum and their opinions have aroused us that violation of history will soon be checked by the general public," he wrote.[14] Beeson distrusted writers who asked him for information because he thought that they misrepresented much of what he provided. For example, when Walter Campbell (who wrote under the name Stanley Vestal), a professor of American literature at the University of Oklahoma, asked him for information for his book *Dodge City: Queen of Cowtowns* in 1949, Beeson asserted his determination never to sell such information for those seeking to profit from fictionalizing the town's history. Only after Campbell assured him that he was an academic scholar and would not profit from his history of the city did Beeson agree to cooperate.[15]

Like the Adams Museum in Deadwood, Beeson touted his museum as an educational facility while at the same time promoting its Wild West aspects to tourists. In 1950 he moved the material to a new larger site just outside the city on a main highway leading into town. The move opened more room for the 6,000 items in the collection and gave visitors easier access. Next Beeson advertised the Corral as presenting "authentic history and articles" and featuring "photographs of the good and bad men and women of the plains," including Bat Masterson, Wyatt Earp, Bill Tilghman, and Luke Short, along with the "true story of Boot Hill." This same promotion appeared routinely in newspaper accounts of the museum. One reporter was fascinated by its piano from the Long Branch Saloon but made special note of its gambling devices, guns, and cowboy relics.[16]

The Beeson Museum's success unexpectedly brought new interest in a city-sponsored museum at Boot Hill. The town's mayor, E. G. Gingrich, worried that the existing Boot Hill display of Doc Simpson's statues failed to live up to the expectations of the growing numbers of tourists, particularly when compared to Beeson's enterprise. "A great many people who have read of Boot Hill stop in Dodge City to see it, or even go out of their way to come by here," he told a reporter in 1935, "and then they are disappointed at what they find." Beeson's offer to donate his collection to the city if construction began heartened the mayor, but attempts to attract New Deal funds earmarked for public improvements failed. The continued lack of money in the Dust Bowl–choked city prevented any action. The outbreak of World War II ended talk of building a museum, despite a 1941 survey finding that Dodge City and its association with the Wild West was the leading reason motorists gave for visiting Kansas.[17]

Interest in building a city museum on Boot Hill revived at the end of the war, partly because of the city commissioners' decision to build an auditorium at the place originally earmarked for the museum. To head off criticism over the decision, new mayor Bert Green assured citizens that the new construction would not interfere with Simpson's existing Boot Hill figures because the cemetery was such a "valuable attraction to City visitors." A few months later the mayor unveiled his vision of what Dodge City's historic commemoration should look like. With no vintage buildings left, he proposed erecting copies of what might have been found in a typical Kansas frontier cowtown. The result would create a "commercially profitable movie set" of the town's original Front Street featuring a corral, a working blacksmith shop selling small "DC" souvenir branding irons, a museum, and a hotel where patrons could buy Dodge City steaks "served on checkered table cloths by costumed waitresses." Each building would be constructed in historic fashion. The mayor saw the price tag as the only drawback to his scheme. Green estimated the cost of the project as $100,000 and said that local businesses would have to pay for the massive project because the city would never do so.[18] Too ambitious and expensive for Dodge City's commercial sector, the mayor's vision stalled and the concept was tabled—at least for the next few years.

Meanwhile a new plan emerged. In January 1947 W. B. "Dad" Rhodes announced his retirement as the overseer of the Boot Hill attraction. Fearing that the site might be abandoned, R. G. Hill Jr., a leading member of the

Dodge City Junior Chamber of Commerce, persuaded fellow members to take responsibility for the site, upgrade the cemetery, and build a museum. When Paul Allen, Jaycee president, and a committee of club members presented the proposal to Mayor Green, he gave the city's blessing to the plan for a museum on Boot Hill. Within a few weeks, the Jaycees moved ahead. Hill drew up a design that called for a 600-square-foot concrete block structure made to look like adobe, so the museum would replicate a frontier-era building. Hill's plans also called for a curio shop, a cowboy wishing well, and a corral. The building's centerpiece was a miniature version of Green's Front Street setting. Hill envisioned a diorama showing the territory from Dodge City to the Rocky Mountains, featuring over a thousand tiny figures of buffalo, cattle, wagons, cowboys, and Indians, plus the historic landmarks crucial in the region's development. A series of glass cases with filled with historic relics would surround the diorama.

Once Hill unveiled his plans, the Jaycees launched a local fund-raising campaign. Going from merchant to merchant, club members raised $4,500—enough to construct the building that spring, but not much else. When it opened a few months later, the Jaycees presented only a small part of Hill's vision. Instead of a massive diorama, the main feature included a small model of an Indian village with a series of wooden figures of Indians and buffalo carved by the museum's first manager and custodian, Roy Hardin.[19]

Now called the Boot Hill Jaycees, the club members justified their role as museum administrators as part of their public service. They saw the facility as an educational tool and a means to strengthen the local tourist industry. Because of their service commitment, the group financed the museum through donations and the sales of souvenirs rather than charging admission. The museum's newsletter announced that its mission was to preserve "the spirit and history of the old west" and "to bring tourists to Dodge City and keep them here as long as possible." To do that its displays emphasized the sensationalism of the cemetery and displayed artifacts and features that matched audience expectations of the Wild West and its associated violence. In 1951 the Jaycees added another room called the "grave room" to the museum. As its primary attraction, an open grave showed a skeleton and the remains of a casket found on the original Boot Hill site. Two years later the Jaycees moved the 1864 Fort Dodge jail house to the site, offering what one later called "a grim relic of the early days of the west."[20]

Despite the group's good intentions, Boot Hill's ersatz graves and its lurid hucksterism offended many, who criticized the displays and called for change. Joe Hulpieu, the furniture store owner who wanted to turn Boot Hill into a historical park that replicated the Santa Fe Trail in miniature, called the graveyard "just a hole in the ground" that needed to be returned to a hill with the existing museum placed underground. Rejecting criticism, the Jaycees claimed that their presentation represented the spirit of the frontier era, not the literal truth. "Some of our more critical neighbors say Boot Hill is a farce," one member wrote. He defended it saying that "whether it is north, south, east or west of the City Hall, it makes no difference. It is still Boot Hill. As the big sign on the cemetery grounds says, it is still a MONUMENT TO THOSE WHO DIED WITH THEIR BOOTS ON."[21]

Ignoring the critics, the Jaycees continued adding new features to the museum. In 1954 its administrators exhibited a steam locomotive. Then they gathered an extensive collection of guns and built a new room to house them, funding both the gun collection and the new construction with money loaned by five Jaycee members. The organization decided to protect its members' investment and founded a nonprofit entity called Boot Hill, Inc., with all Jaycees included as stockholders. The new organization expected to place the museum on a solid business footing in order to plan for future expansion and to deal with the growing numbers of tourists coming to the city because of radio and television exposure from *Gunsmoke*. At that point Mayor Green's old proposal to build a replica of old Front Street still intrigued many Jaycee members, who hoped to start serious planning for the new project.[22]

As the number of visitors increased, the Front Street concept seemed to be a logical addition to the Boot Hill and Beeson museums. Limited in how they could offer visitors an Old West experience, the museums could only exhibit relics, photographs, curios, and dioramas. Many tourists hoped for more. "As usual, we get tourists who still think we're living in the Old West," George Heinrichs, director of the Boot Hill Museum, told a reporter. When they did not get more of the Wild West, criticism followed. "We had Eastern relatives visit who couldn't wait to see Dodge City," one *Globe* reader wrote, "and in thirty minutes they had seen it. Disappointed? You said it." In 1958 the *High Plains Journal* reported that the only building "on the early day townsite left is the one made into a rug cleaning plant by the Dodge City Laundry."[23] Clearly the building had little draw for tourists looking for a western experience in the town. To fill the gaps, the Jaycees decided to give them the next best thing, a replication of the town's notorious Front Street. Dodge City was not alone in this line of thinking. Frontier City outside Oklahoma City and Old Tucson, a movie set constructed in 1940 near Tucson, Arizona, both appealed to the 1950s western craze by offering replications of entire Old West towns.

Dodge City built the replica of Front Street as part of its effort to become the home to the National Cowboy Hall of Fame. The idea for a national shrine devoted to cowboys and the West originated in 1953 with Charles A. Reynolds, the chairman of the board of the R. D. Lee Company in Kansas City. He helped establish a board of trustees consisting of the governors of seventeen western states plus two appointed members from each state. In January 1955 the group met in Denver to set up guidelines for deciding which city should have the honor. During the next month the group received proposals from forty-seven towns, including Abilene, Kansas; Cheyenne, Wyoming; Denver, Colorado; Las Vegas, New Mexico; Prescott, Arizona; North Platte, Nebraska; Oklahoma City, Oklahoma; Colorado Springs, Colorado; and Dodge City. Even Tombstone and Deadwood asked for consideration. Working quickly, a site committee cut the list to ten and after site visits in March 1955 narrowed the field to three finalists: Dodge City, Oklahoma City, and Colorado Springs. The final choice would be made in the following month.[24]

Having received the news, Dodge City business and city leaders began an all-out campaign to get the honor. The movement began with a city-wide meeting of local business leaders, where Larry Yost, the president of Boot Hill, Inc., led a committee to coordinate efforts. Racing against the deadline, Gene Gunner, a local architect, provided architectural plans for an impressive structure with a dining room atop a tower overlooking the city, a two-tier parking garage, and plenty of display space for relics and exhibits. This became a central part of the quickly prepared statement listing the reasons why Dodge City offered the ideal setting for the new hall of fame: "Dodge City is the product of a romantic past, showing a violent record which includes thundering cattle herds, range wars, rampaging buffalo herds, gunfights in the streets, daring marshals and all the other segments which contributed to the history of the old West." The authors pointed out that Dodge City stood alone among "other Old West cities, whether it be claims of cattle bawdiness or gunfighters" or because it was the first to "edify the Cowboy himself." They reminded the location committee that the town had an established national reputation as a shrine to the Old West. "Few cities have been written about as much, or filmed or better known the world over than Dodge City," the statement boasted. "Dodge City is IT whenever a cowboy is thought of or an animal is branded, and whenever one thinks of law and order or the Development of the West is discussed." As evidence it listed twenty-four books, seven movies, and the radio program *Gunsmoke*, soon to become a TV hit.[25]

While the committee wrote the case statement and sent it to the Hall of Fame Trustees, Larry Yost orchestrated a letter-writing campaign to show widespread popular support for Dodge City. He gave the names and addresses of all the trustees and urged letter writers to emphasize the town's national publicity. "Tell the man or men you write to that you have BEEN IN DODGE CITY or SEEN DODGE CITY IN THE MOVIES OR ON TELEVISION, or HAVE HEARD ABOUT DODGE CITY ON THE RADIO."[26] At the same time, the local committee asked other Kansas communities, the governor, and other political leaders to endorse Dodge City's application. They responded enthusiastically as other Kansas communities supported Dodge City— Abilene even withdrew its application in deference to Dodge. Meanwhile the towns of Garden City and Pratt pledged their assistance to Dodge on the condition that it get rid of its "notorious tourist trap, Boot Hill," which the *Garden City Telegram* regarded as "tarnish" on the "monumental project." When this demand infuriated Jess Denious, publisher of the *Dodge City Daily Globe*, the towns retracted it but refused to change their opinion of Boot Hill. The editor of the *Garden City Telegram* commented that if Dodge wanted to continue to "perpetrate that cemetery fraud on the witless public, then I suppose all we can do is to keep warning the gullible."[27]

There is no way to know what effect the Boot Hill kitschiness had on the Hall of Fame trustees' decision. On April 15, 1955, Dodge City opened its final presentation before them with a parade led by the Dodge City Cowboy Band. Representing the interest of the Kansas town was a powerful group headed by Governor Fred Hall, while Dodge City native and U.S. senator from Kansas Andrew Schoepel represented the town. Speaking to the trustees, the governor offered the support for the project of every chamber of commerce in Kansas along with pledges from state labor, agricultural, and individual business associations and assured them that the Kansas legislature would provide a state appropriation. When the presentations by the three cities concluded, a reporter for the *Hutchinson News-Herald* believed that the general consensus among close observers favored Dodge City.[28] This proved to be wrong. On April 17 Oklahoma City won the competition, primarily because of the state's willingness to provide money up front to finance the project.

Dodge City backers cried foul, shouting that Oklahoma money had trumped fame. "We don't believe we have ever seen a bunch of people as mad as Kansans over the decision to sell the memorial to Oklahoma City for cash on the barrelhead," the *High Plains Journal* observed. Those who expressed their disappointment and bitterness were not all from Dodge City either. Letters of sympathy and support flowed into Dodge City from across the state. One supporter from Ashland, representing the National Press Women, called Oklahoma City's prize the "Hall of Shame" and described it as a "sell-out" that was "as cheap as the plot of a third-rate Western movie."[29] The *Kansas City Kansan* called on "the governor, senators, chambers of commerce and hundreds of individuals who plead the cause of Dodge City [to] continue to do so, but to carry on in practical manner by acquiring a site and erecting a Kansas memorial to the cowboy, in the real cowboy capital." Governor Hall agreed. He called the decision a slap in the face to the people of Kansas and urged the citizens of Dodge City to respond by constructing their own memorial in Dodge City.[30]

The response to Hall's call for action came just a few days later. On the evening of April 19, 1955, a crowd of as many as five thousand people gathered at a hastily called mass meeting. As an expression of their anger, some Dodge citizens hung a dummy with a sign reading "A Good Cowboy" next to a placard reading "Judas Sold-Out for Money." At the meeting they listened to a series of speakers, including Dodge City mayor Gordon Morgan and state senator Bill Weigand, who urged them to open a campaign for funds to construct their own shrine. After the meeting a new statewide committee chaired by Harry Stark of Dodge City emerged and set an initial goal of raising $100,000 to construct the memorial. Spurred by strong emotions and existing pledges to the original concept, the local fund reached $50,000 within two weeks.[31] To differentiate itself from the original group, the new one became the Cowboy Capital of the World, Inc., with its headquarters in Topeka.

As so often happened in local historic commemoration activities, serious differences over where to locate the memorial emerged between other members of the state committee and those from Dodge City. In June 1955 the mayor of Dodge City offered the Cowboy Capital of the World committee a site on Boot Hill if it agreed to construct a replica of Old Front Street at the same time.[32] The committee added this proposal to its list of sixteen other potential Dodge City locations. In the fall of 1955 it met in Dodge and toured all of the proposed sites, under the impression that each would be available either as an outright gift or for purchase at a minimal cost. After the tour Dodge City members of the committee refused to consider any site other than Boot Hill. The Boot Hill Jaycees composed the majority of Dodge City representatives, so the move came as no surprise. Larry Yost, as president of Boot Hill, Inc., sent a strongly worded letter to Mayor Gordon Morgan affirming the group's insistence that Boot Hill was the only acceptable site in Dodge City where the "cowboy should be honored." He wrote that if the committee chose any other site his organization would not support the effort and would not allow its museum to become part of it. The members of Boot Hill, Inc., wanted to avoid having two competing tourist attractions in Dodge City and felt an "obligation to the businessmen of Dodge who have helped us so much in the past in providing an attraction for visitors to our city."[33]

Members of the building committee brushed off Boot Hill, Inc.'s strong-arm tactic because it thought neither Boot Hill's location in the city nor its reputation was appropriate for the project. In fact they declared that "a cowboy and his horse has never been found in the heart of a city and that [he] is always looked at as a man in the wide open spaces." Nor did the committee think that Boot Hill was the most hallowed spot for cowboy heritage: "We feel that all history will agree with our thinking that Boot Hill did not become famous because of the reputable and peace loving cowboy. Rather, the name came from those who died with their boots on and was typically the cowhand or outlaw who ran afoul of the law. That is not the typical cowboy."[34] Unfortunately, the committee members failed to offer any viable alternative. After reviewing the seventeen sites, they eliminated all but two: Boot Hill and an old army airbase. Boot Hill remained the most plausible because of the city's pledge to donate the site.

Stymied by their own negative feelings toward the Boot Hill site and the failure to find an alternative, the committee members recommended that the state board suspend planning unless Dodge City presented a more viable site or other Kansas locations could be considered. If neither of these suggestions met approval, they recommended dissolving the state organization and making it a Dodge City project.[35] At its next meeting in Emporia, faced with falling revenues and the Boot Hill impasse, the board acted to shift the project into the hands of the Dodge City contingent, giving it control of the project. In one its first acts the new board moved the headquarters from Emporia to Dodge City. There the chamber of commerce assumed control, appointed town representatives, and furnished office space and administrative staffing.[36]

Now in full authority, the Dodge City–controlled board announced Boot Hill as the official site and began planning how to reenergize the sagging capital campaign. In March 1957 the total amount raised had amounted to only $120,000. The new board opened a new $250,000 campaign for the cowboy memorial. Dodge City leaders made no apologies as they announced their intention to build a tourist attraction. They discussed creating an industry based on the town's place in western history. A "fact" sheet issued to potential donors described the project as having a "broader significance" because it recognized this city's "unique historical background and the great part Dodge City played in the opening of the West and the spread of the United States from ocean to ocean." The new campaign focused on building the Cowboy Shrine, a modest building planned to include a miniature replica of Dodge City and exhibits on peace officers, but gave little attention to reconstructing Front Street.[37]

In just a year that emphasis shifted because of the rising popularity of the television shows *Gunsmoke* and *Wyatt Earp* and the number of tourists those programs brought to Dodge City. During 1957 the Boot Hill Museum boasted 295,000 visitors, the highest in its history, along with its largest revenue and resulting surplus. In September 1957 C. E. Knight, a local businessman, wrote that Dodge needed to capitalize on this new windfall. He believed that the city was "blessed not by nature, but by history with the heritage of the old west" and recognized that eastern tourists arrived with specific visual expectations. "Recent TV programs," he continued, "have added a mental image to the tales of radio, with Dodge City the center of locale." Knight recommended that the town should provide what the visitors wanted to see. "With a nominal investment in cash, talent and sweat, Dodge City could live up to its reputation of TV and radio fame and recreate most of the scenes and activities of the old west." Rather than building a "fancy, marble shrine," he argued, if "the tourist wants to come to Dodge City and pay to see a chapter of Wyatt Earp . . . let's give it to them."[38]

Flush with the success of the Boot Hill Museum, the Jaycees proposed that the Cowboy Capital of the World organization join them so that the two groups could rebuild the Old Front Street replica at Boot Hill. The Cowboy Capital of the World accepted the invitation. They decided Boot Hill, Inc., should manage the replica and agreed that the two corporations should manage future profits jointly. One Dodge City newspaper celebrated the decision. Noting that "pay-as-you-goers are looking for notorious frontstreet," the writer applauded the intention to match tourist expectations. "With out-of-state requests pouring in," Dodge City wisely "decided to put the money raised for a Cowboy Hall of Fame into a replica of Front Street. . . . There's gold in that thar hill north of Wyatt Earp Boulevard and Dodge City had decided to mine it."[39]

Now financed, construction on the replica began in late 1957. Both the January 1958 ceremonial ground-breaking by actor Hugh O'Brian, dressed as his character Wyatt Earp, and the final dedication seven months later by *Gunsmoke* actors Milburn Stone and Amanda Blake on August 1, 1958, demonstrated the town's strong new ties to its television images. Trying to offset the criticism of Boot Hill, organizers promised to make the replica of 1870s Front Street "as authentic as possible." According to the *Dodge City Daily Globe* it would "provide a center of reliable information about the old west to visitors." The row of false front buildings reflected what its organizers hoped would give a Wild West atmosphere. While the structures included the Rath and Wright General Store, a dry goods store, and a dental office, the Long Branch Saloon became its main attraction. Already famous because a version of it appeared on *Gunsmoke*, it featured floor shows and can-can dancers along with Miss Kitty, inspired by the Amanda Blake character from the television series. For some authenticity, Jaycee members furnished the buildings with relics purchased from the Beeson Museum.[40]

The Front Street Replica's immediate success proved that the Jaycees understood the tourists' desires for a western experience. During the opening month of August 1958 the site recorded 90,000 visitors. By the end of the year the number had climbed to an all-time high of 370,076. Gross receipts grew to six times what they had been the previous year. At the beginning of 1959 Don Young Jr., the president of Boot Hill, Inc., and Front Street boasted that the two had become the biggest tourist attraction in

Kansas. Flush with success, the Boot Hill/Front Street operation expanded its services. It added stagecoach rides in 1960 and gunfight reenactments four years later. That same year Boot Hill, Inc., purchased the Beeson Museum and moved it to the complex, allowing Merritt Beeson's daughter to manage it. In 1969 it brought the Hardesty House, an 1878 ranch home, to the site. Two years later the organization added an ice cream parlor and built a new a theater to facilitate larger and more sophisticated stage productions.[41]

Realizing that Front Street's success depended on television programs, particularly *Gunsmoke*, the managers stressed gunfighting, historic characters, and other standard images to meet tourist demands for the Old West experience. In 1960 writer Robert Pearman wrote that, despite knowing that television had exaggerated the violence, the "sweet smell of tourist dollars" persuaded Dodge City's residents to stress its frontier image. Yet whether the legends stemmed from real lawmen such as Earp or fictional ones like Matt Dillon, they led "to the biggest bonanza in free publicity since Barnum gave the world Tom Thumb," he noted. As a result, "Dodge City, where for years the repentant citizens tried to forget the city's frontier sins, is becoming one of the biggest tourist attractions between Williamsburg and Disneyland." George Heinrichs, the executive director of Boot Hill, Inc., affirmed this observation. He told a reporter that the show kept the city in the tourist business and acknowledged that since the program began the average number of tourists had risen from 150,000 to 405,000 in 1971.[42] The generation-long benefits from the show ended with its cancellation in 1975, raising questions about the future of the town's principal tourist attraction and historical commemorative efforts. At least publicly, Heinrichs displayed confidence in continued growth. But declines in attendance—a drop to 280,000 in 1977 and a sharp fall in revenue—called for new efforts to attract tourists.[43]

In 1977 newly hired museum director Jim von Oremp led planning for its post-*Gunsmoke* future. He invited a professional consultant to lead a discussion with the mayor, trustees, chamber of commerce members, and the staff. They decided to fence the property and charge admission in order to raise revenue, prevent vandalism, and ensure better crowd control. Von Oremp increased the number of Long Branch Saloon shows in the hope, as he told a reporter for the *Globe*, that "the history and entertainment will bring people back."[44] When that effort failed he resigned. At that point Boot

The front entrance to the Boot Hill Museum in Dodge City, 2011.
Photograph by Lithistman released under the Creative Commons Attribution–Share Alike 3.0 Unported license.

Hill, Inc., trustees decided to drop their television-based fictional image and redesign the museum as an authentic historic institution. In 1979 the board hired Jim Sherer as the institution's first professional director. He, in turn, recruited Richard Welch from the Studebaker Museum in Indiana to become its first academically trained curator. Together they worked to meet the board's goal of having the museum become nationally recognized through accreditation by the American Association of Museums.[45]

Most of the efforts to build historic credibility involved replacing the hucksterism and television influences that had given the institution its image as a tourist trap. They removed Simpson's concrete casts from the fake Boot Hill cemetery and, despite protests from some board and community members, covered over the open grave that had served as a macabre wishing well for visitors. Next they began to catalogue and document the artifact collections and tried to make the façades on Front Street depict their era accurately. More significantly, they deemphasized the gunfighters and other lurid aspects of the Wild West and shifted attention toward community building and the role of Indians and minorities in the town's past. To underscore their new approach, Sherer and Welch masterminded the construction of a new visitors' center, which included an orientation exhibit gallery, archival space, and a small theater.[46] In 1985, exactly a decade after *Gunsmoke* ended, the American Association of Museums accredited the museum, showing that Dodge City had gained national recognition of its historical legitimacy.

In direct contrast to Deadwood and Dodge City, historic preservation efforts in Tombstone centered on trying to save the large number of frontier-era buildings still standing in order to create the town's historic identity. Led by the new editor of the *Tombstone Epitaph*, Walter Cole, serious talk about preserving the town as a whole began when it lost its role as the county seat. According to a witness at the meeting of town boosters in 1931, the discussion centered around two preservation plans. The first was to make the town a historical monument, prohibit any new construction in the old district, and create an entirely new community nearby. If that failed, the second plan was to find a wealthy benefactor such as John D. Rockefeller Jr. to subsidize Tombstone as a historic park.[47] Neither of these ideas seemed realistic. Throughout the 1930s the group struggled to find some way to preserve the slowly deteriorating buildings.

The passage of the National Historic Landmark Act in 1935 prompted editor Cole to have the National Park Service designate the town as a national monument. With help from U.S. senator Carl Hayden, the *Epitaph* owner arranged a 1936 site visit by William R. Horgan, a Park Service representative. Impressed by the town's history and its array of vintage buildings, he recommended that the Bird Cage Theatre become a National Historic Site, but no action followed at the time.[48] In 1943 Aubrey Neasham, regional supervisor of historic sites, recommended that Tombstone be designated a historic landmark because its large number of endangered sites and buildings helped the town retain "much of its historic flavor." He urged the Park Service to set up an advisory board and create a master plan to preserve and interpret the Tombstone buildings.[49] U.S. involvement in World War II halted action on the report.

While unable to get any federal support, town leaders formed the Southwest Museum Association during the 1930s, whose first goal was to convert the now empty courthouse into a museum. During Ray Krebs's term as mayor, he secured the building by having the town take a fifteen-year lease on it from the county at a cost of one dollar a year. His plan had two goals:

to make it a museum and prevent the historic structure from being used for private commercial purposes.[50] The association hoped to fund the conversion with a state legislative appropriation and asked Arizona governor R. C. Stanford for help. The attorney general saw the proposal as unconstitutional and said that it would be feasible only if the proposed museum represented all of southeastern Arizona. Disappointed, Cole appealed to the governor to tack the appropriation onto a state fair bill, saying: "If Tombstone is to persist as a relic of the early days of the state, it must have some help from the state, itself."[51] Unfortunately, the state offered no support. When Cole moved away in 1938, he left the preservation momentum leaderless.

Although city officials and chamber of commerce members wanted to preserve Tombstone's buildings, little physical restoration took place because nobody had any money. During the Depression and World War II many of the old structures deteriorated further, while townspeople remodeled or razed others. Tombstone's first post office, the Mining Exchange Office, Sheriff's Office, Fly's Photo Studio, and Grand, Cosmopolitan, and Occidental Hotels all marched into oblivion. One of the last vestiges of the Chinese immigrant community, the Quong Wing Sing Emporium, lost its roof and rapidly crumbled. The fourteen-room home of E. B. Gage, once owner of the Grand Central Mine, became the Loma de Plata Guest Lodge. Schieffelin Hall was remodeled, and in 1939 the town's first church, originally opened by Endicott Peabody, fell to the wrecking ball. In 1946 a Douglas businessman leased the long-empty Tombstone Courthouse from the county and tried to remodel it into a three-story hotel. Following the economic recovery after World War II, both long-term and new residents started to voice concern about the growing number of architectural changes. The *Epitaph* reported in 1946 that it was "deluged with communications bemoaning the loss of landmarks to the real estate boom." Alarmed by the damage to what remained of the town's historic environment, Clayton Smith, the latest in a line of *Epitaph* publishers, called for the people of the city to help preserve Tombstone as a historical shrine.[52]

In an unlikely move, D'Estell Izard, a Hollywood movie executive, answered Smith's call for action. A lover of western lore, he became interested in restoring Tombstone while stationed at nearby Fort Huachuca. Izard visited the town several times after 1946 and persuaded longtime residents Ethel Macia and former mayor Ray Krebs and newly arrived citizens such as Edna Landin and Clayton Smith to begin a new restoration effort. Over the next three years the group built a core of local support, assisted by Smith, who used the *Epitaph* to urge community members to help Izard, calling the effort the last chance to save the town's disappearing past.[53]

In October 1949 members of the group presented to business leaders its dream of a Tombstone restored to its original frontier glory. They proposed a completely restored downtown district that would "be authentic in every respect." The plan included redoing building façades, installing wooden awnings, adding hitching posts and water troughs, building board sidewalks, restoring historic buildings such as the OK Corral and Schieffelin Hall, and removing all modern advertising signs, power lines, and telephone wires. Izard estimated the total cost of the completed project at $350,000. Knowing that the plan's success rested on the support of the business community, in the fall of 1949 Izard and his allies began a campaign to build enthusiasm. Concerned about the stigma of hucksterism, they pledged to keep the project free of commercialism by allowing the restored downtown to be free and open to the public.[54]

Yet, to get the support of businesses, Izard returned to the old argument that Tombstone was losing its share of the tourism market by failing to give the "tourist industry what it wants—the Old West." Thousands of people know Tombstone, he told the *Epitaph*: "They have found mental pictures of an old western in their minds, and they expect to see just that when they come to visit." Izard later told a group of business leaders that modern Tombstone was a disappointment to visitors because it had little of the Old West left to show them. With the new restoration program, he promised, Tombstone would boom as the "Williamsburg of the West."[55] Clayton Smith, speaking through the *Epitaph*, was more direct. He described the local economy as being at "low ebb" and warned that without "100% backing" the plan would fail. This talk contradicted the official line of those who claimed they wanted to show "visitors from all parts of the country what an old western town was really like" rather than create a tourist attraction.[56]

In December 1949 the preservationists incorporated as the Tombstone Restoration Commission and announced the goal of making Tombstone "the showcase of the West." They welcomed all of the residents to become voting members. Designed to bridge the private and public sectors, a seven-person board composed the Governance Commission, four elected from the general membership, two appointed by the city, and a commission-appointed historian. The initial members included long-term residents

Ethel Macia (the historian), A. P. Giacoma, Mayor John Giacoma, and Sam Medigovich along with the more recent arrivals Clayton Smith, C. M. Palmer, and Izard as director. On January 5, 1950, the commission opened its campaign to restore Tombstone with a week-long western celebration. Arizona governor Dan Garvey proclaimed it as "Tombstone Restoration Week." He asked all Arizonans to contribute to the new project as a way to recognize Tombstone's role in the state's history. The campaign kickoff included a special restoration issue of the *Epitaph* and reenactments of historic incidents by the local Vigilantes.[57]

The publicity surrounding Tombstone Restoration Week drew interest and criticism. The grassroots nature of the Restoration Commission and its professional approach intrigued federal officials. Frederick Rath, the executive secretary of the National Council for Historic Sites and Buildings, pledged to help Izard with information or expertise if the locals needed either. Erik Reed, the regional archaeologist for the National Park Service, called it a "genuine local project, organized and supported by local people with the objective of true restoration, not primarily designed to attract tourists." He affirmed Rath's belief that it merited the cooperation of the National Park Service and National Council but felt that the "widespread feeling in Arizona of antagonism to Federal authority" made it inadvisable to suggest any National Historic site arrangement. After a visit to Tombstone in April, Reed concluded that Izard's thorough research and strong sense of vision made technical assistance and help in planning unnecessary. The biggest challenge, the archaeologist concluded, was how to raise the large sum of money to support "such an ambitious project."[58]

At the same time, the project drew criticism from some who questioned the basic idea that the experience of the frontier period could be brought into the present. The editor of *Walt Coburn's West Magazine* endorsed the commission's efforts but felt that the Hollywood style reenactors insulted the memory of the real pioneers. "Let's not have any more of those whiskerino vigilante, blank cartridge forces to mock the dead in the boothill graves," he pleaded.[59]

A more scathing comment came from the *New York Times*, which questioned the core idea that architectural restoration could ever replicate the feelings and experiences of actual people from the past. The editor took particular offense at the comparison to Williamsburg, which he believed deserved restoration simply because it "was a gem of Colonial Architecture."

Tombstone, in contrast, "never surpassed the Taj Mahal or even a railroad street in a Pennsylvania coal town. What old Tombstone did have for a few short years was life—loud, roaring and bawdy—and pyrotechnic people. Alas, how does one rebuild or recreate them? If the Tombstoners know how to do that, they have something." The townspeople could dress up as their fathers did in the 1880s, he wrote, but they will never bring back the ghosts of the past.[60]

Community was a grave concern to the Restoration Commission because its plans rested on grassroots fund-raising and support. Ethel Macia, the commission's official historian, acknowledged the situation early and admitted that the plan would "not be able to satisfy everyone" even in terms of historic accuracy. Although the commission hoped for broad support, business leaders and residents still wanted to use contemporary advertising methods and usually favored development. One group felt that the Restoration Commission should build Old Tombstone at a separate location like the movie set Old Tucson. The commissioners resisted because of the extra costs and the loss of authenticity. Izard repeatedly tried to get support, assuring downtown business owners that the commission's concerned only the "external appearance of the town" and pledging that they would have "have nothing to do with any interiors and anything done therein." His assurances failed to build enough support. Erik Reed saw the lack of consensus clearly during his spring 1950 visit to Tombstone. He reported that "many of the local people are either hostile, or indifferent, or else impatient for impossibly quick results."[61]

By the end of the year Restoration Commission president C. M. Palmer admitted that the campaign had failed. Part of the reason, he believed, came from a downturn in the economy when the army decommissioned Fort Huachuca and the military families moved away. The citizens of Tombstone raised only $1,400, barely enough to cover initial expenses and the cost of a six-minute film appealing for funds. Only Schieffelin Hall received any attention, from the Masons. In his annual report Palmer conceded that the original goal of a grassroots fund-raiser was "the product of enthusiasm and not of a clear understanding" of what could be done. Much of this naivete, he confessed, came from the belief that people around the country "were just waiting for the opportunity to contribute to such a project to restore Tombstone." The inexperience with fund-raising carried over into the actual restorations. Palmer admitted that the restoration of buildings such as the OK Corral became a formidable challenge when the workers lacked photographs and other documentation needed before the project begin. He recommended that the commission reconsider its stance on commercialism but at the same time reasserted the idea that tourists come to see a "legitimate" show about the Wild West, a goal that would ultimately be achieved by re-creating the town's historic atmosphere.[62]

Shortly afterward Palmer proposed a stop-gap measure. Rather than pursuing the original massive restoration project, he asked the commission to help attract tourists by focusing on historic interpretation and getting community support "first and foremost." He wrote that citizens must "WEAR WESTERN. There is no alternative." His new plan suggested many ways for people to help. Business owners could put up signs with the old names of their buildings. The town could install historic markers, prepare a guide map, and organize a guide service using the Vigilantes wearing badges, sidearms, boots, and Stetsons as colorful helpers for visitors. The town could also boast of a series of exhibits on mining, gambling, ranches, Mexican American life, Indians, and a diorama of gunfights. Palmer asked merchants to display vintage products from the 1880 if they had them. To set an example the commission exhibited a large collection of assay and mining equipment next to its offices in Schieffelin Hall.[63]

In 1955 Edna Landin succeeded Palmer as the president of the commission. The choice of Landin proved to be a good one. During her five-year tenure she brought new energy, a pragmatic approach, and an aptitude for local politics. Landin moved to Tombstone in 1949 and displayed a remarkable ability to move into the community's social and political power structures. She sat on the City Park and Recreation Board, headed the Tombstone Business and Professional Woman's Club, and in 1957 became the first woman to be elected to the city council. More importantly for the cause of preservation, in the three years before becoming president of the Restoration Commission she served as the president of the chamber of commerce. Landin returned the commission's focus to architectural preservation. Instead of trying to revitalize the earlier plan of trying to fund a massive project with a large-scale campaign, she concentrated her energies on halting the further demolition of historic buildings and searching for public funding to preserve the town's famous courthouse.

Economic changes also worked in Landin's favor. When the U.S. Army announced the reactivation of nearby Fort Huachuca in 1953, new business applications flooded into Tombstone. The possibility of new stores raised concern among Landin and elected officials about demolition and the need to protect what remained of the historic downtown from the threat of modern development. "In a few months," the *Epitaph* warned, "enough changes could be made to create an entirely different town than that for which Tombstone is famous." In February 1954 the mayor and city council instructed the city legal advisor to draft the town's first ordinance to preserve the "western flavor" of the six square blocks of downtown Tombstone. When it passed on April 10, this measure established a bordered restoration zone, with the requirement that all new buildings there conform to the "Tombstone atmosphere as prevailed generally in 1883" and a zoning commission to oversee the process. The regulations limited the height of buildings to twenty feet, restricted construction materials to adobe, frame, or brick, and prohibited any adornments, signs, or outside fixtures not consistent with Old Tombstone.[64] To Clayton Smith of the *Epitaph*, the business community's lack of protest signaled that the town had finally recognized its future rested on "building a tourist industry" based on history. "Mines come and go," he wrote, but "history with its fabulous amount of free advertising is here for keeps."[65]

With the ordinance secured and the downtown's historic integrity protected, Landin turned her energy toward restoring the old county courthouse. The building had become available for preservation after an earlier attempt to convert it into a hotel failed. Then it stood empty, fell into disrepair, and became a major concern for the preservationists, who elected to take it on as their first tangible project. Early in 1954 Landin and the commission persuaded the county to take over the building for the purposes of restoration. With the building secured, Landin started a campaign to provide funds to remove the renovations made by its previous lessee. By 1957 she had raised $60,000 including in-kind construction donations and the city's assistance to reroof the courthouse. The cash was enough to stabilize the structure and restore its first floor. Even though the second floor remained unfinished, in October of that year the commission moved its exhibits and offices out of Schieffelin Hall to the partially refurbished courthouse and opened it to the public.[66]

Having completed the first step in the project, Landin struggled to get state funding to complete it. Despite an initial rebuff by newly elected governor Howard Pyle in 1954, she wrote that Tombstone would ask for a state appropriation because the territorial courthouse was the oldest in the state and its restoration needed "help from all citizens of Arizona." Landin ignored the governor's negative response and contacted Dennis McCarthy, director of the Arizona State Parks Board, stressing the need for the courthouse to be designated a state monument. After months of negotiation, in September 1958 McCarthy notified her that the courthouse would be part of a new first-year plan for inclusion in the new Arizona State Park system. A month later Landin sent McCarthy the town's offer to deed the building to the state, if it agreed to finish the project. Under the agreement, the state allowed the Restoration Commission to keep its bookstore and store in the courthouse. On August 1, 1959, the building became the Tombstone Courthouse State Historic Monument, the third Arizona state park. With state funding contractors removed the rest of the 1946 alterations and completed the second floor. In keeping with Tombstone's Wild West atmosphere, they built a replica of the gallows "with 13 fateful steps" originally used to hang the four Bisbee store robbers in 1884, in the building's courtyard.[67]

Soon after getting the courthouse moved into state hands, Landin learned of the National Park System's renewed interest in Tombstone as a site for national landmark status. She contacted Park Service regional historian Robert Utley, reminding him of the town's earlier consideration as a National Monument. A year later, after Utley visited, she promised the town's fullest cooperation because there "was no question" that the town's landmarks deserved to become "an authentic shrine to our last Frontier of the Old West." At the same time, Landin met with Kenneth Corley, director of Colonial Williamsburg and a friend of John D. Rockefeller, hoping that the benefactor of Williamsburg might likewise help Tombstone. While she got no help from the philanthropist, she did get the approval from the National Park Service. Utley's report supported Tombstone for National Landmark Status on the basis of its being "one of the best preserved specimens of the rugged frontier mining town of the 1870's and 1880's." The historian added that "except for the addition of neon signs and paved streets, it retains much of its frontier flavor and, under the auspices of the Tombstone Restoration Commission, is trying to recapture even more." The National Park Service Advisory Board approved Utley's recommendation, and in September 1962 Arizona governor Paul Fannin dedicated the courthouse as a National Historic Landmark.[68]

Despite its two major victories, the preservation movement in Tombstone split among groups supporting a more commercialized approach, private business interests, and those with more altruistic motives. Beginning with the Bird Cage Theatre and later the OK Corral, private museums turned into tourist attractions had long been a mainstay in Tombstone. As the town's television fame grew, the lines between historic restoration and tourist trap operators gradually blended together. In 1957 Don Dedera, a columnist for the *Arizona Republic* in Phoenix, described the scene accurately when he wrote that "in Tombstone, the unorganized efforts of private owners have brought forth a corrupt carnival of tourist traps. Preservation and restoration, in that town has resulted in a mockery, a caricature of history."[69]

Local circumstances became even more confused when private individuals and groups worked with the Restoration Commission. For example, in 1959 Floyd and Minnie Laughrum moved to Tombstone and purchased the old Nellie Cashman Hotel and the adjacent Wells Fargo office. After two years of restoration they installed an ice cream parlor; furnished the buildings with a variety of pioneer artifacts, including a gun, vintage clothing, and Indian objects; and built a diorama of an undertaker's parlor with wax corpses, a gambling scene with three Chinese card players, and a Navajo hogan.[70] Despite its commercial objectives, some members of the Restoration Commission pointed to this as a good example of historic preservation.

Growing tensions over the ambiguous meanings of restoration erupted in 1962 when the Arizona Highway Department decided to reroute U.S. Highway 80 through the heart of Tombstone's historic district. In 1960 the City Council had requested the change. It wanted the highway to come through downtown because the state would pay the mounting costs of street paving and repair and hoped that it might bring more tourists and business to stores on Fremont Street as well. The plan's chief liability came from the danger that widening the street posed to the integrity of the designated historic district. Shortly after the announcement, two factions began a bitter debate over the decision. On one side, Jeanne Devere argued that the change would force many of the structures on Fremont Street such as Schieffelin Hall and the old city hall to modify their porches. Members of the Vigilantes reenactors group joined her protest. They objected to paving the street because it was historically inaccurate and would force their members who currently "bit the dust" during the shows on Fremont Street to "have to bite the concrete." Members of Devere's faction feared that the street improvement might endanger the town's new status as a National Historic Landmark, so they petitioned the governor to halt the project.[71]

Their opponents, led by Edna Landin, endorsed the rerouting. They argued that Tombstone could not afford to lose any of its tourist trade that might result from a possible rerouting of the highway around the city and pointed out that Vigilant reenactors had performed on the asphalt of the current Highway 80 for the last thirteen years, underscoring the point that the paving of Allen Street with fifteen landmarks had not affected the town's historic designation. Landin further pointed out correctly that the widening of the street would make it conform to the 1880s original plan, which called for an eighty-foot width.[72]

To avoid being caught in the dispute, Governor Fannin called for an analysis by the State Landmarks Committee. It examined studies of the impact that rerouting had on tourism, reread National Park Service guidelines, and polled state courthouse visitors to determine the possible effects on visitation. In December 1962 it issued a report to Fannin supporting the Devere group. "It is the opinion of this committee," it concluded, that "any modern highway construction through the historic portion of Tombstone will damage, impair, and cheapen the historical value of one of Arizona's most important landmarks." The committee recommended further study of the feasibility of a bypass around the city. Reacting to the report, Landin sent Governor Fannin a petition containing 275 signatures, including those of the mayor and fifty business owners, opposing the committee's findings. Fannin, in turn, sent the issue back to the Highway Department, which ruled in favor of Landin's group in January 1963.[73]

The continuing disputes between restoration and commercialization in Tombstone took an even more dramatic turn later that same year when Harold O. Love led a consortium of business investors from Detroit to form Historic Tombstone Adventures. They intended to restore Tombstone using many of the ideas previously outlined by the Restoration Commission in the hope that the old dream of a western Williamsburg would bring substantial profits. The group bought many of Tombstone's main historic attractions, including the Crystal Palace, Fly's Photographic Studio, Schieffelin Hall, the *Tombstone Epitaph*, and the OK Corral. In each case they tried to restore the building as accurately as possible but did not always succeed. To profit from the expected increase in tourism the company built a forty-unit motel overlooking Boot Hill called the Lookout Lodge and established the 26,500-acre Lucky Hills ranch nearby. One of their featured attractions, shown in Schieffelin Hall, was the "Tombstone Historama," a program featuring a revolving scale model of old Tombstone, synchronized with a film narrated by actor Vincent Price. Ultimately the company planned to build a 108-room resort that would serve as a conference center for seminars on the Old West as well as a beginning point for tours into Apache country. The high costs of restoration, however, ended the group's enthusiasm. By the early 1970s Love had bought out all of his associates.[74]

The actions of private enterprises such as Historic Tombstone Adventures and the controversy during the Fremont Street discussions illustrated the weakness of the existing city preservation ordinance on the actual definition of "1883 character" and issues of enforcement graphically. In 1971 Restoration Commission president Theda Medigovich and Jeanne Devere began yet another effort to draft a plan for standard design guidelines and to clarify restoration priorities. In late 1973 the Tombstone Common Council accepted the Restoration Commission's recommended "Plan for the Creation of a Historic Environment in Tombstone, Arizona" as its official preservation code. The plan defined the restoration time frame as 1885, identified and recommended buildings to be preserved based on visitor expectations, and expanded the old restoration boundaries.[75]

By the 1990s Deadwood, Dodge City, and Tombstone had all received national affirmation of their historic significance. Alliances of social, political, and business leaders who viewed authenticity and economics as indistinguishable elements drove the preservation movements in each town. This belief developed because dime novelists, journalists, biographers, and local historians all had appropriated and commodified a specific aspect of their pasts. These writers, along with movie studios and later television producers, created a parade of powerful visual images—gunfights, saloons, dirt streets, dance halls, false front buildings, Boot Hills, and hanging trees—that defined the Wild West. Once readers and viewers became tourists and then customers, each town tried to satisfy their expectations with celebrations, markers, attractions, museums, replicated and vintage buildings, and national recognition.

Yet, as each community discovered, the effort to capture and use an Old West moment based largely on fictional images posed a difficult challenge. Many questions came from having to decide what constituted historical authenticity. Aside from the visual portraits of television and movies, what was the Wild West? Most material evidence of the past such as wagons, hoes, typewriters, switchboards, sewing machines, railroad spikes, wedding dresses, and furniture donated to local museums or historic homes and businesses could be found in any American town. In fact they pointed to postboom modernization—not to the Old West. This was not the West that many leading residents in these towns wanted to preserve. Most of the business owners, museum administrators, city promoters, and restoration advocates, who had economic stakes in the town's collective memory, defined the community's past solely in terms of popular images. Although they had no consensus on a specific definition, they all agreed on one overarching notion: the Wild West, and with it the town's historic identity, had to be preserved. This concept gained its life through local ordinances, official support of museums and restoration activities, and efforts to achieve official recognition. In Tombstone, Deadwood, and Dodge City images informed historic commemoration and preservation and became transformed into reality in the minds and policies of town leaders.

✒ Conclusion

Progressive Era boosters from Tombstone, Deadwood, and Dodge City would be shocked at what their towns had become at the end of the twentieth century. Promoters who had worked long and hard to distance themselves from their seedy boomtown pasts by casting new images of their communities as morally upstanding, family oriented, law-abiding, and economically sound would find a very different picture. Tombstone became an exaggeration of its past. On the city's streets, amid wooden sidewalks and signs pointing out famous gun battles, people could encounter residents dressed as dance-hall girls or gunslingers, buy Old West souvenirs, and have an opportunity to witness daily reenactments of street killings. In Deadwood turn-of-the-century reformers like Edward Senn would be saddened to learn that the town had brought back gambling from the town's past and made it the leading industry. Even more strikingly, Dodge City replicated an entire block of its once-notorious Front Street so that visitors could more fully experience its wild and woolly past. These actions raise the question: how could these memories of gambling, prostitution, drinking, and fighting, once the most embarrassing part of the towns' history, become celebrated moments in their history? The answer lies in each town's effort to reshape its past into virtual reality. Tombstone, Deadwood, and Dodge City all focused on their history as a commercial venture in order to gratify tourists. By 2014 they had succeeded: *True West Magazine* placed both Dodge City and Tombstone on its list of "Top 10 True Western Towns."[1]

During the late twentieth century local boosters across the country relabeled their history as cultural or sustainable heritage tourism. Particularly in communities suffering economic downturns, they sought to use any novel or interesting part of their past to attract visitors. The experiences of Tombstone, Deadwood, and Dodge City illustrate the long process of movement from the actual past to a situation where history has become a franchise. It grew out of a long fascination with the West and its heroes. Americans cherished the frontier West. They saw it as a glorious region that made the United States a special place. Because the West stood at the center of national identity, Americans demanded at least some authenticity in its heroes and settings. This became crucial, something that publishers, showpeople, and later filmmakers and television producers willingly incorporated as they tailored it to create salable products. In their search for authentic heroes, post–Civil War writers looked west to find figures for their stories. There journalists and dime-novel authors found a ready supply of larger-than-life people such as Buffalo Bill, Wild Bill Hickok, Calamity Jane, and other westerners whose lives they used in cheap fiction. By the end of the century Americans' feelings that the frontier era had ended encouraged a new wave of chroniclers to capture the waning spirit of the West by recording their own experiences. Wyatt Earp, Calamity Jane, Bat Masterson, Alfred Henry Lewis, and even Theodore Roosevelt added their recollections to the evolving collective memory of the West.

While dime novelists and journalists searched for heroes during this period, they discovered the perfect settings for their heroes' actions. Lurid accounts of the early boomtowns of Tombstone, Deadwood, and Dodge City established their reputations as sinful, wicked, and dangerous places. That idea likely would have been forgotten had it not been for dime novelists who turned journalists' descriptions into popular fiction. To the dismay of civic boosters who sought to create wholesome images of their towns, the negative reputations got added legitimacy when writers like Alfred Henry Lewis and Bat Masterson gave gunfighters and law officers more attention while embellishing the turbulent boom periods of each town.

Boosters, political and social leaders, and business interests a generation later began to accept and use the sordid memories that they had avoided earlier. This shift came about gradually during the interwar years. Local elites recognized that their towns' embarrassing reputations offered economic opportunities as American hunger for authentic reminders of the Old West grew. At the same time Western movie makers like William S. Hart and Ken Maynard and writers like Walter Noble Burns, William MacLeod Raine, and Stuart Lake discovered that stories of Tombstone, Deadwood, and Dodge City's heroes met this need. Attention by outsiders,

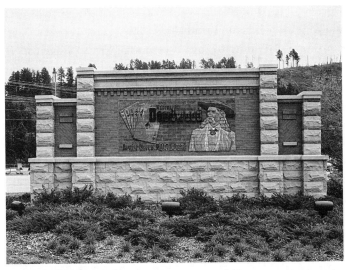

Deadwood welcome sign, 2009.
Photograph by Jimmy Emerson, DVM, released under the Creative Commons
Attribution-NonCommercial-NoDerivs 2.0 Generic (CC BY-NC-ND 2.0) license.

combined with published memoirs and recollections by locals, affirmed that these communities represented an important aspect of America's past.

National publicity gradually brought in a wave of auto tourists who came to each city looking for remnants of the Old West that they had read about or witnessed in theaters. Business leaders in Deadwood and Tombstone, in particular, quickly recognized that exploitation of their original boom period offered a chance to revitalize their depressed economies and perhaps encourage new development.

Civic promoters' realization that their Wild West reputations had market value created a major irony. In each town they had to convince their own communities of the economic benefits that a tourist industry based on Wild West history would bring. To overcome apathy and opposition and arouse community support, promoters in all three towns depended on local newspapers to encourage civic organizations to donate time and money toward commemorating the popular images associated with their boom period. Tourism advocates discovered that events celebrating each town's founding helped raise local support and gain national publicity. By drawing on acts from Wild West Shows, rodeos, and local pageants, event organizers refocused negative past events as forms of entertainment. At the same time they invented traditions such as Deadwood's Days of '76 and Tombstone's Helldorado, and later Dodge City's Dodge City Days, to help the Old West moment become the signature of each town's identity.

After 1930 Hollywood's repeated uses of these towns strengthened their identification with the Old West. Inspired by books like Walter Noble Burns's *Tombstone* and Stuart Lake's *Wyatt Earp: Frontier Marshal*, movie producers issued a series of films about famous characters associated with Deadwood, Dodge City, and Tombstone. In particular, Wyatt Earp and his brothers, Wild Bill Hickok, and Calamity Jane received attention. While the movies brought added notoriety to all three towns, they also strengthened existing images associated with them—saloons, dance halls, prostitutes, gunfighters, gamblers, and general community instability. Television carried these visual portraits to the small screen after World War II to a cold war population eager to celebrate the Old West and American exceptionalism. Both media forms brought tourists to the three towns with strong expectations of what the Old West was and what it should be.

Preservation of the past became intertwined with the tourism industry as local efforts reinforced the entertainment industries' portraits of a romanticized Old West. Local editors, chambers of commerce, and business leaders understood that tourists came to their towns hoping to find authentication of what they had read about or seen in films or on television. From the 1920s on, promoters worked to market Old West sites, collect and display relics in museums, and turn abandoned cemeteries, at least in Dodge City and Tombstone, into visitor attractions. Preservation efforts to authenticate the Old West accelerated in the 1950s after television programs such as *Gunsmoke, The Life and Legend of Wyatt Earp, The Adventures of Wild Bill Hickok*, and *Tombstone Territory* ushered in a new wave of affluent tourists seeking the Old West. Preservation took different forms. While Tombstone sought to restore vintage buildings to save its Old West atmosphere, Dodge City went to the opposite extreme, constructing an entire replica of its old Front Street business section.

By the 1990s the towns had reached their goals through recognition of their status by federal government or professional museum accreditation. In the process the actual meaning of authenticity came into question. Local businesses and chambers of commerce saw commemoration in economic terms and used the romanticized Wild West being advertised by books, movies, and television. They worked to make these images official through preservation ordinances in Deadwood and Tombstone or by providing lands and services as they did in Dodge City. At times the result brought considerable debate, as long-term residents contested the images of writers and Hollywood. They presented their memories of the towns as orderly and relatively nonviolent communities. Nor did the local preservation movements agree on the definition of authenticity. The hucksterism of Boot Hill embarrassed many Dodge City residents. Members of Tombstone's official preservation group, the Tombstone Restoration Commission, argued over what the limits of restoration efforts should be. Complicating efforts to define what authenticity actually meant, a number of private enterprises, such as Historic Tombstone Adventures and Deadwood's Ghosts of Deadwood Gulch Wax Museum, embarked on their own versions of what they believed was the Wild West.

In spite of local disagreements over how much attention to place on the Old West, history in each of the three towns had evolved into a business, through the decades-long interdependency between tourism and commemoration. The free publicity that each town received from popular books, magazines, movies, and television became the driving element in this view for much of the twentieth century. It focused on each town's turbulent era and western heroes, inserting these stereotypical images into the national consciousness. By the late twentieth century the interest in the Old West that fostered the market for the Old West waned as westerns largely disappeared from television and theaters. Dodge City felt the loss of free advertising most keenly and saw a marked decline in tourists without the boost from television. Its Boot Hill Museum, which had benefited from the twenty years of free publicity provided by the television series *Gunsmoke*, experienced a steady decline in visitation after 1975 when CBS canceled the series. From a peak of 400,000 visitors in 1967, attendance declined to just under 51,000 in 1993.[2]

A series of museum directors with business backgrounds tried to boost profits by charging admission. For example, in 1994 Mike Armour, the director of the Boot Hill Museum in Dodge City, installed glass walls inside the period buildings and fired all the costumed interpreters along with the museum's longtime curator. That set off a firestorm in the community and in state newspapers, which charged that the elimination of the museum's professional staff signaled a return to its old days of hucksterism.[3] The controversy raised the issue of whether the city should provide greater support for the museum or allow it to close as a failed business. One of the most eloquent appeals came from Gary Reber, the editor of the *Dodge City Daily Globe*, who argued that the closure of Boot Hill would destroy the town's identity. "Beyond the financial impact Boot Hill has on Dodge City and Ford County," Reber wrote, "Boot Hill is synonymous with Dodge City. The tourist attraction brings in thousands of visitors every year who want a taste of the Old West. . . . Boot Hill is Dodge City."[4] Rocked by the threat to its major tourist attraction, residents rallied. The museum borrowed enough funds to survive and eventually hire a professional staff.

The Dodge City experience illustrated the precarious situation of history once it became a business. The need to survive in the marketplace could push the utilitarian use of the past to extremes. Unlike Dodge City, Tombstone had a collective of historic attractions and museums that operated both privately and publicly, all of which depended on tourism.[5] To remain competitive in the market, the city undertook to franchise its image. In 1996 Raveen Arora, an Indian immigrant who had held a longtime fascination with Tombstone after his father took him to see the film *Gunfight at the O.K. Corral*, made an arrangement with the city council to use the name of the town on a new line of foods and sauces in exchange for a portion of the profits to be reinvested into the community. The Los Angeles–based company, calling itself the Tombstone (1877) Prospecting Company, was a subsidiary of Golden Holdings, Inc., of Santa Fe, California. It offered its customers products such as Epitaph hot seasoning sauce, Boot Hill extra-hot seasoning, Bird Cage hot salsa, Big Nose Kate Dijon-dill sauce, and Johnny Ringo beef jerky. For an element of authenticity, each label featured a few lines about the town and the namesake of the product. The company distributed its line in Tombstone stores and restaurants and nationally through gourmet shops. Customers could order the products by phone by dialing 888-Wyatt Earp.[6]

The main premise of this study has been to show how each of these towns worked to create an Old West identity based on its violent past. It demonstrates how the entertainment business (publishers, Wild West shows, movie studios, and television producers) perpetrated popular images of a romanticized frontier era. Motivated by the economic value of those images and the opportunity to have a special place in history, each town adopted them. These communities accepted their romantic and unruly pasts, hoping to use their old booms to fuel a new ones. That action allowed each of them to create an identity linked to a national myth that confirmed America's uncomplicated beginnings and offered tourists the chance to revisit the Wild West of their imaginations: a place where life was uncomplicated, emotions raw but pure; where the lines between good and evil were clearly drawn. It was also a place based on the personifications of these values—Wild Bill Hickok, Buffalo Bill, Wyatt Earp and his brothers, Doc Holliday, Matt Dillon, and Bat Masterson. Within this virtual realm women like Calamity Jane, Nellie Cashman (a boarding house owner in Tombstone), and Dora Hand (a Dodge City dance hall singer) tempered the raw edge of wildness extremes with their hearts of gold.

Authentication was an intrinsic element in making these images economic realities. Members of the business and social hierarchy produced and directed this validation to gratify tourist expectations for a true Old West experience. Building on the historical legitimacy offered by popular histories and visual images provided by films and television, tourism boosters and commercial interests supported their claims of national distinction and status as historic icons of the Old West by offering physical proof to tourists with personal witnesses, relics, commemorative markers, reenactments, celebrations, and architecture. This authenticated Old West rested on invented notions. As professional historians entered the scene, their constructions of authenticity presented a different meaning of the concept, which, ironically, hearkened back to the much more mundane version of history offered by Progressive Era boosters and turn-of-the century memoir writers.

Basing the past on romanticized images and authenticating it by bringing it into the present bring unforeseen consequences. In Deadwood and Tombstone the abstracted past became so deeply intertwined into the community fabric that life imitates it. Deadwood's decision to relive its gambling past caused the town to boom in 1990 as real-estate values skyrocketed then crashed a year later after the town became saturated with casinos and the Homestake Mine in Lead laid off miners when gold prices fell. At the same time, the new construction had changed the historic district to such an extent that it threatened its National Historic Landmark status. In addition, retail shopping declined. The city had to double its police force as crime rates jumped dramatically.[7]

In 1991 three Tombstone residents challenged the city's 1879 ordinance banning firearms within city limits. When the group received support from the National Rifle Association in 1992, the city council changed the ordinance, allowing the public to carry guns. Following the repeal, the town suddenly found itself a mecca for gun-toting tourists. After an incident when a visitor drew a real weapon during a street reenactment, the Vigilantes decided to perform only in an amphitheater. Meanwhile bars and restaurants, fearing real violence, now have customers check arms at the door, as had happened in many western towns a century earlier. Deadwood and Tombstone have become places where fantasy overlaps reality. "I could see me living in the Old West," a western-attired pistol-wearing tourist told a reporter for the *Arizona Daily Star* in 1996, "if there was reincarnation, that's when I want to be reincarnated from."[8] A Deadwood hotel owner echoed that sentiment. He supported Deadwood's decision to bring back gambling as inevitable because of its heritage as a western icon. "The Old West is alive with gambling, with dance-hall girls, people drinking and smoking cigars and all the things we've outlawed," he told a reporter. "It's got to happen someplace."[9]

The Wild West identity of each of the three towns served the economic needs of their white, middle-class professional, and business classes. By reshaping the memory and cultural experience of a transient working class into a romanticized ideal and community myth, they achieved the goal of gaining national significance and a notable place in America's past. Among the many ironies of this appropriation of the memory of a lower class for its economic and social value was the myth's lack of room for each town's present underclasses. The only minority people traditionally represented in public commemorations such as parades and reenactments were Indians and Chinese, both groups associated with the frontier past but no longer a presence inside any of the three towns. African Americans and Mexican Americans were largely invisible. In the early twenty-first century this situation edged toward radical change in Dodge City. Since the early 1990s Mexican American workers, attracted to well-paid jobs in the city's meat-packing and food-packaging industries, have altered the demographic mix. By 1996 half of the students in the town's schools were Hispanic. As a newly emerging Mexican American middle class brings a different culture and historic sensibilities, it stands to reason that it will either ignore the Old West or insist on a place next to Wyatt Earp.[10]

☞ Notes

ABBREVIATIONS USED IN THE NOTES

ADLAPR   Arizona Department of Library, Archives and Public Records
AMA   Adams Museum Archives
BHF   Boot Hill File
BHMA   Boot Hill Museum Archives
DCC   Deadwood Chamber of Commerce Records
DPA   Deadwood Preservation Archives
DPR   Deadwood Preservation Records
KHC   Kansas Heritage Center
SCUAL   Special Collections, University of Arizona Library
TCSHPA   Tombstone Courthouse State Historical Park Archives

INTRODUCTION

1. *Arizona Daily Star*, October 10, 2015.
2. *Arizona Daily Star*, October 21, 2015, and January 26, 2016.
3. *Arizona Daily Star*, March 28, 2016.
4. Whipple, *Study Out the Land*, 59, 61.
5. Slotkin, *Fatal Environment* and *Gunfighter Nation*; Nash, *Nervous Generation*; Wrobel, *End of American Exceptionalism* and *Global West*; Bruner, *Culture on Tour*; and McCormack, *Imaging Tombstone*.
6. Christensen, *Red Lodge*; Elliott, *Custerology*; McCormack, *Imaging Tombstone*; Dykstra and Manfra, *Dodge City*; Palmer, "Quivira, Coronado, and Kansas."
7. Calder, *There Must Be a Lone Ranger*, xii.
8. Benjamin, *Reflections*, 221.
9. Boorstin, *Image*; MacCannell, *Tourist*; Cohen, "Sociology of Tourism."
10. Moscardo and Pearce, "Historic Theme Parks," 477.
11. Slotkin, *Fatal Environment* and *Gunfighter Nation*; Wrobel, *End of American Exceptionalism* and *Global West*; Rothman, *Culture of Tourism*; Bruner, *Culture on Tour*.

CHAPTER 1

1. Fabian, "History for the Masses," 227.

2. Marietta and Rowe, *Troubled Experiment*.

3. Noel, *Villains Galore*, 169–71.

4. Parker, *Gold in the Black Hills*, 65–68.

5. Jackson's *Custer's Gold* chronicles the 1874 Black Hills expedition; for Custer's defeat, see Utley, *Cavalier in Buckskin*, chapter 6.

6. Larson, *Red Cloud*, 205–207; Lazarus, *Black Hills, White Justice*, 89–93; Kappler. "Fort Laramie Treaty," Article 12, 1002 (quotation).

7. Paul, *Mining Frontiers*, 180; Parker, *Deadwood*, 32, 60.

8. Anderson, "Deadwood."

9. Quoted in Paul, *Mining Frontiers*, 181.

10. Parker, *Deadwood*, 43, 58.

11. Ibid., 101, 228–29.

12. Mandat-Grancy, *Cow-boys and Colonels*, 134.

13. Richardson, "Trip to the Black Hills," 755.

14. *Manitowoc Pilot*, March 8, 1877.

15. Quoted in Parker, *Deadwood*, 207.

16. *New York Times*, August 13, 1877.

17. *Frank Leslie's Illustrated*, October 6, 1877.

18. Wheeler, *Deadwood Dick*, 3, 5–6.

19. Johannsen, *House of Beadle and Adams*, 1:260.

20. *New York Times*, May 4, 1879.

21. *Deadwood Daily Pioneer-Times*, August 16, 1923.

22. Underhill, "Tombstone Discovery," 44–67.

23. Myers, *Last Chance* 33; Marks, *And Die in the West*, 45.

24. Barra, *Inventing Wyatt Earp*, 95.

25. Marks, *And Die in the West*, 61–62; Myers, *Tombstone Story*, 43–45.

26. *Arizona Quarterly Illustrated* (July 1880).

27. The newest and best account of these events is Isenberg, *Wyatt Earp*. For earlier views, see McClintock, *Arizona*, 482; Lockwood, *Pioneer Days*; and Marks, *And Die in the West*.

28. Hall, "Remaking of an Old Bonanza," 239; "Tombstone Mining History," in William F. Staunton Papers, Box 2, Folder 2, Special Collections, University of Arizona Library (hereinafter SCUAL).

29. *Chicago Tribune*, February 7, 1880, Noon Papers, Arizona Historical Society, 3–4.

30. Quoted in West, "Saloon in Territorial Arizona," 61.

31. Bishop, "Across Arizona," 498.

32. Wheeler, *Deadwood Dick's Dream*, 5, 12.

33. Badger, *Old Boy of Tombstone*, 3, 6.

34. Lawson, *Dashing Diamond Dick*, 1–2.

35. Dykstra, *Cattle Towns*, 55–58; Wright, *Dodge City*, 138.

36. Quoted in Dykstra, *Cattle Towns*, 60.

37. Ibid., 62; Vestal, *Dodge City*, 83; Wiggins, "Dodge City," 51.

38. Dykstra, *Cattle Towns*, 85–106, 340.

39. Dykstra, "Overdosing on Dodge City," 509; Dykstra, *Cattle Towns*, 144.

40. Dykstra, *Cattle Towns*, 112–48.

41. *Dodge City Times*, September 1, 1877.

42. Quoted in Wright, *Dodge City*, 144.

43. *Washington (D.C.) Evening Star,* January 1, 1878.

44. *Scribner's Monthly* (March 1880): 769.

45. *New York Times,* June 17, 1878.

46. *New York Times*, May 10, 1883.

47. *New York Times*, May 11, 1883. Shillingberg's *Dodge City* gives a solid analysis of the cattle-boom era.

48. *New York Times,* June 9 and June 11, 1883.

49. Simms, *Dandy of Dodge*, 1–2.

50. Raine, *Famous Sheriffs*, 1–2.

51. Lake, *Wyatt Earp*, 138–39.

52. Lake, *Wyatt Earp*, 242 (quotation); Sonnichsen, "Tombstone in Fiction," 63.

53. Denning's *Mechanic Accents*, 47–61, demonstrates how the dime novels used class ideas to portray their characters; Jones, *Dime Novel Western*, 8.

54. *Deadwood Daily Pioneer-Times*, November 11, 1914.

55. Niven, "English Schoolboy," 349–51 (quotation on 350).

56. Waxman, "I Learned about America," 53.

57. Young, *Hard Knocks*, 1.

58. Shearer, *J. R. Bowman's Illustrated Transcontinental Guide*, 68–71, 358–59.

59. Clavin's *Dodge City* illustrates that exciting stories about the "heroes" continue to the present.

CHAPTER 2

1. Faragher, *Daniel Boone*, 331–32.

2. Jones, *Dime Novel Western*, 3; Folson, *American Western Novel*, 35–59.

3. For examples of the violence, see Bird, *Nick of the Woods*, 1, 65–66; and Webber, *Jack Long*, and *Old Hicks*. See also Dahl, *Robert Montgomery Bird*, 55.

4. Peters, *Life and Adventures of Kit Carson*; Sabin, *Kit Carson Days*, 506 (quotation).

5. Denning, *Mechanic Accents*, 31; Smith, *Virgin Land*, 92–96; Jones, *Dime Novel Western*, 4–6; Bold, *Selling the Wild West*, xii–xiii; Johannsen, *House of Beadle and Adams*, 1:3; Noel's *Villains Galore* traces the rise of weekly serials.

6. Jones, *Dime Novel Western*, 6.

7. Johannsen, *House of Beadle and Adams*, 1:33.

8. Jones, *Dime Novel Western*, 8.

9. Bold, *Selling the Wild West*, 3.

10. Robinson, "The Dime Novel Is Dead," 64.

11. Judson, *Red Warrior*, 1.

12. Hamilton, *Single Hand*, 18.

13. Steckmesser, *Western Hero*, 110.

14. Quoted in Rosa, *They Called Him Wild Bill*, 17.

15. *St. Louis Democrat*, April 4, 1867.

16. Rosa, *Wild Bill Hickok*, 101.

17. *Atchison (Kansas) Champion*, February 1, 1867; *Springfield (Missouri) Patriot*, January 31, 1867. Both papers are quoted in Rosa, *Wild Bill*, 26-27.

18. Monaghan's *Great Rascal*, 3–7; Rosa's *Wild Bill Hickok*, 161–63; and Rosa's *They Called Him Wild Bill* together give a solid account of Hickok's life.

19. Sell and Weybright, *Buffalo Bill and the Wild West*, 106. For the most recent account of Hickok's show business career, see Warren, *Buffalo Bill's America*, 69–81.

20. *Saline County (Kansas) Journal*, January 18, 1872.

21. Quoted in Russell, *Lives and Legends*, 207.

22. Quoted in Jones, *Dime Novel Western*, 62; Cody, *Life of Buffalo Bill*, 333; Warren, *Buffalo Bill's America*, 185.

23. Young, *Hard Knocks*, 202–208.

24. Rosa, *Wild Bill Hickok*, 179.

25. Senn, *Deadwood Dick*, 3.

26. McClintock, *Pioneer Days*, 129.

27. Etulain, *Life and Legends of Calamity Jane*, 3–4.

28. Wheeler, *Deadwood Dick on Deck*, 23.

29. McLaird's *Wild Bill Hickok and Calamity Jane* gives the most thorough analysis of this topic. He and other scholars agree that there was no romantic involvement between the two.

30. McLaird, *Calamity Jane*, 5.

31. Senn, *Deadwood Dick*, 10.

32. Quoted in McLaird, *Wild Bill Hickok and Calamity Jane*, 88.

33. Kuykendall, *Frontier Days*, 191.

34. Etulain's *Life and Legends*, 196–99, discusses her burial. His book and McLaird's *Calamity Jane* give the most up-to-date and authoritative discussions of her life.

35. Roosevelt's *Ranch Life* and Branch's *The Cowboy* both deal with this idea at length. See also Wrobel, *End of American Exceptionalism*, 29–41.

36. Wister, *Roosevelt*, 29.

37. Quoted in Branch, *The Cowboy*, 193. For an insightful analysis of Roosevelt, Remington, and Wister's ideas about the West, see White, *Eastern Establishment*. Scharnhorst's *Owen Wister* is the most recent analysis of his work.

38. Adams, *Log of a Cowboy*; Siringo, *Texas Cowboy*.

39. Smith, *Virgin Land*, 112.

40. *Topeka Daily Capital*, January 3, 1915.

41. Lewis, "Confessions," 7.

42. Ibid., 7–8.

43. *San Francisco Examiner*, August 2, 1896. Isenberg's *Wyatt Earp* examines Earp's writing effectively.

44. *San Francisco Examiner*, August 7, 1896.

45. Earp to Maule, May 24, 1927, Burns Papers, Box 3, Folder 1, SCUAL.

46. Walters to Burns, March 16, 1928, Burns Papers, Box 3, Folder 1, SCUAL (quotation); Isenberg, *Wyatt Earp*, 107–10.

47. Breakenridge to Burns, January 31, 1928, Burns Papers, Box 3, File 1, SCUAL.

48. Raine, "Helldorado," 11, 13; Breakenridge, *Helldorado*, 11 (quotation).

49. Dearment, *Gunfighter*, 70–72; DeArment, *Bat Masterson*, 371.

50. Little, "Round Table," 439.

51. Adams, *Log of a Cowboy*, 192.

52. Lewis, *Sunset Trail*, vii, x.

53. Ibid., 234.

54. Masterson, *Famous Gunfighters*, 5.

55. Ibid., 65.

CHAPTER 3

1. Hamer, *New Towns*, 85; Nelson, *After the West Was Won*, 82–112; Murphy's *Mining Cultures* shows how western cities identified strongly with civil solidarity after the frontier era.

2. Estlemen's *Wister Trace* analyzes these developments effectively.

3. Dodge City Business Club, *Dodge City*, 17.

4. Baldwin, *Black Hills Illustrated*, 92–93.

5. Quoted in Hattich, *Tombstone*, 17, 21.

6. Baldwin, *Black Hills Illustrated*, 92.

7. Dodge City Business Club, *Dodge City*, 23.

8. Hattich, *Tombstone*, 44.

9. Baldwin, *Black Hills Illustrated*, 92.

10. Dodge City Business Club, *Dodge City*, 17.

11. Morris, "Dodge City," 97.

12. Baldwin, *Black Hills Illustrated*, 92.

13. Morris, "Dodge City," 90.

14. Hattich, *Tombstone*, 25–26.

15. Deadwood Board of Trade, *Deadwood*; *Deadwood Times*, January 12, 1883.

16. *Arizona Graphic*, February 10, 1900.

17. Morris, "Dodge City," 91.

18. Dodge City Business Club, *Dodge City*, 7.

19. Baldwin, *Black Hills Illustrated*, 92.

20. Young, *Dodge City*, 146.

21. Morris, "Dodge City," 89.

22. *Dodge City Times*, Spring 1888.

23. *Arizona Graphic*, February 1, 1900.

24. Rosen, *Pa-Ha-Sa-Pah*, 399–401.

25. Tallent, *Black Hills*, v, 101, 356.

26. Wright, *Dodge City*, 6, 33, 299–300.

27. Ibid., 327.

28. Wrobel's *End of American Exceptionalism* discusses these ideas thoroughly.

29. *Overland Monthly* 67 (March 1916): 243–45 (quotations), 251; *Black Hills Weekly*, January 17, 1927.

30. *Black Hills Weekly*, July 3, 1930.

31. *Sunset* 61 (December 1928): 4.

32. *Black Hills Weekly*, February 19, 1930; July 3, 1930.

33. Bechdolt, *When the West Was Young*, 309.

34. *Tombstone Epitaph*, August 5, 1926.

35. Earp to Maule, May 24, 1927, Burns Papers, Box 3, File 2, SCUAL.

36. Flood to Burns, March 26, 1927, Burns Papers, Box 3, File 2; Burns to Maule, June 14, 1927, Burns Papers, Box 7, File 1, SCUAL.

37. Burns to Maule, June 15, 1927, Burns Papers, Box 7, File 1, SCUAL.

38. Isenberg, *Wyatt Earp*, 199–218.

39. Burns to Maule, June 15, 1927, Burne Papers Box 7, File 1; and Doubleday & Co. to Earp, July 7, 1927, Burns Papers, Box 7, Folder 1, SCUAL.

40. Burns, *Tombstone*, 387–88. Dworkin's *American Mythmaker* is the newest analysis of Burns's work.

41. Raine, "Helldorado," 9.

42. *Tombstone Epitaph*, November 15, 1928; *Sunset* 61 (December 1928): 4.

43. *Tombstone Epitaph*, February 7, 1929; March 14, 1929.

44. Walters, *Tombstone's Yesterdays*, 9, 11.

45. *Tombstone Epitaph*, June 16, 1927.

46. *Tombstone Epitaph*, July 7, 1927.

47. Clum, "It All Happened in Tombstone," 54–55.

48. Foy and Harlow, *Clowning through Life*, 98.

49. Ibid., 104, 158.

50. Lake to Ira Rich Kent, February 13, 1930, Kent Papers, Huntington Library.

51. Kent to Lake, October 15 and 23, 1930, Lake Papers, Huntington Library.

52. Lake, *Wyatt Earp*, 138–39, 243.

53. *Tombstone Epitaph*, March 3, 1932.

54. *Dodge City Daily Globe*, January 14, 1929.

55. *Dodge City Daily Globe*, February 29, 1932; Beeson to Houghton Mifflin, October 27, 1931, Beeson Papers, Box 1a, Boot Hill Museum Archives (hereinafter BHMA).

56. *Dodge City Daily Globe*, October 25, 1922; April 6, 1922.

57. *Dodge City Daily Globe*, April 16, 1922; July 23, 1929 (quotation); September 26, 1922 (quotation); *Dodge City Journal*, May 31, 1928.

58. *Dodge City Daily Globe*, April 25, 1929; April 23, 1932; August 17, 1929.

59. *Deadwood Daily Pioneer-Times*, August 16, 1923.

60. Brown and Willard, *Black Hills Trails*, i.

61. Bennett, *Old Deadwood Days*, 4.
62. Nash, *Nervous Generation*, 81 (quotation); Wrobel's *Global West* and Slotkin's *Gunfighter Nation* consider the shifting national moods and the roles of ideas about the Old West during this era.

CHAPTER 4

1. Rothman's *Devil's Bargains*, 10–28, and Philpott's *Vacationland*, 3–23, lay out many of the challenges that tourism entails for communities.
2. Butler, *History of Tombstone Mines*.
3. i2 Environmental Consultants, *Tombstone Heritage*, 154.
4. Parker, *Deadwood*, 102–103.
5. Ibid., 212–13; quoted in Faehnrich, "Edward L. Senn," 28.
6. *Deadwood Telegram*, September 2, 1924.
7. Aikman, "Deadwood the Dreadful," 342–43.
8. *Dodge City Daily Globe*, October 31, 1921.
9. Quoted in *Dodge City Journal*, May 2, 1929.
10. Worster's *Dust Bowl* analyzes these events effectively.
11. Pomeroy, *In Search of the Golden West*, 127–30.
12. *Deadwood Daily Pioneer-Times*, April 7, 1923; *Black Hills Weekly*, February 19, 1930.
13. *Tombstone Prospector*, May 1, 1916; *Arizona Daily Star*, September 6, 1925, and October 22, 1942; quoted in *Dodge City Daily Globe*, April 21, 1922.
14. *Dodge City Daily Globe*, May 10, 1922. See also Carson, "Goggles and Side Curtains," 38.
15. Ayers, "Lawrence County Roads," 9–15.
16. Deadwood Business Club, *Souvenir Book*, no pagination.
17. Jakle, *Tourist*, 124–26; *Tombstone Epitaph*, January 16 and August 14, 1921.
18. Lancaster, "Great American Hotel," 102.
19. *Dodge City Daily Globe*, January 3 and June 8, 1922.
20. *Tombstone Epitaph*, December 19, 1920; September 1, 1927.
21. Jakle, *Tourist*, 152–53; Carson, "Goggles and Side Curtains," 110; *Deadwood: What to See*, no pagination (quotation); *Dodge City Daily Globe*, October 21, 1922.
22. *Tombstone Epitaph*, October 7, 1923.
23. *Deadwood Daily Telegraph*, September 9 and August 11 1923.
24. *Dodge City Weekly*, February 21, 1924; *Deadwood Telegram*, September 1, 1927.
25. *Black Hills Weekly*, April 25, 1929; *Tombstone Epitaph*, April 11, 1927.
26. *Tombstone Epitaph*, January 20, 1922; *Black Hills Weekly*, May 10, 1928.
27. *Deadwood Daily Telegram*, September 19, 1923; Flagg, *Boulevards All the Way*, 95.
28. Finger, *Adventure under Sapphire Skies*, 113–14; *New York Times*, February 21, 1929.
29. *Black Hills Weekly*, March 6, 1930.
30. *Black Hills Weekly*, July 10, 1930; quoted in *Tombstone Epitaph*, January 14, 1923.
31. *Tombstone Epitaph*, March 14, 1920.

32. *Tombstone Epitaph*, March 3, 1927.

33. *Tombstone Epitaph*, April 25, 1929.

34. *Dodge City Journal*, April 30, 1925.

35. *Dodge City Journal*, March 9, 1922.

36. *Deadwood Daily Telegram*, September 9, 1923.

37. *Deadwood Pioneer Times*, April 13, 1930.

38. Quoted in *Deadwood Pioneer Times*, September 6, 1923.

39. *Deadwood Daily Telegram*, September 23, 1923.

40. *Deadwood Daily Pioneer-Times*, September 23, 1922.

41. *Tombstone Epitaph*, September 19, 1924.

42. Gardiner to Burns, November 16, 1927, Burns Papers, Box 3, Folder 1, SCUAL.

43. *Tombstone Epitaph*, April 12, 1928.

44. *Tombstone Epitaph*, November 15, 1928.

45. *New York Times*, February 21, 1929; *Tombstone Epitaph*, February 21, 1929.

46. *Tombstone Epitaph*, February 25, 1932.

47. *Black Hills Weekly*, March 13, 1930; P. D. Peterson, *Through the Black Hills and Bad Lands of South Dakota*, p. 84.

48. *Dodge City Daily Globe*, November 18, 1926.

49. *Dodge City Daily Globe*, February 21, 1924.

50. Frothingham, *Trails through the Golden West*, 27.

51. *Dodge City Journal*, April 30, 1925.

52. Finger, *Adventure under Sapphire Skies*, 113.

53. *Tombstone Epitaph*, February 19 (quotation) and April 22, 1922; Holbrook, "Guy Who Named Tombstone," 746–47.

54. *Commoner*, December 4, 1934.

55. Gardiner, *Main Street through Arizona*, 11.

56. *Tombstone Epitaph*, June 13, 1920.

57. *Arizona Daily Star*, December 13, 1925.

58. *Tombstone Epitaph*, January 29. 1922. See also *Tombstone Daily Prospector*, December 22, 1922.

59. *Tombstone Epitaph*, February 22, 1922; *Tombstone Daily Prospector*, December 22, 1922.

60. *Souvenir of the Birdcage*, Arizona State University, Arizona Collection, Tempe.

61. *Dodge City Journal*, April 30, 1925; Frothingham, *Trails through the Golden West*, 27 (quotation).

62. Finger, *Adventure under Sapphire Skies*, 113.

63. *Dodge City Journal*, January 4, 1929; *Deadwood Daily Pioneer-Times*, November 22, 1914.

64. *Black Hills Weekly*, August 1, 1929; *Tombstone Epitaph*, January 29, 1922.

65. *Deadwood Daily Pioneer-Times*, February 1, 1920.

66. Clark, "Society of Black Hills Pioneers," 1.

67. *Black Hills Weekly*, March 6, 1930.

68. *Deadwood Daily Pioneer-Times*, January 23, 1924.

69. *Deadwood Telegram*, December 7, 1923.

70. *Deadwood Telegram*, December 7, 1923; January 28, 1924; July 11, 1924; *Deadwood Daily Pioneer-Times*, July 11, 1924; "Points of Outstanding Interest," Deadwood Chamber of Commerce, Deadwood (quotation).

71. *Tombstone Epitaph*, November 10, November 24, and December 8, 1927; April 11, 1929.

72. *Dodge City and Ford County, Kansas*, 113–14.

73. *Dodge City Journal*, August 10, 1922; October 7, 1926 (quotation); August 11, 1927.

74. Deadwood Promotional Pamphlet, 1929, Deadwood Public Library; Wright, *Dodge City*; Tombstone Promotional Pamphlet 9, SCUAL; Cole to Douglas Martin, October 17, 1961, Cole Papers, SCUAL.

CHAPTER 5

1. Robert Eagan Papers, Box 1, Notebook 1, Western History Department, Denver Public Library.

2. *Tombstone Epitaph*, April 1, 1926; August 2, 1928.

3. *Ford County Globe*, February 4, 1879.

4. *Hays Sentinel*, May 31, 1879.

5. *Dodge City Daily Globe*, April 2, 1925.

6. Dodge City Commission Journals, July 1 and July 15, 1925, Kansas Historical Society, Topeka.

7. Quoted in *Dodge City Daily Globe*, April 2, 1927; Dodge City Commission Minutes, April 20, 1927, Robert Eagan Papers, Denver Public Library.

8. *Dodge City Globe*, September 21, 1927.

9. *Dodge City Journal*, July 5, 1928.

10. *Dodge City Journal*, March 28, 1928.

11. Quoted in *Dodge City Globe*, March 26, 1931. See also Ida Rath, "Dr. O. H. Simpson," Boot Hill File, Kansas Heritage Center, Dodge City.

12. *Dodge City Globe*, February 9, 1932.

13. *Dodge City Globe*, May 11, 1931.

14. *Dodge City Globe*, March 2, 932.

15. *Dodge City Globe*, April 5, 1932.

16. Quoted in *Dodge City Globe*, May 9, 1932, and March 4, 1971; unidentified clipping, n.d., Lois Bryson Collection, 1989, Box 59, Boot Hill Museum Archives, Dodge City.

17. *Dodge City Journal*, April 28, 1932; Dodge City Commission Meeting Minutes, Journal 1, April 27, 1932, Kansas Historical Society, Topeka.

18. *Dodge City Journal*, June 6, 1932.

19. *Dodge City Journal*, September 14, 1935.

20. *Dodge City Journal*, October 10, 1935.

21. *Dodge City Journal*, October 10, 1935; February 21, 1947 (quotation).

22. *Dodge City Journal*, July 26, 1937.

23. Carey, *Thrilling Story* (quotation); *Dodge City Journal*, September 14, 1937.

24. Unidentified clipping, n.d., Boot Hill Research File, Boot Hill Museum Archives; *Dodge City Journal*, December 19, 1935 (quotation).

25. *Dodge City Daily Globe*, July 10, 1936.

26. Bechdolt, *When the West Was Young*, 277–78.

27. Moy, *Tombstone Epitaph Annual Resource Edition*, March 6, 1925.

28. *Tombstone Epitaph*, March 6, 1925.

29. *Tombstone Epitaph*, June 26, 1925.

30. Ibid. See also Traywick, *Tombstone's Boothill*, 4.

31. *Arizona Daily Star*, March 22, 1925.

32. Moy, *Tombstone Epitaph Annual Resource Edition*, 22. A local family had taken most of the original wooden grave markers for fuel years earlier. Carr, *The West Is Still Wild*, 53.

33. *Tombstone Epitaph*, May 26, 1932.

34. *Tombstone Epitaph*, May 26 and November 11, 1932; unidentified clipping, April 6, 1933, Tombstone Ephemeral File, Arizona Department of Library, Archives, and Public Records, Phoenix (hereinafter ADLAPR).

35. *Tombstone Epitaph*, January 1, 1931.

36. *Tombstone Epitaph*, May 26, 1932.

37. Quoted in unidentified clipping, August 14, 1934, Tombstone Ephemeral File, ADLAPR; *San Antonio Evening Herald* quoted in *Tombstone Epitaph*, April 9, 1936.

38. *Tombstone Epitaph*, April 9, 1937; *Souvenir of Tombstone*, Pamphlet 14, SCUAL.

39. *San Diego Union*, November 20, 1937; *Arizona Daily Star*, March 13, 1925.

40. Andy Anderson Biographical File, Arizona Historical Society.

41. Unidentified clipping, Tombstone ephemeral file, November 22, 1936, ADLAPR; *Arizona Daily Star*, February 10, 1929; William Du Puy, "Tombstone Quickens to the New Deal," *New York Times Magazine*, April 1, 1934.

42. Unidentified clipping, Tombstone ephemeral file, November 22, 1936, ADLAPR; quoted in *Tombstone Epitaph*, July 29. See also *Arizona Daily Star*, July 30, 1937; *Arizona Republic*, October 3, 1937.

43. Quoted in *Tombstone Epitaph*, April 7 and April 21, 1937.

44. *Tombstone Town Tattler*, n.d., Pamphlet 9, SCUAL.

45. Miller, "Here Lie the Bodies," 18; Brimmer, "Boothill Graveyards," 12, 15.

46. *Tombstone Epitaph*, June 29, 1944.

47. *Tombstone Epitaph*, November 11, 1946; July 22, 1949; Brimmer, "Boothill Graveyard," 17; *Fiftieth Anniversary Helldorado Program*, 1979, 20, SCUAL: Nunnelly, "A Descriptive List of the More Than 250 Graves in Boothill," SCUAL.

48. *Black Hills Daily Times*, July 17, 1878; *Deadwood Daily Pioneer-Times*, January 14, 1924.

49. Quoted in Rosa, *Wild Bill Hickok*, 206. See also *Black Hills Daily Times*, April 20 and 27, 1880.

50. *Black Hills Daily Times*, August 5 and 9, 1879; McClintock, *Pioneer Days*, 112–13

(quotations); Young's *Hard Knocks*, 223, claims that only the left side of the body was petrified.

51. *Black Hills Daily Times*, April 27, 1880; September, 21, 25, 1883.
52. Unidentified clipping, n.d., Hickok File, Adams Museum Archives, Deadwood (hereinafter AMA).
53. Quoted in Rezzato, *Mount Moriah*, 32.
54. *Deadwood Daily Pioneer-Times*, August 23, 1901.
55. Unidentified clipping, n.d., Hickok File, AMA.
56. Quoted in *Belle Fourche Bee*, August 6, 1903. See also Etulain, *Life and Legends*, 198.
57. *Deadwood Daily Pioneer-Times*, July 23, 1903.
58. Johnson, "Touring the Black Hills," 163 (quotation); and Bellamy and Seymour, *Guide to the Black Hills*, 26–27 (quotation).
59. *Deadwood Telegram*, August 29, 1923, and *Kimball Graphic*, October 19, 1923.
60. Peterson, *Through the Black Hills*, 87–88; Bellamy and Seymour, *Guide to the Black Hills*, 26; Price, *Black Hills*, 106; Coursey, *Beautiful Black Hills*, 100.
61. Deadwood Chamber of Commerce Records, File 96.1.30, Deadwood Preservation Archives (hereinafter DPA).
62. Price, *Black Hills*, 109; Coursey, *Beautiful Black Hills*, 111; Peterson, *Through the Black Hills*, 88.
63. Tharp, "Looking Back at the Old West."
64. Henry Alsberg to Lisle Reese, November 3, 1937; Byron Cane to Clerk and Recorder, December 12, 1937; Archer Gilfillan to Camille Yuill, November 8, 1937, Deadwood Chamber of Commerce Records, File 96.1.30, DPA.
65. Perrigoue to Gilfillan, December 6, 1937, DPA.
66. Peterson, *Through the Black Hills*, 88; quoted in *Deadwood Telegram*, August 11, 1924. For a recent treatment of dude ranches and tourism, see Johnson, "Romancing the Dude Ranch."
67. *Deadwood Daily Pioneer-Times*, July 11, 1924.
68. Ibid.
69. Cooper, "Another Redskin Bit the Dust!" 106.
70. *Black Hills Weekly*, July 15 and July 30, 1938.
71. Perrigoue to Pankow, January 8 and March 7, 1940 (quotations), Chamber of Commerce Records, File 96.1.23, DPA.
72. Chamber of Commerce Annual Report, 1941, DPA; *Black Hills Weekly*, September 19, 1941 (quotation).
73. Chamber of Commerce Minutes, April 25, 1950, Chamber of Commerce Records, File 96.1.7, DPA.
74. *Black Hills Weekly*, June 17, 1953.
75. *Black Hills Weekly*, June 24, 1953.
76. Chamber of Commerce Activities in Review, n.d., File 96.1.11, 4, DPA.
77. Cooper, "Another Red Skin Bit the Dust!" 106.
78. Finger, *Adventure under Sapphire Skies*, 119–20.

CHAPTER 6

1. Wrobel, *End of American Exceptionalism* and *Global West*.
2. Russell, *Wild West*; and Slotkin, *Myth of the Frontier*, 74–84.
3. Schwarz, "Wild West," 659.
4. *Dodge City Daily Globe*, December 21, 1921; October 11, 1922.
5. *Dodge City Journal*, October 12, 1922; *Dodge City Daily Globe*, October 10, 1922.
6. *Dodge City Journal*, October 12, 1922; *Dodge City Daily Globe*, October 10, 1922.
7. *Dodge City Daily Globe*, October 9, 1922; *Dodge City Journal*, October 5, 1922.
8. *Dodge City Journal*, October 26, 1922.
9. *Dodge City Daily Globe*, March 31, 1924.
10. *Hutchinson Gazette*, October 23, 1922.
11. *Dodge City Journal*, October 14, 1922.
12. *Black Hills Pioneer*, June 29, 1924.
13. *Deadwood Daily Pioneer-Times*, May 27, June 5, and July 9, 1924.
14. *Deadwood Daily Pioneer-Times*, June 17, 20, 25, and 29, 1924.
15. *Deadwood Daily Pioneer-Times*, June 29, July 9 and 26, 1924.
16. *Deadwood Daily Pioneer-Times*, July 20, 1924. See also *Deadwood Daily Telegram*, July 24, 1924.
17. *Deadwood Daily Pioneer-Times*, July 3, 1924.
18. *Deadwood Daily Pioneer-Times*, July 30, 1924.
19. *Deadwood Daily Telegram*, June 26, 1924.
20. *Deadwood Daily Telegram*, August 11, 1924.
21. *Deadwood Daily Telegram*, August 14, 1924.
22. *Deadwood Daily Pioneer-Times*, July 18, 1924.
23. *Deadwood Daily Pioneer-Times*, July 24, 1924.
24. *Deadwood Telegram*, August 19, 1924.
25. Ibid.; *Deadwood Daily Pioneer-Times*, August 19, 1924.
26. Nell Perrigoue and Mary Ann Wood, "Deadwood's Historic Mining Court: The Trial of Jack McCall," n.d., Folder 96.1.24, DPA; Souvenir Program, "The Trial of Jack McCall for the Killing of Wild Bill Hickok," n.d., n.p., Deadwood Public Library.
27. *Deadwood Daily Pioneer-Times*, August 24, 1924.
28. *Deadwood Daily Pioneer-Times*, August 24, 25, and 29, 1924.
29. *Tombstone Epitaph*, June 27, 1929.
30. Pat Hayhurst to Toohey, May 5, 1934. Tombstone Research File, ADLAPR.
31. William Kelly to Walter Cole, August 22, 1929, Folder 19, Kelly Papers, SCUAL.
32. *Tombstone Epitaph*, May 30, 1929.
33. *Bisbee Review*, June 13, 1929; R. B. Krebs to Kelly, June 3, 1929, Folder 1, Kelly Papers, SCUAL.
34. Kelly to Walter Cole, August 22, 1929, Folder 19, Kelly Papers, SCUAL.
35. Quoted in *Tombstone Epitaph*, June 27, 1929; "Suggested Program for Tombstone's Helldorado," Folder 1, Kelly Papers, SCUAL.
36. George C. Pound to Kelly, June 30, 1929, Folder 5, SCUAL.

37. Clyde Zerby to Kelly, July 6, 1929, Folder 5 (quotation); Clum to Kelly, Folder 9, SCUAL.
38. Kelly, press release, n.d., Folder 3, and Kelly to Walter Noble Burns, August 27, 1929, Folder 8, Kelly Papers, SCUAL.
39. Kelly to E. D. Rockwell, June 30, 1929, Folder 16, SCUAL.
40. Kelly press release, n.d., Folder 3, SCUAL.
41. "Helldorado," *Progressive Arizona* 4 (October 1929): 16 (quotation); *Los Angeles Times Sunday Magazine*, December 8, 1929; *New York Herald Tribune*, October 27, 1929.
42. *Tombstone Epitaph*, August 29, 1929.
43. *Tombstone Epitaph*, September 12, 1929. See also Kelly to Fred McSparron, September 8, 1929, Folder 6, Kelly Papers, SCUAL.
44. Kelly to Francis Crabbe, October 5, 1929, Folder 6, Kelly Papers, SCUAL.
45. Quoted in *Tombstone Epitaph*, September 12 and September 26, 1929. See also Agreement of Citizens, n.d., Folder 1, SCUAL.
46. *Arizona Daily Star*, October 13, 1971.
47. *Tombstone Epitaph*, June 6, 1929.
48. *Tombstone Epitaph*, June 27 and July 25, 1929.
49. *Arizona Daily Star*, November 20, 1929; *Tombstone Epitaph*, September 12, 1929.
50. *Arizona Daily Star*, September 5, 1929; *Graham County Guardian*, September 19, 1929.
51. *Tombstone Epitaph*, September 12, 1929.
52. *El Paso Times*, October 28, 1929.
53. Clum, *Helldorado*, 5.
54. Kelly to Ted Shipley, October 7, 1929, Folder 7, Kelly Papers; Kelly to Yuma Indian Band, October 8, 1929, Folder 13, SCUAL; Clum, *Helldorado*, 5.
55. *Phoenix Republican*, October 26, 1929.
56. *Douglas Dispatch*, October 26, 1929; Clum, "Helldorado," 11.
57. *Arizona Daily Star*, October 15, 1929; Harriet Hankin to Kelly, September 24, 1929, Folder 6 Kelly Papers, SCUAL; *Bisbee Review*, October 18, 1929.
58. Clum, *Helldorado*, 4–5, 8–9.
59. *Arizona Daily Star*, October 27, 1929; *Phoenix Gazette*, October 28, 1929.
60. Kelly to Walter Cole, April 4, 1930, Folder 19, Kelly Papers, SCUAL.
61. "Pioneer Days in Kansas," program in scrapbook 7747, Box 80, BHMA.
62. James L. Pogue, "The Last Round-Up," transcript in Last Round Up files, BHMA.
63. *Dodge City Journal*, October 10, 31, 1929. See also Invitation letter, n.d., Last Round-Up file, Kansas Heritage Center, Dodge City (hereinafter KHC).
64. *Dodge City Daily Globe*, October 14, 1929.
65. *Dodge City Daily Globe*, October 24, 1929.
66. *Dodge City Daily Globe*, October 21 and 30, 1929.
67. *Dodge City Daily Globe*, October 22, 1929.
68. *Black Hills Weekly*, March 6, 1930.

69. *Deadwood Daily Pioneer-Times,* July 14 and August 1, 1924.

70. J. C. Hihawk to President, July 16, 1938, Days of '76 files, DCC; Gib La Beau to Larry Hanson, January 17, 1972, DCC.

71. For discussions of early rodeo, see Wooden and Ehringer, *Rodeo in America,* 7–16; Fredericksson, *American Rodeo,* 6–20; *Black Hills Weekly,* September 29, 1929; Deadwood Chamber of Commerce Minutes, March 31, May 19 and 26, 1931, Box 96.1.7, DPA.

72. Quoted in *Black Hills Weekly,* September 29, 1929; Kenneth Ellis to Deadwood Chamber of Commerce, September 8, 1938, File 96.1.3; Jack Paige to Perrigoue, June 8, 1944; Perrigoue to Paige, July 26, 1944, File 96.1.21, DPA.

73. *Rapid City Journal,* June 21, 1953.

74. *Black Hills Weekly,* July 25, 1929. See also McClintock, *Pioneer Days,* 133–34; Deadwood Business Club Minutes, March 6, 1928, DPA, 1929.

75. *Black Hills Weekly,* May 9, 1941; Perrigoue to Donald Severn, October 22, 1942, Potato Creek Johnny File, DPA.

76. *Tombstone Epitaph,* June 5, 1930.

77. Helldorado Program, 1930, SCUAL.

78. *Tombstone Epitaph,* August 14, 1930 (quotation) and November 6, 1930.

79. *Los Angeles Times,* April 26, 1931.

80. *Tombstone Epitaph,* August 14, 1931.

81. *Tombstone Epitaph,* September 1 and 28, 1932.

CHAPTER 7

1. Rothman's *Devil's Bargains* and Philpott's *Vacationland* develop this idea effectively.

2. For insights on the role of film and television in twentieth-century American society, see Slotkin, *Gunfighter Nation,* 231; Bluestone, "Changing Cowboy"; Cawelti, *Six Gun Mystique;* Mitchell, *Westerns;* Etulain and Riley, *Hollywood West;* and Rollins and O'Connor, *Hollywood's West.*

3. Perrigoue to Ray Hoadly, September 29, 1941, Folder 96.1.23, DPA.

4. Films about Wild Bill and Calamity Jane appeared often during the 1940s and 1950s. The most recent was *Wild Bill* (1995) produced by Warner Electra.

5. *Dodge City Globe,* December 27, 1916. Other films featuring the city were *The Plainsman* (Lippert, 1936), *Santa Fe* (Columbia, 1951), *Masterson of Kansas* (Columbia, 1954), and *Gunfight at Dodge City* (Mirisch, 1959).

6. Sarf, *God Bless You,* 37–67; Tuska, *American West in Film,* 175–80.

7. Hart, *My Life,* 198; *Tombstone Epitaph,* October 27, 1927; Hayne, *Autobiography of Cecil B. DeMille,* 352.

8. Hayne, *Autobiography of Cecil B. DeMille,* 234–37, 306; Earp to Hart, July 7, 1923, William S. Hart Letters, Los Angeles Museum of Natural History; Walsh, *Each Man in His Time,* 103; Bogdanovich, *John Ford,* 84–85.

9. Hart, *My Life,* 233, quoted in *Dodge City Daily Globe,* November 6, 1929.

10. *Tombstone Epitaph,* March 20, 1921; *Deadwood Daily Pioneer-Times,* January 6,

1927; *Dodge City Daily Globe*, December 4, 1923.

11. *Deadwood Daily Pioneer-Times*, August 18, 1926.

12. *Deadwood Daily Pioneer-Times*, August, 13, 14, and 18, 1926.

13. Kelly to Fox Studios, Folder 18, Kelly Papers; Maynard to Tombstone Chamber of Commerce, October 9, 1929, SCUAL.

14. Breakenridge to Kelly, October 13, 1929; City Council to Maynard, October 125, 1929, SCUAL.

15. Bert Bell to Paramount Studios, May 13, 1932, Movie File, DCC; Perrigoue to Paramount Production Department, April 22, 1936, DCC (quotation).

16. *Dodge City Daily Globe*, December 4, 1923.

17. *Deadwood Daily Pioneer-Times*, July 27 and 28, 1923.

18. Unidentified clipping, n.d., File 96.1.20, DPA.

19. Grabia quoted in unidentified clipping, n.d., File 96.1.20, DPA; Mayor's Proclamation, Ewing Movie File, DCC.

20. *Dodge City Globe*, October 4, 1938; George Shaffer to Dodge City Chamber of Commerce, October 13, 1938, Warner Brothers Collection, 1988.2.44, Document Box 55e, BHMA.

21. Minutes, Dodge City Premier Committee, December 1938, BHMA.

22. Ibid.

23. Dunkley to Warner Brothers Pictures, January 7, 1939, *Dodge City*, Warner Brothers Collection, 1988.2.44, BHMA.

24. Dunkley to Hubbard, February 10, 1939, BHMA.

25. *Dodge City Globe*, February 21, 1939; Sutton, "Dodge City, Kansas," 45, 47.

26. Dunkley to Grimsley, March 11, 1939, *Dodge City*, Warner Brothers Collection, 1988.2.44, BHMA.

27. Dunkley to Skidmore, March 14, 1939, BHMA; *Dodge City Journal*, March 2, 1939.

28. *Dodge City Journal*, March 16, 1939; *Dodge City Daily Globe*, April 1, 1939.

29. Zierold, *Moguls*, 245; Sutton, "Dodge City, Kansas," 54; *Dodge City Daily Globe*, August 2, 1939; June 13, 1939; press release, April 1, 1939, Warner Brothers Collection, Box 55e, BHMA.

30. *Dodge City Daily Globe*, April 3. See also May 27, 1939; July 26, 1990.

31. *New York Times*, April 9, 1939; Sutton, "Dodge City, Kansas," 56.

32. "Revival in Tombstone," 94–95; "Tombstone, Arizona," *Parade Magazine* (May 4, 1947); i2 Environmental Consultants, *Tombstone Heritage*, 37–39, 154.

33. Lee, *Guns, Gals, Gold, Guts*, 248; Anonymous, *Some History of Lawrence County*, 569–70.

34. State Board of Agriculture, *36th Biannual Report, 1947–48*, 253; Bureau of Government Research, *Comprehensive Planning Survey*, 6.

35. Nash, *American West*, 242.

36. *Black Hills Weekly*, May 2, 1947; *Dodge City Daily Globe*, July 28, 1953.

37. Kamman, *Mystic Cords*, 548–49; Slotkin, *Gunfighter Nation*, 347–53.

38. Vestal, *Dodge City*; Myers, *Last Chance*; Casey, *Black Hills*; Peattie, *Black Hills*.

39. *Tombstone Epitaph*, September 12 and 19, 1946; October 28, 1948.

40. *Arizona Daily Star*, October 24, 1948.

41. Frank Leslie, "The Biggest Show in the West," October 10, 1949, Western Ways Collection, Box 82, File 1603, Arizona Historical Society. See also *Tombstone Epitaph*, October 27, 1949.

42. *Tombstone Epitaph*, September 7, 1950.

43. *Dodge City Globe*, November 11 and 16, 1957; March 23, July 26, 1960.

44. Barson, "TV Westerns," 57–64; Parks, *Western Hero*.

45. *Arizona Daily Star*, May 5, 1961; John Gilchriese, "Governor Fannin's Address at the Dedication of Tombstone as a National Historical Site," September 30, 1962, Pamphlet 5, SCUAL.

46. *Tombstone Epitaph*, March 12, 1959.

47. Barson, "TV Westerns," 60; Hutton, "Celluloid Lawman,"

48. Barabas and Barabas, *Gunsmoke*, 152.

49. Weeks to Howard Meigan, December 15, 1952, *Gunsmoke*, Correspondence File, 1988.2.66, Document Box, 55i, BHMA.

50. Cave to Sidney Garfield, January 29, 1953, *Gunsmoke* Correspondence File, 1988.2.66, Document Box 55i, BHMA.

51. Weeks to Bud Tenerani, July 10, 1956, BHMA.

52. *Kansas City Times*, August 1, 1958.

53. Pearman, "Earp, Dillon and Co.," 68; *Dodge City Daily Globe*, November 11, 1959; Bassett to Pearman, March 31, 1960, Publicity News Stunts File, 1988.2.24, Document Box 55c, BHMA.

54. *Tombstone Epitaph*, February 19, 1959, and March 23, 1961;. See also Hollister, "Trip to a Tough Town," 13.

55. *Tombstone Epitaph*, September 3, 1959.

56. David Dole to R. E. Driscoll, June 6, 1951, and Leo Burnett Co. to George Hunter, June 7, 1959, File 96.1.7, DPA.

57. *Black Hills Weekly*, June 27, 1951. See also Hoadly Dean press release, June 11, 1951, File 96.1.25, DPA.

58. *Dodge City Globe*, January 27, 1958.

59. *Dodge City Globe*, September 18, 1958. See also Mitchell Ferguson to Merchants and Tourism Publicity Committee, n.d.; George Weeks to Ron Roberts, September 23, 1958, CBS Publicity Jaunt File, 1988, 2.18, Document Box 55c, BHMA.

60. George Voss to CBS, n.d., *Gunsmoke* Correspondence File 1988.2.7, Document Box 55i, BHMA.

61. Thad Sandstorm to Frank Stanton, President, CBS, March 11, 1976, Document Box 55i, BHMA; Barabas and Barabas, *Gunsmoke*, 124–25; *Topeka Daily Capital*, April 3, 1976.

62. *Tombstone Epitaph*, April 2, 1959.

63. Minutes, Chamber of Commerce Meeting, May 17, 1949, 96.1.7, DPA.

64. *Chicago Tribune*, June 25, 1961.

65. Minutes of the Deadwood Chamber of Commerce, May 17, 1949, 96.1.7, DPA; *Tombstone Epitaph*, April 27 and May 4, 1950.

66. *Tombstone Epitaph*, September 23, 1949; March 3, 1951.

67. Olsson, *Welcome to Tombstone*, 77–78.

68. *Tombstone Epitaph*, August 8, 1955.

69. *Tombstone Epitaph*, April 5, 1962.

70. *Tombstone Epitaph*, October 10, 1963; Helldorado Program, 1964, SCUAL.

71. *Tombstone Epitaph*, July 25, 1963.

72. Barabas and Barabas, *Gunsmoke*, 130.

73. *Tombstone Epitaph*, June 29 and October 19, 1961.

74. *Tombstone Epitaph*, May 5 and 8, 1961.

75. Quoted in *Tombstone Epitaph*, July 16, 1953.

76. *Tombstone Epitaph*, December 16, 1954.

77. Helldorado Program, 1957 and 1965, SCUAL; *Tombstone Epitaph*, August 22, 1975.

78. *Howdy*, 154; "Welcome to the Twin Cities of the Black Hills," 1961, Deadwood and Lead Chambers of Commerce, South Dakota Historical Society Archives; Tombstone promotional pamphlets, SCUAL.

79. *Tombstone Epitaph*, January 1, 1959; and *Black Hills Weekly*, August 3, 1955.

80. *Tombstone, Arizona, Community Profile*; *Tombstone Epitaph*, September 27, 1962 (quotations).

81. Robertson to Bassett, March 25, 1960, Publicity Clippings and Correspondence File 1988.2.48, Document Box 55f, BHMA (quotations); Mike Chegwyn to Robert Eagan, January 5, 1981, Robert Eagan Papers, Box 6, Denver Public Library; Waters, *Earp Brothers*, 3 (quotation), 41.

82. *Tombstone Epitaph*, April 20, 1961 (quotations); *Black Hills Weekly*, April 1, 1958.

CHAPTER 8

1. *Deadwood Telegram*, August 2, 1926; February 10, 1927; *Black Hills Weekly*, September 15, 1927.

2. *Black Hills Weekly*, October 2, 1930, and October 9, 1930.

3. *Black Hills Weekly*, October 9, 1930.

4. *Black Hills Weekly*, June 29, 1934; *Rapid City Journal*, February 19, 1950 (quotation).

5. "Deadwood: Historic Gold Camp," unidentified clipping, n.d., South Dakota State Archives; "Points of Outstanding Interest . . . City of Deadwood," 1934, File 96.1.24, DPA.

6. *Black Hills Weekly*, July 12, 1961; Deadwood site designation report, n.d., Deadwood Preservation Records, South Dakota State Archives (quotations).

7. National Register of Historic Places Inventory—Nomination Form 1966, 2, South Dakota State Archives.

8. *Lead-Deadwood Daily Call*, September 16, 1972; *Rapid City Journal*, February 22, 1975.

9. State Historical Preservation, "Report on Historic Preservation and Restoration in Deadwood," 1–3; Dennis, "Gambling as a Tool."

10. *Dodge City Daily Globe*, December 12, 1929; April 21, 1930.

11. *Dodge City Daily Globe*, June 25, 1930. For fears of losing their frontier past in western towns, see Athearn, *Mythic West*, 43–63.

12. Beeson, "Museum" transcription in Beeson Papers, Box 1B, BHMA (quotation); *Dodge City Daily Globe*, January 11, 1933.

13. Beeson to Mrs. Earp, January 16, 1934, quoted in Beeson to Frank Warren, June 6, 1934, Beeson Papers, Box 1A, 1996.24.1, BHMA; *Dodge City Daily Globe*, January 30, 1935 (quotation).

14. Beeson, "Beeson Museum," January 24, 1939, Beeson Papers, Box 1B, BHMC.

15. Beeson to Walter Campbell, June 6, 1951; Campbell to Beeson, June 13, 1951, Beeson Papers, Box 1A, BHMA.

16. *The Corral* promotional pamphlet, n.d., Box 1B, BHMA.

17. *Dodge City Daily Globe*, January 18, 1935 (quotation); March 3, 1942.

18. *Dodge City Daily Globe*, April 26, 1946.

19. *Dodge City Daily Globe*, February 28, March 14, 21, and May 27, 1947; Boot Hill, Inc., Annual Report, 1953, 2, Jaycee Scrapbook 7968M, BHMA; "Operations of Boot Hill Museum and Front Street," Jaycees Records, 7754, 2, Box 81, BHMA.

20. "Operations of Boot Hill Museum and Front Street," Jaycee Records, 7754, 2, Box 81, BHMA. See also "Digest in the Field of Trade Promotion," Dodge City Jaycees, Scrapbook 79966d; *Boot Hill Bulletin*, August 23, 1954, Boot Hill File Box 59A; Boot Hill Museum, Inc., Annual Report, 1953, 3, Jaycee Scrapbook 7968M, BHMA.

21. *Dodge City Daily Globe*, November 3, 1952; *Boot Hill Bulletin*, August 23, 1954, Boot Hill File Box 59A, BHMA.

22. "Operations of Boot Hill Museum and Front Street," Jaycee Records, 7754, 2, Box 81, BHMA; *Boot Hill Bulletin*, August 23, 1954, Boot Hill File Box 59A, BHMA.

23. Unidentified clipping, n.d., and *Dodge City Daily Globe*, n.d., Boot Hill Research File, KHC, Dodge City.

24. *High Plains Journal*, February 10 and March 20, 1955.

25. "Cowboy Hall of Fame: Dodge City," Cowboy Shrine File, 1988.2.10, Document Box 55B, BHMA.

26. "Dodge City the Cowboy Capital," typescript, BHMA.

27. *Garden City Telegram*, clipping, n.d., BHMA.

28. *Hutchinson News-Herald*, April 16, 1955.

29. *High Plains Journal*, April 28, 1955; Ruth McMillion to Dodge City Chamber of Commerce, April 18, 1955, Cowboy Shrine File—1955, 1988.2.10, Document Box 55B, BHMA.

30. *Kansas City Kansan*, April 18, 1955; *Kansas City Times*, April 19, 1955.

31. *Dodge City Daily Globe*, April 30, 1955.

32. Building and Location Committee, Cowboy Capital, Inc., to Citizens and Voters of Ford County, February 29, 1956, Cowboy Capital Collection, May 1, 1956, to 1959, 1988.2.17, Document Box 55C, BHMA.

33. Yost to Gordon Morgan, December 12, 1955, BHMA.

34. Building and Location Committee, Cowboy Capital, Inc., to Citizens and Voters of Ford County, February 29, 1956, Cowboy Capital Collection, May 1, 1956, to 1959, 1988.2.17 Document Box 55C, BHMA.

35. Building and Location Committee, Cowboy Capital, Inc., to Directors, Cowboy Capital Project, n.d., BHMA.

36. George Weeks to John Barrow and Associates, June 19, 1956, Cowboy Capital Collection, BHMA.

37. *Dodge City Daily Globe*, March 22, 1956; Vaughn Kimball to John Drake, October 2, 1956, Cowboy Capital Collection, May 1, 1956, to 1959, 1988.2.17, Documents Box 55C, and "Facts" (quotations), BHMA.

38. *Dodge City Daily Globe*, September 17, 1957.

39. Unidentified clipping, n.d., Front Street Project, 1958, Box 59A, BHMA.

40. *Dodge City Daily Globe*, December 14, 1957. See also Boot Hill Museum, Inc., Annual Report, 1958, 7, Jaycee Scrapbook 7968M, BHMA.

41. Annual Report, 1958, BHMA; *Dodge City Daily Globe*, February 29, 1959.

42. Pearman, "For Fifteen Years," 35; Denney, "The Town 'Gunsmoke' Made Prosperous," 27.

43. *Topeka Daily Capital*, April 3, 1976; *Wichita Eagle*, May 26, 1978.

44. *Dodge City Daily Globe*, December 14, 1977. See also *Wichita Eagle*, May 26, 1978.

45. Byrne-Dodge, "Requiem for a Tourist Trap," 64.

46. Ibid.

47. *Los Angeles Times*, April 26, 1931.

48. Cole to Douglas Martin, October 17, 1931, Cole Papers, SCUAL; Hosmer, *Preservation Comes of Age*, 368; Horgan, "Report on Tombstone, Az," October, 1936; ADLAPR.

49. Neasham, Special Report on the Proposed Historic Site of Tombstone, Arizona, May, 1941, Arizona State Park Archives, State Historic Preservation Office (quotation); Arizona Sites Survey Department, "The Advance of the Frontier," 1943, 72 FA 13.2, ADLAPR.

50. *Arizona Daily Star*, May 2, 1933; *Douglas Daily Dispatch*, November 2, 1931.

51. *Tombstone Epitaph*, February 4, 1937; Cole to Governor Stanford, February 4, 1937; Arizona Governor's Files, Box 9, F10, ADLAPR (quotation).

52. *Tombstone Epitaph*, March 14, 1946.

53. Radio Interview Transcript, KSUN, Bisbee, February 7, 1950. Tombstone Courthouse State Historic Park Archives; *Tombstone Epitaph*, October 13, 1949.

54. *Tombstone Epitaph*, October 6, 1949 (quotation); January 26, 1950.

55. *Tombstone Epitaph*, October 6 and October 13, 1949.

56. Radio Interview Transcript, KSUN, Bisbee, February 7, 1950, Tombstone Courthouse State Historical Park Archives (hereinafter TCSHPA).

57. *Tombstone Epitaph*, February 7, 1950.

58. Rath to Izard, February 14, 1950, TCSHPA; Reed to Director, May 23, 1950, TCSHPA.

59. Quoted in *Tombstone Epitaph*, January 26, 1950.

60. *New York Times*, January 24, 1950.

61. *Tombstone Epitaph*, February 12, 1953; Radio Interview Transcript, KSUN, Bisbee, February 7, 1950, TCSHPA; Reed to Director, May 23, 1950, TCSHPA.

62. C. M. Palmer, Annual Report of Tombstone Restoration Commission, December 21, 1950, TCSHPA. See also *Tombstone Epitaph*, July 6 and December 28, 1950; Edna Landin to Governor Howard Pyle, January 12, 1954, Governor's Files, Box 120c, F17, ADLAPR.

63. C. M. Palmer, "A Few Suggestions for Tombstone Restoration," January 1, 1951, TCSHPA.

64. *Tombstone Epitaph*, February 18, 1954, and April 4, 1954; Tombstone Restoration Zoning Ordinance, No. 146, Tombstone File, TCSHPA. See also Landin to Governor Pyle, February 23, 1954, Governor's Files, Box 120c, F17, ADLARP; Garrett and Garrison, *Plan for the Creation*, 25.

65. *Tombstone Epitaph*, April 1, 1954.

66. Barnes, "Tombstone," 7; Landin to Governor Pyle, February 26, 1954, Governor's Files, Box 120c, F17, ADLAPR; Helldorado Program, 1979, SCUAL.

67. Pyle to Landin, January 18, 1954, quoted in Landin to Pyle, February 26, 1954, Governor's Files, Box 120c, F17, ADLAPR; Landin to McCarthy, October 27, 1958, TCSHPA; *Tombstone Epitaph*, March 30, 1961 (quotation).

68. Landin to Utley, February 2, 1958, TCSHPA, quoted in Landin to Roy Appleman, May 30, 1959, TCSHPA; Appleman to Landin, June 9, 1959, TCSHPA; Utley, Report on National Survey of Historic Sites, March 18, 1958, Arizona State Park Archives, State Historic Preservation Office, Phoenix (quotations).

69. *Arizona Republic*, November 18, 1957.

70. *Tombstone Epitaph*, July 27, 1961; February 11, 1962.

71. Quoted in *Tombstone Epitaph*, September 20, 1962. See also Beatrice Ordnez to Governor Fannin, November 27, 1962, Fannin Papers, State Parks File, ADLAPR; Jeanne Devere to Arthur Lee, December 6, 1962, Fannin Papers, ADLAPR.

72. Landin to Governor Fannon, September 5, 1962, ADLAPR.

73. State Landmark Committee to Fannin, December 15, 1962, Governor's Papers, ADLAPR. See also Landin to Fannin, December 26, 1962, ADLAPR; Fannin to Landin, December 12, 1962, ADLAPR; *Arizona Republic*, January 5, 1963.

74. *Arizona Daily Star*, February 1, 1964; Barnes, "Tombstone," 8; "Tombstone's Love," *True West* 30 (March 1983): 30.

75. Garrett and Garrison, *Plan for the Creation*, 39–57.

CONCLUSION

1. *True West Magazine* 61:2 (February 2014): 70, and 62:2 (February 2015): 82.

2. *Wichita Eagle*, May 29, 1969; *Dodge City Daily Globe*, February 24, 1994.

3. *Dodge City Daily Globe*, March 2, 1994; *Hutchinson News*, March 6, 1994.

4. *Dodge City Daily Globe*, March 4, 1994.

5. In 1980 over 75 percent of the Tombstone workforce depended directly on tourism. Wallace, Cox, and Hitzeman, *Tombstone*, 16; Wallace, Cox, and Hitzeman, *Tourists in Tombstone*.

6. *Arizona Republic*, May 24, 1996.

7. *Rapid City Journal*, May 16, 1990.

8. *Arizona Daily Star*, August 19, 1996.

9. *Pierre Daily Capital Journal*, April 30, 1990.

10. *New York Times*, January 29, 1998.

✐ Bibliography

ARCHIVAL SOURCES

Deadwood

Adams Museum Archives, Deadwood, South Dakota
    Accessions Register
    Calamity Jane File
    Hickok, Wild Bill, File
Days of '76 Museum Files, Deadwood, South Dakota
Deadwood Chamber of Commerce, Deadwood, South Dakota
Deadwood Preservation Archives, Deadwood, South Dakota
Deadwood Public Library, Deadwood, South Dakota
    Deadwood Collection, Oral History Records
South Dakota State Archives, Pierre, South Dakota
Preservation Office Records, Deadwood Files

Dodge City

Boot Hill Museum Archives, Dodge City, Kansas
    Beeson, Merritt, Papers
    Boot Hill Jaycee Records
    Boot Hill Research Files
    Bryson, Lois, Collection
    Cowboy Shrine Records
    Gunsmoke Correspondence File
    Last Round-Up Files
    Warner Brothers Collection
Denver Public Library, Western History Department, Denver, Colorado
    Eagan, Robert, Papers
Kansas Heritage Center, Dodge City, Kansas
    Boot Hill File
    Gunsmoke Files

Last Round-Up File
Tourism File
Kansas Historical Society, Topeka
    Dodge City Files
Los Angeles Museum of Natural History, Los Angeles, California
    Hart, William S., Letters

Tombstone

Arizona Department of Library, Archives, and Public Records, Phoenix, Arizona
    Arizona Governor Files
    Tombstone Ephemeral File
Arizona Historical Foundation, Arizona State University, Phoenix, Arizona
    Goldwater, Barry, Papers
Arizona Historical Society, Tucson, Arizona
    Anderson, Andy, Biographical File
    Noon, Adolphus Henry, file
    Tombstone Ephemera File
    Western Ways Collection
Arizona State Park Archives, State Historic Preservation Office, Phoenix
Arizona State University, Arizona Collection, Department of Archives and Manuscripts, Tempe, Arizona
Huntington Library, San Marino, California
    Lake, Stuart, Papers
Tombstone Courthouse State Park Archives, Tombstone, Arizona
University of Arizona, Tucson, Arizona: Special Collections
    Burns, Walter Noble, Papers
    Cole, Walter, Papers
    Cosulich, Bernice, Papers
    Hancock, John C., File
    Kelly, William, Papers
    Staunton, William F., Papers

INTERVIEWS

Smith, Darken, interview with Kevin M. Britz. Dodge City, Kansas, October 14, 1998.
Wolf, Mark, interview with Kevin M. Britz. Deadwood, South Dakota, July 22, 1996.

BOOKS, ARTICLES, THESES, AND DISSERTATIONS

Adams, Andy. *The Log of a Cowboy*. Boston: Houghton Mifflin Company, 1903.
Aikman, Duncan. *Calamity Jane and the Lady Wildcats*. New York: Blue Ribbon Books, 1927.
———. "Deadwood the Dreadful." *American Mercury* 12, no. 47 (November 1927): 342–43.

Anderson, Harry. "Deadwood: An Effort at Stability." *Montana The Magazine of Western History* 20, no. 1 (January 1970): 41–47.

Anderson, Joseph. *Buried Hickok.* College Station, Tex.: Creative Publishing Company, 1980.

Anonymous. *Some History of Lawrence County.* Pierre, S.Dak.: State Publishing Company, 1891.

Arizona and Its Resources, Phoenix: Reuch and Rich, 1899.

Athearn, Robert. *The Mythic West in Twentieth-Century America.* Lawrence: University of Kansas Press, 1986.

Ayers, George. "Lawrence County Roads and How It Was Done." *Pahasapa Quarterly* 5 (December 1915): 9–15.

Badger, Joseph E., Jr. *The Old Boy of Tombstone; or, Wagering a Life on a Card.* New York: Beadle's Dime Library, 1883.

Baldwin, George, ed. *The Black Hills Illustrated: A Terse Description of Conditions Past and Present of America's Greatest Mineral Belt.* Deadwood: Association. 1904.

Barabas, SuZanne and Gabor Barabas. *Gunsmoke: A Complete History and Analysis of the Legendary Broadcast Series.* Jefferson, N.C., and London: McFarland and Company, 1990.

Barnes, Elinor J. "Tombstone: An Adventure into History." *Arizona Review of Business and Public Administration* 14, no. 10 (October 1965): 4–9, 23.

Barra, Allen. *Inventing Wyatt Earp: His Life and Many Legends.* New York: Carrol and Graf Publishers, 1998.

Barson, Michael. "The TV Westerns." In *TV Genres,* edited by Brian G. Rose, 57–71. Westport, Conn., and London: Greenwood Press, 1985.

Barthel, Diane. *Historic Preservation: Collective Memory and Historical Identity.* New Brunswick, N.J.: Rutgers University Press, 1996.

Barthes, Roland. *Mythologies.* New York: Hill and Wang. 1998.

Baur, John. *Health Seekers of Southern California.* San Marino, Calif.: Huntington Library, 1959.

Bechdolt, Frederick R. *When the West Was Young.* New York: Century Company, 1922.

Bellamy, Paul E., and G. D. Seymour. *A Guide to the Black Hills.* Rapid City, S.Dak.: Black Hills Transportation Company, 1927.

Benjamin, Walter. *Illuminations: Essays and Reflections.* Edited by Hannah Arendt. New York: Schocken Books, 1968.

———. *Reflections: Essays, Aphorisms, Autobiographical Writings.* Edited by Peter Demetz. New York: Harcourt Brace Jovanovich, 1978.

Bennett, Estelline. *Old Deadwood Days.* Lincoln: University of Nebraska Press, 1982 (reprint of 1928 edition).

Bird, Robert Montgomery. *Nick of the Woods; or, Jibbenainosay: A Tale of Kentucky.* Philadelphia: Carey, Lea and Blanchard, 1837.

Bishop, William Henry. "Across Arizona in 1883." *Harper's New Monthly Magazine* 65, no. 10 (March 1883): 489–90.

Blodgett, Peter J., ed. *Motoring West: Automobile Pioneers, 1900–1909.* Norman: University of Oklahoma Press, 2015.

Bluestone, George. "The Changing Cowboy: From Dime Novel to Dollar Film." *Western Humanities Review* 14, no. 2 (Summer 1960): 331–37.

Bodner, John. *Remaking America: Public Memory, Commemoration, and Patriotism in the Twentieth Century.* Princeton, N.J.: Princeton University Press, 1992.

Bogdanovich, Pete. *John Ford.* Berkeley: University of California Press, 1978.

Bold, Christine. *Selling the Wild West: Popular Western Fiction, 1860–1960.* Bloomington and Indianapolis: Indiana University Press. 1987.

Boorstin, Daniel. *The Image: A Guide to Pseudo-Events in America.* New York: Vintage Books, 1992.

Boyer, Mary G. *Arizona in Literature.* Glendale, Calif.: Arthur H. Clark Company, 1935.

Branch, Douglas. *The Cowboy and His Interpreters.* New York: Cooper Square Publishers, 1926.

Breakenridge, William. *Helldorado: Bringing the Law to the Mesquite.* Boston: Houghton and Mifflin, 1928.

Brimmer, Leonora. "Boothill Graveyard." *Arizona Highways* 24, no. 1 (January 1948): 12–17.

Britz, Kevin. "'Boot Hill Burlesque': The Frontier Cemetery as Tourist Attraction in Tombstone, Arizona, and Dodge City, Kansas." *Journal of Arizona History* 44, no. 3 (Autumn 2003): 211–42.

———. "Deadwood's Days of '76." *South Dakota History* 40, no. 1 (Spring 2010): 52–84.

———. "Tombstone, Arizona." In *American Tourism: Constructing a National Tradition,* edited by J. Mark Souther and Nicholas Dagen Bloom, 261–69. Chicago: Columbia College, 2012.

———. "'A True to Life Reproduction': The Origins of Tombstone's Helldorado Celebration." *Journal of Arizona History* 42, no. 1 (Winter 2001): 369–408.

Brown, Dona. *Inventing New England: Regional Tourism in the Nineteenth Century.* Washington, D.C: Smithsonian Institution Press, 1995.

Brown, Jesse, and A. M. Willard. *The Black Hills Trails: A History of the Struggles of the Pioneers in the Winning of the Black Hills.* Rapid City. S.Dak.: *Rapid City Journal,* 1924.

Bruner, Edward M. *Culture on Tour: Ethnographies of Travel.* Chicago: University of Chicago Press, 2005.

Buntline, Ned. *Wild Bill's Last Trail.* New York: Street and Smith, 1894.

Bureau of Government Research. *A Comprehensive Planning Survey of Dodge City. Kansas.* Lawrence: University of Kansas, 1950.

Burnett, William R. *Saint Johnson.* New York: MacVeagh, 1930.

Burns, Walter Noble. *Tombstone: An Iliad of the Southwest.* Garden City, N.Y.: Doubleday, Page and Company. 1927.

Butler, B. S. *History of Tombstone Mines.* Bulletin 143. Phoenix: Arizona Bureau of Mines, January 1, 1938.

Butler, Thomas, ed. *Memory, History, Culture, and the Mind.* Oxford: Basil Blackwell, 1989.

Byrne-Dodge, Teresa. "Requiem for a Tourist Trap." *Americana* 11, no. 6 (January/ February 1984): 62–66.

Calder. Jenni. *There Must Be a Lone Ranger.* London: Hamish Hamilton, 1974.

Carey, Henry. *The Thrilling Story of Famous Boot Hill.* Dodge City, Kans.: Brick Printers, 1937.

Carr, Harry. *The West Is Still Wild.* Boston and New York: Houghton Mifflin, 1932.

Carson, Gerald. "Goggles and Side Curtains." *American Heritage* 18, no. 3 (April 1967): 32–39, 108–109.

Carson, Lewis W. *Ben, the Trapper; or, The Mountain Demon: A Tale of the Black Hills.* New York: Beadle and Adams, 1875.

Casey, Robert. *The Black Hills and Their Incredible Characters.* New York: Bobbs-Merrill, 1949.

Cawelti, John. *Adventure, Mystery and Romance: Formula Stories as Art and Culture.* Chicago: University of Chicago Press, 1976.

———. *The Six Gun Mystique.* 2nd ed. Bowling Green, Ohio: Bowling Green State University Press, 1984.

Christensen, Bonnie. *Red Lodge and the Mythic West: Coal Miners to Cowboys.* Lawrence: University Press of Kansas, 2002.

Clark, Cushman. "The Society of Black Hills Pioneers." In *Some History of Lawrence County.* Pierre, S.Dak.: State Publishing Company, 1891.

Clavin, Tom. *Dodge City: Wyatt Earp, Bat Masterson, and the Wickedest Town in the American West.* New York: St. Martin's Press, 2017.

Clements, Eric. "Boom and Bust in the Mining West." *Journal of the West* 35, no. 4 (October 1996): 40–54.

Clum, John. *Helldorado, 1879–1929.* Tombstone: *Tombstone Epitaph,* 1930.

———. "It All Happened in Tombstone." *Arizona Historical Review* 2, no. 3 (October 1929): 46–72.

Cody, William. *The Life of Buffalo Bill or, The Life and Adventures of William F. Cody, as Told by Himself.* Santa Barbara, Calif.: Narrative Press, 2001.

Cohen, Eric "Rethinking the Sociology of Tourism." *Annals of Tourism Research* 6, no. 1 (January-March 1979): 18–35.

———. "The Sociology of Tourism." *Annual Review of Sociology* 10 (1984): 373–92

Connerton, Paul. *How Societies Remember.* Cambridge: Cambridge University Press, 1989.

Cooper, Courtney Ryley. "Another Redskin Bit the Dust!" *Saturday Evening Post* 2, no. 5 (August 2, 1930): 32, 106.

Coursey, O. W. *Beautiful Black Hills.* Mitchell, S.Dak.: Educator Supply Company, 1926.

————. *Wild Bill*. Mitchell. S.Dak.: Educator Supply Company, 1926.

Crockett, David. *A Narrative of the Life of David Crockett Written by Himself.* Philadelphia: E. L. Carey and A. Hart, 1834.

Dahl, Curtis. *Robert Montgomery Bird.* New York: Twayne Publishers, 1963.

Davis, Susan. *Parades and Power, Street Theatre in Nineteenth Century Philadelphia.* Philadelphia: Temple University Press, 1986.

Deadwood Board of *Trade. Deadwood, Metropolis of the Black Hills.* Deadwood: Board of Trade, 1892.

Deadwood Business Club. *Deadwood of Today.* Deadwood: Deadwood Business Club, 1903.

————. *Souvenir Book of Deadwood, Lawrence County, South Dakota.* Deadwood: *Deadwood Daily Pioneer Times,* 1915.

Deadwood: What to See and How to Do It. Pamphlet. Deadwood: n.p., n.d.

DeArment, Robert K. *Bat Masterson: The Man and the Legend.* Norman: University of Oklahoma Press, 1979.

————. *Gunfighter in Gotham: Bat Masterson's New York City Years.* Norman: University of Oklahoma Press, 2013.

Denney, James. "The Town 'Gunsmoke' Made Prosperous." *Grit* (October 8, 1972): 27.

Denning, Michael. *Mechanic Accents: Dime Novels and Working-Class Culture in America.* London: Verso, 1987.

Dennis, Michelle. "Gambling as a Tool for Funding Small Town Preservation: A Case Study of Deadwood, South Dakota." MA thesis, University of Oregon, 1995.

Dinan, John A. *The Pulp Western: A Popular History of the Western Fiction Magazine in America.* No. 2.1.0. Evans Studies in the Philosophy and Criticism of Literature. San Bernardino, Calif.: Borgo Press, 1983.

Dodge City and Ford County, Kansas, 1888: A Brief Statement of Its Climate, Soil, Products, Business, Opportunities, School and Church Privileges. Dodge City, Kans.: *Dodge City Tunes,* Spring Edition, 1888.

Dodge City Business Club. *Dodge City and Ford County, Kansas: A History of the Old and a Story of the New.* Larned, Kans.: Tucker-Vernon Publishing Company, 1911.

DuFran, D. Dee Dora. *The Low Down on Calamity Jane.* Stickney, S.Dak.: Argus Printers, 1981 (reprint of 1932 edition).

Du Puy, William A. "Tombstone Quickens to the New Deal: Hope of Silver Stirs the Mining Camp Where 'Two-Gun' Men Ran Wild 50 Years Ago." *New York Times Magazine* (April 1, 1934): 23.

Durham, Phillip. "A General Classification." *Huntington Library Quarterly* 17, no. 3 (May 1954): 287–89.

Dworkin, Mark J. *American Mythmaker: Walter Noble Burns and the Legends of Billy the Kid, Wyatt Earp, and Joaquin Murrieta.* Norman: University of Oklahoma Press, 2015.

Dykstra, Robert R. *The Cattle Towns.* Lincoln: University of Nebraska Press, 1968.

Dykstra, Robert R., and Ann Manfra. *Dodge City and the Birth of the Wild West.* Lawrence: University Press of Kansas, 2016.

———. "Overdosing on Dodge City." *Western Historical Quarterly* 27, no. 4 (Winter 1996): 505–14.

Eco, Umberto. *Travels in Hyperreality.* New York: Harcourt, Brace and Company, 1973.

Ellis, Edward S. *The Fighting Trapper; or, Kit Carson to the Rescue: A Tale of Wild Life on the Plains.* New York: Frank Starr, 1874.

———. *On the Plains; or, The Race for Life: A Story of Adventure among the Black Hills.* New York: Beadle and Adams, 1863.

———. *Seth Jones, or, The Captives of the Frontier.* New York: Beadle and Company, 1860.

Estleman, Loren D. *The Wister Trace: Assaying Classic Western Fiction.* 2nd ed. Norman: University of Oklahoma Press, 2014.

Etrick, Carl. *Dodge City Semi-Centennial Souvenir.* Dodge City: Etrick Publishers, 1921.

———. *The Last Round Up.* Dodge City: Carl Etrick Printers, 1929.

Etulain, Richard. "Bronco Billy, William S. Hart, and Tom Mix." In *The Hollywood West: Lives of Film Legends Who Shaped It,* edited by Richard M. Etulain and Glenda Riley, 1–19. Golden, Colo.: Fulcrum Publishing, 2001.

———. "The Historical Development of the Western." In *The Popular Western: Essays Toward a Definition,* edited by Richard Etulain and Michael T. Marsden, 17–26. Bowling Green, Ohio: Bowling Green University Popular Press, 1974.

———. *The Life and Legends of Calamity Jane.* Norman: University of Oklahoma Press, 2014.

———. "Riding the Point: The Historical Development of the Western." In *The Popular Western: Essays toward a Definition,* edited by Richard Etulain and Michael T. Marsden. Bowling Green, Ohio: Bowling Green Popular Press, 1974.

———. *Telling Western Stories: From Buffalo Bill to Larry McMurtry.* Albuquerque: University of New Mexico Press, 1999.

Etulain, Richard, and Michael T. Marsden, eds. *The Popular Western: Essays toward a Definition.* Bowling Green, Ohio: Bowling Green University Press, 1974.

Etulain, Richard, and Glenda Riley, eds. *The Hollywood West: Lives of Film Legends Who Shaped It.* Golden, Colo.: Fulcrum Publishing, 2001.

Fabian, Ann. "History for the Masses: Commercializing the Western Past." In *Under an Open Sky: Rethinking America's Western Past,* edited by William Cronon, George Files, and Jay Gitlin, 223–38. New York and London: W. W. Norton and Company, 1992.

Faehnrich, Denise. "Edward L. Senn: Deadwood's Fiery Crusader." MA thesis, University of South Dakota, 1997.

Faragher, John Mack. *Daniel Boone: The Life and Legend of an American Pioneer.* New York: Henry Holt and Company, 1992.

Filler, Louis. "Wolfville." *New Mexico Quarterly Review* 13, no. 1 (1943): 35–49.

Finger, Charles. *Adventure under Sapphire Skies*. New York: William Morrow and Company, 1931.

Flagg, James. *Boulevards All the Way—Maybe*. New York: George Doran Company, 1925.

Folson, James K. *The American Western Novel*. New Haven, Conn.: College and University Press, 1966.

Ford County Historical Society. *Dodge City and Ford County, Kansas, 1870–1920: Pioneer Histories and Stories*. Dodge City: Ford County Historical Society, 1996.

Foy, Eddie, and Alvin F. Harlow. *Clowning through Life*. New York: E. P. Dutton and Company, 1928.

Franz, Joe B., and Julian Choate, Jr. *The American Cowboy: The Myth and Reality*. Norman: University of Oklahoma Press, 1955.

Fredericksson, Kristine. *American Rodeo: From Buffalo Bill to Big Business*. College Station: Texas A&M Press, 1981.

French, Philip. *Westerns: Aspects of a Movie Genre*. New York: Viking Press, 1974.

Frothingham, Robert. *Trails through the Golden West*. New York: Robert M. McBride and Company, 1932.

Furlong, Leslie. "Gold Dust and Buckskins: An Analysis of Calamity Jane as a Symbol of Luck and Womanhood in the Black Hills." PhD dissertation, University of Virginia, 1993.

Gardiner, A. H. *The Main Street through Arizona*. Tombstone: Tombstone Commercial Club, 1924.

Garrett, Billy, and James W. Garrison. *Plan for the Creation of a Historic Environment in Tombstone, Arizona*. Tombstone: Tombstone Restoration Commission, 1972.

Gillis, John, ed. *Commemorations: The Politics of National Identity*. Princeton, N.J.: Princeton University Press, 1994.

Glassberg, David. *American Historic Pageantry: The Uses of Tradition in the Early Twentieth Century*. Chapel Hill: University of North Carolina Press, 1990.

Goodstone, Tony, ed. *The Pulps*. New York: Chelsea House Publishers, 1970.

Guinn, Jeff. *The Last Gunfight: The Real Story of the Shootout at the O.K. Corral and How It Changed the American West*. New York: Simon and Schuster, 2011.

Halbwachs, Maurice. *The Collective Memory*. New York: Harper and Row, 1980.

Hall, Sharlot. "The Remaking of an Old Bonanza." *Out West* (December 1906): 239–40.

Hamer, David. *New Towns in the New World: Images and Perceptions of the Nineteenth-Century Urban Frontier*. New York: Columbia University Press, 1990.

Hamilton, William J. *Single Hand, the Comanche Attila; or, The Chaparral Rangers*. New York: Beadle and Adams, 1872.

Hart, William S. *My Life East and West*. New York: Benjamin Blom, 1968 (reprint of 1929 edition).

Harvey, Charles. "The Dime Novel in American Life." *Atlantic Monthly* 100, no. 7 (July 1907): 37–45.

Hattich, William. *Tombstone, in History, Romance and Wealth*. Tombstone: *Daily Prospector*, 1903.

Hayne, Donald, ed. *The Autobiography of Cecil B. DeMille*. Englewood Cliffs, N.J.: Prentice-Hall, 1959.

Herbert, Frank. *40 Years Prospecting and Mining in the Black Hills*. Rapid City, S.Dak.: *Rapid City Journal*, 1921.

Hobsbawn, Eric, and Terrence Ranger, eds. *The Invention of Tradition*. London: Cambridge University Press, 1983.

Holbrook, Stewart H. The Guy Who Named Tombstone." *American Mercury* 58, no. 246 (June 1944): 742–47.

Hollister, George. "Trip to a Tough Town." *Desert Magazine* 31, no. 2 (February 1968): 12–13.

Hosmer, Charles B., Jr. *Preservation Comes of Age: From Williamsburg to the National Trust, 1926–1949*. Charlottesville: University of Virginia Press, 1981.

Howdy. Dodge City: Strange and Hetzel Publishing, 1954.

Hutton, Paul. "Celluloid Lawman: Wyatt Earp Goes to Hollywood." *American West* 21, no. 3 (May–June 1984): 58–65.

i2 Environmental Consultants. *The Tombstone Heritage: A Description of Dominant Trends*. Phoenix: Office of Economic Planning and Development, 1974.

Ingraham, Prentiss. *Wild Bill, the Pistol Dead Shot; or, Dagger Don's Double*. New York: Beadle and Adams, 1882.

———. *Wild Bill, the Pistol Prince*. New York: Beadle and Adams, 1891.

Isenberg, Andrew C. *Wyatt Earp: A Vigilante Life*. New York: Hill and Wang, 2014.

Jackson, Donald. *Custer's Gold: The United Cavalry Expedition of 1874*. New Haven, N.J.: Yale University Press, 1966.

Jackson, Joseph Henry. "Speaking of Books." *Sunset* 61, no. 6 (December 1928): 4–6.

Jakle, John A. *The Tourist: Travel in Twentieth-Century North America*. Lincoln: University of Nebraska Press, 1985.

James, Ronald M. *Virginia City: Secrets of a Western Past*. Lincoln: University of Nebraska Press, 2012.

James, Ronald M., and Susan A. James. *A Short History of Virginia City*. Reno: University of Nevada Press, 2014.

Johannsen, Albert. *The House of Beadle and Adams and Its Nickel and Dime Novels: The Story of a Vanished Literature*. 2 vols. Norman: University of Oklahoma Press, 1950.

Johnson, Adrienne Rose. "Romancing the Dude Ranch, 1926–1947." *Western Historical Quarterly* 43, no. 4 (Winter 2012): 438–61.

Johnson, A. I. "Touring the Black Hills." *Pahasapa Quarterly* 9, no. 2 (June 1920).

Johnson, Stanley. "Top 10 True Western Towns of 2014." *True West* 61, no. 2 (February 2014): 68–84.

Jones, Billy M. *Health Seekers in the Southwest*. Norman: University of Oklahoma Press, 1967.

Jones, Daryl. "Clenched Teeth and Curses: Revenge and the Dime Novel Outlaw Hero." In *The Popular Western: Essays Toward a Definition*, edited by Richard

Etulain and Michael Marsden, 10–23. Bowling Green, Ohio: Bowling Green University Press, 1978.

———. *The Dime Novel Western.* Bowling Green, Ohio: Popular Press, 1978.

Judson, Edward. *The Red Warrior; or, Stella Delorme's Comanche Lover.* New York: Beadle and Adams, 1879.

Kammen, Michael. *Mystic Cords of Memory: The Transformation of Tradition in American Culture.* New York: Vintage Books, 1993.

Kappler, Charles J. "Fort Laramie Treaty." In *Indian Affairs: Laws and Treaties,* comp. Charles J. Kappler, 2:998-1003. 2 vols. Washington, D.C.: Government Printing Office, 1903–1904.

Kelly, William. "Helldorado!" *Progressive Arizona* 9, no. 4 (October 1929): 16, 28–29.

Kent, Thomas. *Interpretation and Genre: The Role of Generic Perception in the Study of Narrative Texts.* Lewisburg, Pa.: Bucknell University Press, 1986.

Kravetz, Robert E. *Health Seekers in Arizona.* Phoenix: Academy of Medical Sciences of the Maricopa Medical Society, 1988.

Kuykendall, W. L. *Frontier Days: A True Story of Striking Events on the Western Frontier.* N.p.: J. M. and H. L. Kuykendall, 1917.

Lake, Stuart. "Straight Shooting Dodge." *Saturday Evening Post* 202, no. 43 (April 26, 1930): 12–13.

———. *Wyatt Earp: Frontier Marshal.* New York: Houghton Mifflin Company, 1931 (reprint 1994).

Lancaster, Paul. "The Great American Motel." *American Heritage* 33, no. 4 (June/July 1982): 100–108.

Landin, Edna. "A Legend Lives." *Desert Magazine* 28, no. 1 (January 1965): 30–31.

Larson, Robert W. *Red Cloud: Warrior-Statesman of the Lakota Sioux.* Norman: University of Oklahoma Press, 1997.

Larson, Rupert. "Exploring a Once Wild and Woolly Town." *Progressive Arizona* 4, no. 5 (May 1927): 15–20, 29–30.

Lawrence County Historical Society. *Some History of Lawrence County.* Pierre, S.Dak.: State Publishing Company, 1981.

Lawson, W. B. *Dashing Diamond Dick; or, The Tigers of Tombstone.* New York: Street and Smith,1898.

Lazarus, Edward. *Black Hills, White Justice: The Sioux Nation versus the United States, 1775 to the Present.* New York: HarperCollins, 1991.

Lee, Bob, ed. *Gold, Gals, Guns, Guts.* Deadwood and Lead: Deadwood and Lead '76 Centennial, 1976.

Lee, Shebby. "Traveling the Sunshine State: The Growth of Tourism in South Dakota, 1914–1939." *South Dakota History* 19, no. 2 (Summer 1989): 194–223.

Leuchtenberg, William. *The Perils of Prosperity, 1914–1932.* Chicago: University of Chicago Press, 1958.

Lewis, Alfred Henry. "The Confessions of a Newspaper Man." *Human Life* (August 1906).

———. *Faro Nell and Her Friends.* New York: G. W. Dillingham Company, 1913.

————. *Sandburrs*. New York: Frederick A. Stokes Company, 1898.

————. *The Sunset Trail*. New York: A. S. Barnes and Company, 1905.

————. *Wolfville*. New York: Frederick A. Stokes Company, 1897.

————. *Wolfville Days*. New York: Frederick A. Stokes Company, 1902.

————. *Wolfville Folks*. New York: D. Applegate and Company, 1908.

Lipsitz, George, ed. *Time Passages: Collective Memory and American Popular Culture*. Minneapolis: University of Minnesota Press, 1990.

Little, E. C. "The Round Table of Dodge City." *Everybody's Magazine* 7, no. 5 (November 1902): 432–39.

Lockwood, Frank. *Pioneer Days in Arizona*. New York: Macmillan Company, 1932.

Love, Nat. *The Life and Adventures of Nat Love, Better Known in the Cattle Country as Deadwood Dick*. New York: Arno Press, 1968 (reprint of 1907 edition).

Lowenthal, David. *The Past Is a Foreign Country*. Cambridge: Cambridge University Press, 1985.

Lowther, Charles. *Dodge City, Kansas*. Philadelphia: Dorrance and Company, 1940.

MacCannell, Dean. *The Tourist: A New Theory of the Leisure Class*. New York: Schocken Books, 1976.

Maguire, Horatio N. *The Black Hills and American Wonderland*. Lakeside Library, 4th series, no. 82. Chicago: Donnelly, Lloyd and Company, 1877.

Mandat-Grancy, Edmond. *Cow-boys and Colonels: Narrative of a Journey across the Prairie and over the Black Hills of South Dakota*. London/New York: J. B. Lippincott Company, 1963 (facsimile of 1887 edition).

Manzo, Floumey D. "Alfred Henry Lewis: Western Story Teller." MA thesis, Texas Western College, 1966.

————. "Alfred Henry Lewis: Western Storyteller." *Arizona and the West* 10, no. 1 (Spring 1968): 5–24.

Marchand, Roland. *Advertising the American Dream: Making Way for Modernity, 1920–1940*. Berkeley: University of California Press, 1985.

Marietta, Jack D. and G. S. Rowe. *Troubled Experiment: Crime and Justice in Pennsylvania, 1682–1800*. Philadelphia: University of Pennsylvania Press, 2006.

Marks, Paula. *And Die in the West: The Story of the OK Corral Gunfight*. Norman: University of Oklahoma Press, 1989.

Masterson, Bat. *Famous Gunfighters of the Western Frontier* (1907). Olympic Valley, Calif.: Outbooks, 1978.

Mazzanovich, Anton. *Trailing Geronimo*. Los Angeles: Gem, 1926.

McClintock, James H. *Arizona: The Nation's Youngest Commonwealth with a Land of Ancient Culture*. Chicago: S. J. Clarke Publishing Company, 1916.

McClintock, John S. *Pioneer Days in the Black Hills*. Deadwood: John S. McClintock, 1939.

McCormack, Kara. *Imaging Tombstone: The Town Too Tough to Die*. Lawrence: University Press of Kansas, 2016.

McGrath, Roger. *Gunfighters, Highwaymen, and Vigilantes: Violence on the Frontier*. Berkeley: University of California Press, 1984.

McLaird, James. "Calamity Jane and Wild Bill: Myth and Reality." *Journal of the West* 37, no. 2 (April 1998): 23–32.

———. "Calamity Jane: The Life and the Legend." *South Dakota History* 24, no. 1 (Spring 1994): 1–18.

———. *Calamity Jane: The Woman and the Legend.* Norman: University of Oklahoma Press, 2005.

———. *Wild Bill Hickok and Calamity Jane: Deadwood Legends.* Pierre: South Dakota State Historical Society, 2008.

McNeil, Alex. *Total Television: A Comprehensive Guide to Programming from 1948 to the Present.* New York: Penguin Books. 1991.

Meringlo, Denise D. *Museums, Monuments, and National Parks: Toward a New Genealogy of Public History.* Amherst: University of Massachusetts Press, 2012.

Michael, Elliott. *Custerology: The Enduring Legacy of the Indian Wars and George Armstrong Custer.* Chicago: University of Chicago Press, 2007.

Miller, Joseph. "Here Lie the Bodies." *Arizona Highways* 14, no. 3 (March 1938): 18–19, 28–29.

Miller, Nyle H., and Joseph W. Snell, eds. *Why the West was Wild.* Topeka: Kansas State Historical Society, 1963.

Mitchell, Lee Clark. *Westerns: Making the Man in Fiction and Film.* Chicago: University of Chicago Press, 1996.

Monaghan, Jay. *The Great Rascal: The Life and Adventures of Ned Buntline.* Boston: Little, Brown and Company, 1952.

Morris, D. M. "Dodge City, Kansas." *Kansas Magazine* (September 1910): 89–97.

Moscardo, Gianna M., and Philip L. Pearce. "The Concept of Authenticity in Tourist Experiences." *Australian and New Zealand Journal of Sociology* 22, no. 1 (March 1986): 121–32.

———. "Historic Theme Parks: An Australian Experience in Authenticity." *Annals of Tourism Research* 13, no. 3 (1986): 467–79.

Moy, Frank. *Tombstone Epitaph Annual Resource Edition.* Tombstone, 1925.

Murbayer, Nell, "Saga of the Rootin' Tootin' Boothill Cemetery." *Magazine Tucson* 4, no. 7 (September 1951): 16–17.

Murdock, David Hamilton. *The American West: The Invention of a Myth.* Cardiff, UK: Welsh Academic Press, 2001.

Murphy, Mary. *Mining Cultures: Men, Women, and Leisure in Butte, 1914–41.* Urbana/Chicago: University of Illinois Press, 1997.

Myers, John Myers. *The Last Chance: Tombstone's Early Years.* New York: Dutton, 1950.

Nash, Gerald. *The American West in the Twentieth Century.* Albuquerque: University of New Mexico Press, 1977.

Nash, Roderick. *The Nervous Generation: American Thought, 1917–1930.* Chicago: Rand McNally and Company, 1970.

Nelson, Paula M. *After the West Was Won: Homesteaders and Town-Builders in Western South Dakota, 1900–1917.* Iowa City: University of Iowa Press, 1986.

Newson, Thomas. *Drama of Life in the Black Hills.* St. Paul, Minn.: Dodge and Larpenter, 1878.

Niven, Frederick. "An English Schoolboy and Deadwood Dick." *Living Age* 306 (August 7, 1920): 348–51.

Noel, Mary. *Villains Galore: The Heyday of the Popular Story Weekly.* New York: Macmillan Company, 1954.

Norkunas, Martha. *The Politics of Public Memory: Tourism, History and Ethnicity in Monterey, California.* Albany: State University of New York Press, 1993.

Olsson, Jan Olof. *Welcome to Tombstone.* London: Elek Books, 1956.

"Over Sunday in New Sharon." *Scribner's Monthly* 19, no. 5 (March 1880): 769–72.

Palmer, Daryl W. "Quivira, Coronado, and Kansas: A Formative Chapter in the Story of Kansans' Collective Memory." *Kansas History* 35, no. 4 (Winter 2012–13): 250–65.

Palmer, Dorothy G. "Ethel Maria: First Lady of Tombstone." *Arizona Highways* 34, no. 4 (April 1958): 30–34.

Para, Madeline Perrin, and Bert M. Fireman. *Arizona Pageant: A Short History of the 48th State.* Tempe: Arizona Historical Foundation, 1975.

Parker, Watson. *Deadwood: The Golden Years.* Lincoln: University of Nebraska Press, 1981.

———. *Gold in the Black Hills.* Norman: University of Oklahoma Press, 1966.

Parks, Rita. *The Western Hero in Film and Television.* Ann Arbor, Mich.: UMI Research Press, 1981.

Parsons, George. *The Private Journal of George Whitwell Parson.* Phoenix: Works Project Administration, 1939.

Patten, William G. *Dismal Dave's Dandy Pard; or, The Clew to Captain Claw: A Story of the Black Hills.* New York: Beadle and Adams, 1879.

Paul, Rodman Wilson. *Mining Frontiers of the Far West, 1848–1880.* Albuquerque: University of New Mexico Press, 1963.

Pearman, Robert, "Earp, Dillon and Co." *New York Times Magazine,* October 19, 1958.

———. "For Fifteen Years Dodge City Was a Mean Town." *Kiwanis Magazine* (July 1960): 35–37.

Pearson, Edmund. *Dime Novels; or, Following an Old Trail in Popular Literature.* Boston: Little, Brown and Company, 1929.

Peattie, Roderick, ed. *The Black Hills.* New York: Vanguard Press, 1952.

Pelzer, Louis. *The Cattleman's Frontier: A Record of the Trans-Mississippi Cattle Industry from Oxen Trains to Pooling Companies, 1850–1890.* Glendale, Calif.: Arthur H. Clark Company, 1936.

Peters, DeWitt C. *The Life and Adventures of Kit Carson, the Nestor of the Rocky Mountains, from Facts Narrated by Himself.* New York: W. R. C. Clark and Company, 1858.

Peterson, P. D. *Through the Black Hills and Bad Lands of South Dakota.* Pierre, S.Dak.: J. Fred Olander Company, 1929.

Philpott, William. *Vacationland: Tourism and Environment in the Colorado High Country.* Seattle: University of Washington Press, 2013.

Pomeroy, Earl. *In Search of the Golden West: The Tourist in Western America.* Lincoln: University of Nebraska Press.

Price, S. Goodale. *Black Hills: Land of Legend.* Los Angeles: DeVorss and Company, 1935.

Raine, William MacLeod. *Famous Sheriffs and Western Outlaws.* New York: Garden City Publishing Company, 1929.

———. "Helldorado." *Liberty* (July 16, 1927): 9, 11–13.

Raine, William MacLeod, and Will C. Barnes. *Cattle.* New York: Garden City Publishing Company, 1930.

Randolph, J. H. *Kit Carson, the Guide; or, Perils of the Frontier.* New York: Frank Starr, 1869.

Ravitz, Abe. *Alfred Henry Lewis.* Boise State University Western Writers Series, no. 32. Boise, Idaho: Boise State University, 1962.

"The Resurrection of Tombstone." *Harper's Weekly* 46, no. 2369 (May 17, 1902): 626.

"Review: The Sunset Trail." *Critic* 47 (November 1905): 477.

"Review: The Sunset Trail." *Dial* 38 (June 1905): 392.

"Revival in Tombstone." *Time Magazine* 46, no. 21 (November 19, 1945): 94–95.

Reynolds, Quentin. *The Fiction Factory or from Pulp Row to Quality Street.* New York: Random House, 1955.

Rezzato, Helen. *Mount Moriah: The Story of Deadwood's Boot Hill.* Rapid City, S.Dak.: Fenwyn Press, 1989.

Rich, Harold. *Fort Worth: Outpost, Cowtown, Boomtown.* Norman: University of Oklahoma Press, 2014.

Richardson. Leander. "A Trip to the Black Hills." *Scribner's Monthly* 13, no. 6 (April 1877): 755.

Robinson, Henry Morton. "The Dime Novel Is Dead But the Same Old Hungers Are Still Fed." *Century Magazine* 116, no. 1 (May 1928): 60–67.

Rockfellow, John. "A Day in Old Tombstone." *Progressive Arizona* 2, no. 3 (March 1926): 27–28.

———. *Log of an Arizona Trailblazer.* Tucson: Acme Printing, 1933.

Rollins, Peter C., and John E. O'Connor, eds. *Hollywood's West: The American Frontier in Film, Television, and History.* Lexington: University Press of Kentucky, 2005.

Roosevelt, Theodore. *Ranch Life and the Hunting Trail.* New York: Century Publishers, 1889.

Rosa, Joseph. *They Called Him Wild Bill: The Life and Adventures of James Butler Hickok.* Norman: University of Oklahoma Press, 1964.

———. *Wild Bill Hickok: The Man and His Myth.* Lawrence: University of Kansas Press, 1996.

Rosen, Rev. Peter. *Pa-Ha-Sa-Pah or the Black Hills of South Dakota.* St. Louis: Nixon-Jones Printing Company, 1895.

Rothman, Hal. *The Culture of Tourism, the Tourism of Culture: Selling the Past to the Present in the American Southwest.* Albuquerque: University of New Mexico Press, 2003.

———. *Devil's Bargains: Tourism in the Twentieth Century.* Lawrence: University Press of Kansas, 1998.

Russell, Don. *The Lives and Legends of Buffalo Bill.* Norman: University of Oklahoma Press, 1960.

———. *The Wild West: A History of the Wild West Shows.* Fort Worth: Amon-Carter Museum of Western Art, 1970.

Sabin, Edwin L. *Kit Carson Days: 1809–1868.* Chicago: A. C. McLurg and Company, 1914.

Samuel, Raphael. *Theaters of Memory.* London: Verso, 1994.

Sara, Delia. *Silver Sam; or, The Mystery of Deadwood City.* New York: Beadle and Adams, 1878.

Sarf, Wayne Michael. *God Bless You, Buffalo Bill.* New York: Associated University Presses and Cornwall Books, 1983.

Savage, William, Jr. *The Cowboy Hero: His Image in American History and Culture.* Norman: University of Oklahoma Press, 1979.

Scharff, Virginia. *Woman and the Coming of the Motor Age.* New York: Free Press, 1991.

Scharnhorst, Gary. *Owen Wister and the West.* Norman: University of Oklahoma Press, 2015.

Schwarz, Joseph. "The Wild West: Everything Genuine." *Journal of Popular Culture* 3, no. 4 (Spring 1970): 656–65.

Sell, Harry Blackman, and Victor Weybright. *Buffalo Bill and the Wild West.* Basin, Wyo.: Big Horn Books (for Buffalo Bill Historical Center), 1979.

Senn, Edward. *Deadwood Dick and Calamity Jane: A Thorough Sifting of Facts from Fiction.* Deadwood, S.Dak.: Edward Senn, 1939.

———. *Wild Bill Hickok: Prince of Pistoleers, a Tale of Facts and Not Fiction and Romance.* Deadwood, S.Dak.: Edward Senn, 1939.

Shadley, Ruth. *Calamity Jane's Daughter: The Story of Maude Weir, a Story Never Told Before.* Caldwell, Idaho: Caxton Printers, 1996.

Shearer, Frederick, ed. *J. R. Bowman's Illustrated Transcontinental Guide to Travel from the Atlantic to the Pacific Ocean and Pacific Tourist and Guide across the Continent.* New York: J. R. Bowman, 1883.

Shillingberg, William B. *Dodge City: The Early Years, 1872–1886.* Norman: Arthur H. Clark Co., 2009.

Simms, A. K. *The Dandy of Dodge; or, Rustling for Millions.* New York: Beadle and Adams, 1888.

Siringo, Charles. *A Texas Cow Boy; or, Fifteen Years on the Hurricane Deck of a Spanish Pony.* Chicago: Rand, McNally and Company, 1886.

Slotkin, Richard. *The Fatal Environment: The Myth of the Frontier in the Age of Industrialization.* New York: Atheneum, 1985.

————. *Gunfighter Nation: The Myth of the Frontier in Twentieth Century America.* New York: HarperCollins, 1993.

————. *The Myth of the Frontier in the Age of Industrialism, 1800–1890.* New York: Athenaeum, 1985.

————. *Regeneration through Violence: The Mythology of the American Frontier, 1600–1860.* Hanover, N.H.: Wesleyan University Press, 1973.

Smith, Henry Nash. *Virgin Land: The American West as Symbol and Myth.* New York: Vintage Books, 1950.

Smith, Waldo R. "Is the Old West Passing?" *Overland Monthly* 67, no. 3 (March 1916): 243–51.

Sollid, Roberta Beed. *Calamity Jane: A Study in Historic Criticism.* Helena: Montana Historical Society Press, 1995.

Sonnichsen, C. L. "Tombstone in Fiction." *Journal of Arizona History* 9, no. 2 (Summer 1968): 59–76.

Souther, J. Mark, and Nicholas Dagon Bloom, eds. *American Tourism: Constructing a National Tradition.* Chicago: Columbia College Chicago, 2012.

Spencer, Mrs. William Loring. *Calamity Jane: A Story of the Black Hills.* New York: Cassell and Company, 1887.

State Board of Agriculture. *36th Biennial Report, 1947–1948.* Topeka: State Printer. 1948.

State Historical Preservation. "Report on Historic Preservation and Restoration in Deadwood" (July 1990). South Dakota State Archives. Pierre, South Dakota.

Steckmesser, Kent Ladd. *The Western Hero in History and Legend.* Norman: University of Oklahoma Press, 1965.

Stephens, Ann S. *Malaeska, the Indian Wife of the White Hunter.* New York: Beadle and Company, 1860.

Stevenson, Elizabeth. "Who Was Calamity Jane? A Speculation." In *Figures in a Western Landscape: Men and Women of the Northern Rockies.* Baltimore: Johns Hopkins University Press, 1994.

Stokes, George. *Deadwood Gold: A Story of the Black Hills.* New York: World Book Company, 1926.

Sulentic, Joe. *Deadwood Gulch: The Last Chinatown.* Deadwood: ABC Business Supply, 1991.

Sullivan, Larry E., and Lydia Cushman Schurman. *Pioneers, Passionate Ladies, and Private Eyes: Dime Novels, Series Books and Paperbacks.* New York: Haworth Press, 1996.

Sutton, Fred, and A. B. McDonald. *Hands Up.* Indianapolis: Bobbs-Merrill Company, 1927.

Sutton, Susan L. "Dodge City, Kansas: Hollywood for a Day." *Under Western Skies* 4 (October 1988): 45–56.

Tallent, Annie. *The Black Hills; or, The Last Hunting Ground of the Dakotahs.* St. Louis: Nixon-Jones Printing Company, 1899.

Tefertiller, Casey. *Wyatt Earp: The Life behind the Legend.* New York: John Wiley and Sons, 1997.

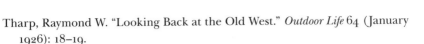

Tharp, Raymond W. "Looking Back at the Old West." *Outdoor Life* 64 (January 1926): 18–19.

"Tombstone, Arizona." *Overland* (second series) 8, no. 11 (November 1886): 483–85.

"Tombstone, Arizona." *Parade Magazine* (May 4, 1947): 17.

Tombstone, Arizona, Community Profile. Phoenix: Department of Economic Planning and Development, 1972.

"The Tombstone Mines, Arizona." *Engineering and Mining Journal* 51 (June 9, 1904).

Traywick, Ben. *Tombstone's Boothill.* Tombstone: Red Marie's Bookstore, 1994.

Turner, Tressa. "Life and Works of Alfred Henry Lewis." MA thesis, University of Texas at Austin, 1936.

Turner, Victor, and Edward Brunner, eds. *The Anthropology of Experience.* Urbana/ Chicago: University of Illinois Press, 1986.

Tuska, Jon. *The American West in Film: Critical Approaches to the Western.* Westport, Conn.: Greenwood Press, 1985.

Underhill, Lonnie, ed. "The Tombstone Discovery: The Recollections of Ed Schieflelin and Richard Gird." *Arizona and the West* 20, no. 1 (Spring 1979): 37–76.

United States Department of the Interior. *Plan for the Interpretation of Deadwood, South Dakota.* Denver: National Park Service, 1992.

Utley, Robert M. *Cavalier in Buckskin: George Armstrong Custer and the Western Military Frontier.* Norman: University of Oklahoma Press, 1988.

Vestal, Stanley. *Dodge City: Queen of Cowtowns.* New York: Bantam Books, 1953.

Wallace, Marian, William Cox, and Andrea Hitzeman. *Tombstone, Arizona: Economic Base Analysis.* Papers in Community Development, no. 6. Tucson: University of Arizona Cooperative Extension Service, 1980.

———. *Tourists in Tombstone: The Nature of Tourism in Tombstone.* Papers in Community and Rural Development, no. 8. Tucson: University of Arizona Cooperative Extension Service, 1980.

Walsh, Raoul. *Each Man in His Time: The Life Story of a Director.* New York: Farrar, Straus and Giroux, 1974.

Walters, Lorenzo. *Tombstone's Yesterdays: True Chronicles of Early Arizona.* Tucson: Acme Press, 1928.

Warner, W. Lloyd. *The Living and the Dead: A Study of the Symbolic Life of Americans.* New Haven: Yale University Press, 1959.

Warren, Louis. *Buffalo Bill's America: William Cody and the Wild West Show.* New York: Alfred A. Knopf, 2005.

Waters, Frank. *The Earp Brothers of Tombstone.* New York: Clark N. Potter, 1960.

Waxman, Percy. "I Learned about America from Deadwood Dick." *Reader's Digest* 38, no. 227 (March 1941): 53–55.

Webber, Charles W. *Jack Long; or, Shot in the Eye A True Story of Texas Border Life.* New York: H. Graham, 1846.

———. *Old Hicks, the Guide; or, Adventures in the Comanche Country in Search of a Gold Mine.* New York: Harper, 1848.

West, Elliot. "The Saloon in Territorial Arizona." *Journal of the West* 13, no. 3 (July 1974): 60–65.

———. "Wicked Dodge City." *American History Illustrated* 17, no. 1 (June 1982): 22–31.

Wheeler, Edward L. *Deadwood Dick on Deck; or, Calamity Jane, the Heroine of Whoop-Up; or, A Story of Dakota.* New York: Beadle and Adams, 1878.

———. *Deadwood Dick's Dream; or, The Rivals of the Road: A Mining Tale of Tombstone.* New York: Beadle and Adams, 1881.

———. *Deadwood Dick, the Prince of the Road; or, The Black Rider of the Black Hills.* New York: Beadle and Adams, 1877.

———. *Rosebud Rob; or, Nugget Ned, the Knight of the Gulch.* New York: Beadle and Adams, 1879.

———. *Wildcat Bob, the Boss Bruiser; or, The Border Bloodhounds.* New York: Frank Starr, 1877.

Whipple, T. K. *Study Out the Land.* Berkeley: University of California Press. 1943.

White, Edward G. *The Eastern Establishment and the Western Experience: The West of Frederic Remington, Theodore Roosevelt, and Owen Wister.* New Haven: Yale University Press, 1968.

Wiggins, Owen H. "Dodge City." MA thesis, Colorado State College, Greely, Colorado, 1938.

Willett, Edward. *The Gray Hunter; or, The White Spirit of the Apaches: A Tale of the Arizona Mountain Placers.* New York: Beadle and Adams, 1879.

Wilson, R. Michael. *Crime and Punishment in Early Arizona.* Las Vegas, Nev.: Stage Coach Books, 2004.

———. *Frontier Justice in Early America.* Guilford, Conn.: Globe Pequot, 2007.

Wilstach, Frank. *Wild Bill Hickok: Prince of Pistoleers.* Garden City, N.Y.: Doubleday and Page, 1926.

Wister, Owen. *Roosevelt.* New York: Macmillan, 1930.

Wooden, Wayne S., and Gavin Ehringer. *Rodeo in America.* Topeka: University of Kansas Press, 1996.

Worster, Donald. *Dust Bowl: The Southern Plains in the 1930s.* Oxford: Oxford University Press, 1979.

Wright, Robert M. *Dodge City: The Cowboy Capital and the Great Southwest in the Days of the Wild Indian, the Buffalo, the Cowboy, Dance Halls, Gambling Halls, and Bad Men.* Wichita: Wichita Eagle Press, 1913.

Wrobel, David M. *The End of American Exceptionalism: Frontier Anxiety from the Old West to the New Deal.* Lawrence: University of Kansas Press, 1993.

———. *Global West: American Frontier Travel, Empire, and Exceptionalism from Manifest Destiny to the Great Depression.* Albuquerque: University of New Mexico Press, 2013.

Young, Frederick. *Dodge City: Up through a Century in Story and Pictures.* Dodge City: Boot Hill Museum, 1972.

Young, Harry. *Hard Knocks: A Life Story of the Vanishing West.* Chicago: Laird and Lee, 1915.

Zierold, Norman. *The Moguls.* New York: Avon Books, 1969.

☞ Index

Page references in *italic type* indicate illustrations.

"Deadwood Dick," 4, 40, 41, 126; and
　Calamity Jane, 41; *Deadwood Dick,
　the Prince of the Road* (Wheeler),
　19, 40; *Deadwood Dick's Dream; or,
　Rivals of the Road* (Wheeler), 24;
　Deadwood violence, 18; in dime
　novels, 40; in film, 149; popularity
　of, 18; in Tombstone, 24; Wheeler
　series, 18
Deadwood Stage, The (film), 153–54
Dean, Eddie, 160
Dedera, Don, 205
de Havilland, Olivia, 149, 157
DeMille, Cecil B., 149, 150, 153
Denious, Jess, 5, 139, 156, 190
Deputy, The (TV show), 164
Devere, Jeanne, 205, 207
Devine, Andy, 164, 168
dime novels, 19, 31, 33, 43, 116, 178;
　end of, 44, 53; and films, 148;
　popularity of, 34–35, 37; tourism
　and, 19; western image, 30, 31, 56,
　57
Dobie, J. Frank, 62
Dodd, Thomas, 173
Dodge City (film), 149, *159*
Dodge City, Kan., 5, 25, 28, 65, 66,
　77; and Bat Masterson, 29, 48–49;
　Boot Hill, 91–103, *97*, 116; cattle
　drives, 4, 25, 43; *Dodge City* (film)
　premiere, 155–60; Dodge City
　Cowboy Band, 190; Dodge City
　Days, 16, 163; in film, 149–51;
　Front Street, 5, 188–89, 209;
　Gunsmoke (TV show), 165–68, 171;
　Last Round-Up, 4, 89, 126, 138,
　140, 163; museums, 184–87, 196,
　196, 213; and National Cowboy
　Hall of Fame, 189–92; Pageant
　of Progress, 119, 121; "Peace
　Commission," 28; Real Estate
　Board, 93; Saddle Club, 163;
　tourism, 7, 9, 53, 74–76, 89, 115,
　120–21, 174, 176, 183, 193–95;
　Townsite Company, 92; violence,
　20, 26–28, 68; weapons ban,
　26–27; western identity, 11, 27,

47, 63, 64, 67, 146, 211; and Wyatt
　Earp, 20, 29, 60, 65, 165
Dodge City Daily Globe, 74, 139, 184; on
　Boot Hill Museum, 213–14; and
　Gunsmoke image, 194; tourism, 75,
　93, 99, 151, 168; and Wyatt Earp,
　65
Drago, Harry, 176
Drunkard, The (play), 162
Duncan, Annie ("Tombstone
　Nightingale"), 136
Durham, George, 66
Dust Bowl, 98, 186
Dykstra, Robert R., 8

Earp, Hobart, 174
Earp, Josephine, 64
Earp, Morgan, 22
Earp, Wyatt, 43, *45*, 50, 56, *65*,
　175; Breakenridge and Raine,
　97; Burns bio, 47, 60; in Dodge
　City, 26, 28, 48, 65; in film and
　television, 149–51, 154, 159, 162,
　165, 168–69, 193–94, 213; Lake
　bio, 20, 29, 64–65, 67, 140, 183–
　84, 212; mythology, 13, 185–86,
　195, 215; reputation, 176–77;
　writings of, 45
Earp Brothers of Tombstone, The
　(Waters), 176
Eastman, Richard, 168
Edison, Thomas, 148
Elliott, Michael, 8
Ellis, Edward (author), 34
El Paso Herald, 78
Escapule, Dusty, Mayor, 3
Everybody's Magazine, 48
Ewing, Ray L., 155, 180

Fabian, Ann, 12
Fannin, Paul, 165
Fastest Gun Alive (TV show), 164
Federal Road Act (1916), 75
Federal Writers' Project, 111
Filson, John, 32
Finger, Charles, 77, 86, 116
Flint, Timothy, 32